Sarah Raven's
COMPLETE
CHRISTMAS
FOOD & FLOWERS

Photography by Jonathan Buckley

B L O O M S B U R Y

With love and thanks to my twin sister
Jane, for all her help and inspiration

Introduction

We all remember the Christmases of our childhood, as if – for a few days – a spell had been cast over the household. In my family we always used to stay with my aunt in Westmorland. Every year was reassuringly the same – a vast, sprayed-white Christmas tree in the curve of the stairs in the hall, beautiful rooms which smelled of hyacinths, piles of presents under the tree, and meal after meal of delicious food. My aunt is an exceptional cook and as well as the usual Christmas food, we had a series of family favourites such as smoked salmon loaf, beef olives and Mrs Titley's éclairs. There was a sense of glowing attention paid to us, and yet it all felt as if it had appeared from thin air.

A couple of decades later, with a young family of my own, it was my turn to play the host and it dawned on me: the reason for this feeling of harmony had been that someone else was doing all the work. To begin with I felt intimidated by the prospect of a houseful of people coming to stay for several days, having to manage all the different personalities, the decorations, the food, the drink, the presents, the money. Stress levels were high until I realised that pre-planning – pinning down most of the meals and thinking through the flowers and decorations well in advance – would free me up to join in and have a good time.

Since then, I've learnt that a light and effortless effect is rarely achieved by wafting in thinking wouldn't it be nice... I have come to realise that there are several stages to a good Christmas, which I've tried to reflect in this book. First comes a long gentle build up, time to put my larder in order and get ahead. Then there's a sparkly opening, which means, if I'm feeling energetic, throwing a Christmas party for friends and neighbours. A few days before Christmas, it's time to make it all look nice, to create a wreath for the front door, to decorate the tree and to make a bumper, long-lasting table centre from 'Paper White' narcissi, hyacinths or amaryllis.

In our house, the family gathers on Christmas Eve and (as breezily as possible) I bring out communal dishes of blinis and smoked salmon, bagna cauda or a pungent cheese fondue, all floated on a sea of flavoured vodka or champagne. This is of course followed by the big *Ta-ra!* of Christmas Day, where we dine on the best stuffed bird (my side of the family favours goose, my husband's turkey, so we alternate) and a chunky-textured, treacly Christmas pudding. After that things calm down a bit and there is the refreshing, cooler after-Christmas week, which is a time for eating simpler food – salads, soups and lots of delicious leftovers. New Year's Eve is the final jamboree, not quite as set in stone as Christmas, but every bit as high-spirited. We usually play masses of games (and try not to start the new year with too much of a hangover).

If you consciously divide your Christmas holiday into phases, it will be much nicer for you and your guests. That claustrophobic and rather deadening feeling of 'Oh no, not *another* massive meal' can be avoided and you can play the event like a conductor, alternating the trombones (a splash of rich, celebratory food) with a quiet passage on the flutes and strings (a crisp, clean-tasting winter salad or a warming soup made from leftovers). Giving a clear rhythm to the meals should help you avoid feeling overwhelmed and will hopefully allow you to re-summon the bright, magical qualities of Christmas, not by floating through them as a child would, but by planning them – and then hugely enjoying them – as a grown up.

Of course, a bit of precision planning is needed. Lists, dates, quantities, sequences, menus and advance ordering may all sound like hard work, but they will be worth it: they will make people think you've hardly lifted a finger. And a feeling of ease and of lightness is all at Christmas – in the flowers, in the decorations, in the food and in the drink. You'll find a lot of silveriness in this book, much more than the traditional reds and greens – because silver is to me the colour of a happy Christmas. Have a lovely time.

Sarah Raven Perch Hill, East Sussex

A Christmas timetable

If you have a weekend or two to spare in the run up to Christmas, use it for getting ahead in a leisurely way. Select a few things from the list below to prepare in advance:

August

Harvest and dry:
Allium heads (page 65)

September

Harvest and make:
Christmas rowan berry (or redcurrant) jelly (page 25)
Damson cheese (page 26)
Quince cheese (page 28)
Apricot and almond compote (page 28)
Apricot and apple chutney (page 29)
Damson vodka or gin (page 41)

Harvest and dry:
Clematis seed heads (page 71)
Borlotti and other beans (pages 73 and 82)
Agapanthus seed pods (pages 65 and 82)
Globe artichokes (page 82)

Plant for forcing:
Hyacinths (pages 46 and 49)
Crocus (page 50)
Miniature iris (page 54)
Anemones (page 56)

October

Harvest and make:
Sloe vodka or gin (page 41)
Rosehip syrup (page 43)

Harvest and dry:
Chinese lanterns (pages 73 and 85)
Leaves for silver birch grove (page 120)

November

Make:
Christmas cake (pages 19 and 20)
Christmas pudding (page 21)
Mincemeat (pages 22 and 24)
Prunes in Armagnac (page 29)
Rose Turkish delight (page 34)

Plant for forcing:
'Paper White' narcissus (page 53)
Amaryllis (page 59)

Early December   Make:
Cranberry and orange compote (page 26)
Cranberry and juniper jelly (page 26)
Nut caramel cartwheel (page 32)
Lemon, cranberry or chilli vodka (pages 41 and 43)
Pink grapefruit cordial (page 43)

Make and freeze:
Mrs Titley's sticky buns (page 145)
Cornmeal rolls (page 146)
Oatmeal rolls (page 210)
Walnut bread (page 153)
Potted shrimps (page 152)
Christmas bagna cauda sauce (page 157)
Stuffings (pages 180 and 185–7)
Smoked haddock chowder (page 209)
Ham and Cumberland sauce (page 220)
Mary's smoked haddock Florentine (page 223)
Carbonnade of beef (page 241)

Mid-December   Make:
Marzipan and royal icing for decorating Christmas cake
(pages 20 and 21)
Banbury cakes (page 22)
Mince pies (page 24)
Candied peel, fruit or ginger dipped in chocolate (page 31)
Peppermint creams dipped in chocolate (page 31)
Fruit and nut chocolate cartwheel (page 32)
Strawberry or raspberry white chocolate truffles (page 32)
Easy chocolate truffles (page 34)
Florentines (page 36)
Orange, cranberry and walnut biscuits (page 36)
Gingerbread house and biscuits for the tree (pages 39 and 40)
Homemade granola (page 147)
Blood orange granita (page 149)
Madeira cake for trifle (page 200)

Planning Ahead

The Christmas larder

Whether you love it or hate it, Christmas is exhausting, and if you're the host, the more you can get done in advance the better. That is not my natural mentality – I am a real last-minute queen – but for Christmas, even I try to get a few things under my belt beforehand. With some of the cooking and preparations done early, you'll have a more enjoyable, less manic time.

In the case of Christmas cake, mincemeat and pudding, everything needs time to mature and marinate in the alcohol. The fruit and nuts absorb the other flavours, and overall the taste becomes deeper and richer with storing. There are other foods that aren't necessarily improved by being made early but are fine if cooked and stashed away in your Christmas larder, such as Banbury cakes and mince pies (see pages 22 and 24), the building blocks of a gingerbread house (see page 39) and cranberry and orange compote (see page 26).

If you think ahead, you can also make some of your presents. In a world where time is short, there are few food-loving adults who wouldn't be happy with a hamper of sweet or savoury jams and chutneys (see pages 25–9), homemade chocolates (see pages 32–4), biscuits (see page 36), or flavoured vodkas (see pages 41–3). Give a selection, rather than lots of one thing, and if there are children around, get them involved in making peppermint creams (see page 31) and designing the wrapping. These then make ideal presents for grandparents and teachers at the end of term.

It's also a good idea to make friends with a cheese seller and ask him to keep a few round, split-chestnut whole Brie boxes for you. These aren't very robust, but make lovely-looking hampers. Shallow wooden fruit or vegetable crates also look okay if you've made enough to fill them, but there's something particularly appealing about the round, shallow shape of the Brie box. Line it with pretty paper, bright-coloured tissue or fabric, fill it, and enclose in a length of cellophane. To stand alone, or as part of the hamper, the much smaller, deeper Camembert boxes also work well (see picture on page 30). If they smell strongly of cheese, put one or two drops of lavender, eucalyptus or citrus oil on to the wood and all will be perfect! You can decorate these and fill them with candied fruit or peel and crystallised ginger dipped in chocolate (see page 31), truffles (see pages 32–4) or Turkish delight (see page 34).

Christmas cake

Christmas cake is at its best eaten with a slice of crumbly Lancashire or Stilton cheese. Have it, instead of a pudding, to finish one of your Christmas meals. (See pages 20–1 for decorating ideas.)

For a 23cm round or 20cm square cake:

- **100g glacé cherries**
- **100g good-quality candied peel (see page 31), chopped**
- **225g currants**
- **225g sultanas**
- **225g stoned raisins, roughly chopped**
- **200g dried apricots (ideally undyed), stoned and soaked**
- **Zest and juice of 1 lemon**
- **2 tablespoons brandy**
- **275g plain flour**
- **Pinch of salt**
- **½ teaspoon ground cloves**
- **½ teaspoon ground cinnamon**
- **½ teaspoon mixed spice**
- **½ teaspoon freshly grated nutmeg**
- **225g unsalted butter**
- **225g light soft brown sugar**
- **6 eggs, beaten**
- **50g whole almonds, roughly chopped if you wish**
- **50g hazelnuts, halved**
- **A little cold milk**

Line the base of a 23cm round or 20cm square tin with greaseproof paper rubbed with a trace of sunflower oil, or a silicone mat, cut to size, and tie a double layer of brown paper, a little higher than the rim of the tin, around the outside.

Wash and dry the glacé cherries and put into a large bowl with the candied peel, all the fruit, the lemon zest and juice, and brandy. Allow this to stand, turning the fruit occasionally, for at least 2 hours, or overnight if possible.

Preheat the oven to 180°C/gas mark 4.

Sift the flour with the salt and spices. Cream the butter and sugar until light and soft and add the beaten eggs, one at a time, stirring well between each addition. (If the mixture begins to curdle while you are adding the eggs, sprinkle in a handful of the sifted flour. Even if it does curdle, don't panic – you'll just have a heavier cake.)

Once you have added the eggs, mix in the flour and fold in the fruit mixture, the nuts and a couple of tablespoons of milk. Spoon the mixture into the prepared tin.

Put the cake into the preheated oven for 1 hour; then lower the heat to 170°C/gas mark 3 and bake for another 2 hours, or until a skewer pushed into the centre of the cake comes out clean. Cool it in the tin; then turn it out and double wrap with greaseproof paper, and put it in an airtight tin until you want to decorate it.

It's fine to store the cake for up to 8 weeks, but beyond that, it will start to dry out a bit.

Glazed fruit Christmas cake

This is the simplest, and I'd say the best, way of decorating your Christmas cake. Just pile up the top with nuts and dried fruit, doing away with fancy icing.

For glazing a 23cm round or 20cm square cake:

A mixture of nuts such as pecans, Brazils, walnuts, almonds, whole
3–4 tablespoons apricot jam
Splash of brandy
Natural-colour glacé cherries
Dried fruit such as prunes, apricots and figs, stoned and soaked
Mixture of crystallised fruits such as pineapple and ginger

Toast the nuts for a few minutes in a medium oven (190°C/gas mark 5) until they're crisp but not brown.

Sieve the apricot jam into a small saucepan to get rid of the lumps of fruit. Add a splash of brandy and heat the mixture over a low heat, stirring well to combine thoroughly. Then, using a pastry brush, glaze the top of the cake with it. Arrange your selection of fruit and nuts on top and when everything is in place, glaze again. The jam acts as delicious edible glue.

Marzipan

I tend not to ice my Christmas cake, but if you've got the time, and your family likes marzipan and icing, making both is quite a jolly occupation, ideal for doing with children. Don't buy marzipan ready made: it's very easy to make and homemade will be much tastier. The marzipan layer serves a purpose: it stops the pure white icing discolouring.

This recipe makes enough to cover the top of a 20cm square or 23cm round cake. My advice is not to do the sides (you can ice these without the marzipan underneath), but if you do want to, then double the quantities below.

For 450g:

110g icing sugar
110g caster sugar
225g ground almonds
1 teaspoon lemon juice
1 teaspoon vanilla extract
1 egg, beaten
2 tablespoons apricot jam, sieved

Sift the icing sugar into a mixing bowl and add the caster sugar and ground almonds. Add the lemon juice and vanilla extract and mix together. Stir in the beaten egg and work together until you have a smooth paste. Don't be tempted to overdo this, as if you do, too much oil will be released from the almonds and it will discolour your icing quite quickly. Roll the paste into a ball, cover and chill in the fridge for half an hour or until needed.

To cover the cake, dust your work surface with sifted icing sugar. Roll out the paste ball into a square or circle slightly larger than the top of the cake.

Warm the apricot jam and, using a pastry brush, paint it on to the top of your cake (if you want a very flat top you can turn the cake upside down). Lay the square or circle of almond paste on the apricot jam and press down gently, using a rolling pin to get rid of any air bubbles, and smooth the top.

Trim the edge of the almond paste and put the cake in a cool place for at least 2 days for the paste to dry out before you ice it.

Royal icing

For those who really want to go to town: the perfect, pure-white, pristine finish to a classic Christmas cake. This recipe makes enough to cover a 20cm square or 23cm round cake with a generous layer of icing.

Decorate the iced cake with whatever you fancy – more icing shapes, ribbon or some sugared or silvered almonds.

For about 900g:
4 egg whites
900g icing sugar, sifted
1 tablespoon lemon juice
2 teaspoons glycerine
 (available from chemists)

Whisk the egg whites in a large bowl until they are frothy but not stiff. With a wooden spoon, gradually beat in half the sifted icing sugar. Add the lemon juice and glycerine and then beat in the remaining sugar.

Cover the bowl with cling film and leave for 30 minutes until any bubbles have burst. With royal icing, bubbles always come to the surface, so if you start to cover the cake too soon, you won't get a smooth finish and will have to pop the bubbles with a pin, which takes ages.

Spoon the icing on to the top of a cake covered with marzipan and use a palette knife (occasionally dipping it into very hot water) to smooth it evenly over the top and the sides of the cake.

Leave the icing to dry for about 24 hours before decorating.

Christmas pudding

The Sunday before Advent (five Sundays before Christmas) is 'Stir-up Sunday', the traditional moment to make your Christmas pudding, mincemeat and Christmas cake.

This recipe, adapted from Constance Spry, makes a pudding with great texture and flavour, including whole almonds and masses of dried fruit. It's the one my mother has always used. As children, we had this stuffed full of coins. Add these just before you eat it on Christmas Day (see page 199).

For 2 medium-sized puddings or 1 very large pudding (for 15–20):
225g self-raising flour
350g fresh white breadcrumbs
450g currants
450g sultanas
450g raisins
350g suet (vegetarian or meat)
110g chopped candied peel
 (see page 31)
50g slivered almonds
1 Bramley apple, grated
Zest and juice of 1 orange
1 teaspoon mixed spice
½ teaspoon freshly grated
 nutmeg
1 teaspoon salt
6 eggs, beaten
300ml brown ale or milk
450g light brown sugar

Mix all the ingredients together. Lightly oil two medium-sized (1.5 litre) pudding basins or one large (2.5 litre) one and fill with the mixture. Cover with a double layer of greaseproof paper, secure with string and then either boil or steam.

If boiling, for each pudding use a huge saucepan with a cushion of crumpled foil in the bottom. Sit the pudding basin in the saucepan on the cushion and fill to two-thirds of the way up the pudding basin with boiling water. Cover tightly and simmer for

5–6 hours, topping up with boiling water when necessary. If steaming, put the basin in a double saucepan or steamer and steam for 5–6 hours, again topping up the water when necessary. Allow them to cool.

Then re-cover the puddings with another double layer of greaseproof paper, secured with string. Cover them with aluminium foil (don't use foil next to the pudding, as the fruits will react to the foil) or muslin and store them in a cool larder, fridge or freezer until you need them.

Before serving, boil or steam the puddings for another 3 hours (see page 199).

Mincemeat with damsons and cobnuts

This recipe makes the best of all mincemeats, with the extra flavour of sloe gin and the crunch of cobnuts. It's from Peter Weeden, head chef of the Paternoster Chop House. Peter was brought up in Kent, loves foraging and is a great champion of the Kentish cobnut, which is bigger, plumper and sweeter than the more common hazelnut.

If you can't find cobs, use hazels instead, but if they're dried, soak them overnight in water. This will plump them up. If you can't find damsons, substitute cranberries or prunes, or even chunky plum jam. If using jam, reduce the amount of sugar in the recipe by half.

This recipe makes enough for 15–20 Banbury cakes (see right) or the same number of mince pies (see page 24).

For 450g:
80g cobnuts, halved
100g damsons or cranberries, or half-and-half cranberries and ready-soaked pitted prunes
50g demerara sugar
50g raisins
75g currants
75g suet (vegetarian or meat)
Juice of ½ lemon
1 apple, peeled, cored and diced
A slug of damson gin (or sloe gin, whisky or brandy)

Mix all the ingredients together in a bowl. You can use this mixture straight away, but it's even better left for a while – 4–6 weeks – to mature and marinate.

Ladle the mincemeat into large screwtop jars that have been sterilised by being boiled in a pan of water for 10 minutes or run through the dishwasher. Alternatively, keep it in a sealed bowl, somewhere cool – the alcohol content makes it safe to store – until you want to use it.

Banbury cakes

I love a Banbury cake, with its crumbly puff pastry. They're best eaten with double cream or with not-too-cold Lancashire cheese. You can use this recipe to make Eccles cakes too. Traditionally round (although some insist they should be oval), these are made with shortcrust pastry, not flaky pastry.

For 15–20 cakes:
500g puff pastry (bought, but made with butter)
450g mincemeat with damsons and cobnuts (see left)
1 egg white
A little caster sugar

Preheat the oven to 200°C/gas mark 6.

Roll out the pastry really thinly (5mm) and, using a cutter, cut out 10cm-diameter rounds. With each round, put a heaped dessertspoon of mincemeat mixture into the centre, gather up the pastry so that it makes a shape like a Shakespearean purse (see opposite), pinch it firmly together and cut off the excess. Turn the little cake upside down and flatten it slightly. Cut three quite deep slits in the top. Mix the egg white with some caster sugar and, using a pastry brush, glaze the cakes. Put them on a silicone mat on a baking tray.

Cook the cakes for 10 minutes in the preheated oven to get a lovely crisp, crystallised finish.

Once they've cooled, freeze them, or store them in a sealed tin: kept airtight, they will be fine for up to a month.

Traditional mincemeat

Here's a delicious recipe for traditional mincemeat. Don't buy mincemeat – homemade is a hundred times tastier.

This recipe makes enough for about 50 mince pies.

For about 1.5kg:
**100g good-quality candied peel
  (see page 31), chopped
350g dessert apples, peeled,
  cored and chopped
125g sultanas
125g dates
125g 'no-soak' dried apricots,
  stoned
125g seedless raisins
125g currants
50g blanched almonds, roughly
  chopped
½ teaspoon freshly grated
  nutmeg
1 teaspoon mixed spice
½ teaspoon ground ginger
175g soft brown sugar
175g suet (vegetarian or meat)
Zest and juice of 1 lemon
4 tablespoons brandy**

Put the candied peel into a large mixing bowl with the chopped apples. Put the sultanas, dates, apricots and raisins into a food processor and pulse briefly. Add this to the mixing bowl with the currants, almonds, spices, sugar and suet, and the lemon zest and juice. Mix well and cover. Leave overnight.

Stir the mixture and add the brandy. Spoon into dry jars that have been sterilised by being boiled in a pan of water for 10 minutes or run through the dishwasher. Cover with wax discs and screwtop lids. Store in the cool for at least 4 weeks before using. The mincemeat is best used within 3 months.

Mince pies

You're going to eat mince pies at some point over Christmas, so make lots with your own mincemeat in a quiet moment and freeze them, preferably uncooked. Mini ones – made in a canapé tray – are brilliant for eating at a Christmas party, particularly with a dollop of brandy butter (see page 199) placed inside the pastry case lid before they're heated through.

For about 25 pies:
**Mincemeat (see page 22 or
  traditional recipe, left)
Cream cheese, soft goats'
  cheese, clotted cream or
  full-fat crème fraîche (optional)
Caster sugar, to taste
1 egg, beaten, for egg wash
1 tablespoon icing sugar, for
  dusting**

For the pastry:
**Pinch of salt
500g plain flour, sifted
250g unsalted butter or half-and-
  half butter and lard
Zest of 2 oranges
1 tablespoon icing sugar (optional)
2 egg yolks
Ice-cold water**

Preheat the oven to 220°C/gas mark 7.

To make the pastry, add the salt to the sifted flour. Rub the butter – or butter and lard – into the flour lightly with your fingers, or pulse in a food processor, until the mixture resembles breadcrumbs. Stir in the orange zest (and a little icing sugar if you want a sweeter pastry). Mix the egg yolks with a very little ice-cold water, and add just enough to bring the mixture together in a ball. Cover the pastry and allow it to rest for half an hour in the fridge.

Flour your work surface and roll out the pastry. Using a cutter, make rounds slightly bigger than you need

to fill the dimples in your tart tin and cut the same number of slightly smaller rounds for the tops. Line the tart tin with the larger rounds and put about a dessertspoon of mincemeat in each. If you want to, add a teaspoon of cream cheese, soft goats' cheese, clotted cream or full-fat crème fraîche, slightly sweetened, on top. (You can't freeze the mince pies if you use light or less than full-fat cream cheese or crème fraîche.)

Wet your fingers with water and lightly dampen the edge of each round before putting the top on and gently pressing the edges together. Make two small slits in the top to let the steam escape, and lightly brush with a little egg wash.

Freeze the pies in their tin at this stage, or bake in the preheated oven for 15 minutes. Mince pies also freeze well once cooked, but try to avoid reheating them more than once, as they dry out easily. They can be cooked from frozen, but will need about 5 minutes' more cooking. Allow them to cool in the tin for a few minutes, before transferring them on to a cake rack to cool a little.

Serve warm, dusted with icing sugar, or store in an airtight tin for up to a month.

Fruit chutneys, compotes and cheeses

Christmas rowan berry (or redcurrant) jelly

A delicious, fragrant red berry jelly, with a lovely soft texture and a spicy taste. Eat it with any red meat or game – venison, jugged hare, rabbit, grouse or partridge – and try it with bread and a slice of Stilton cheese. You need to make it in late summer or early autumn, when, particularly in the woods and hedgerows of northern England and Scotland, tart and delicious rowan berries are abundant. If you can't find these, then use redcurrants.

For 4 small jars:
**900g rowan berries
(or redcurrants)
900g Bramley apples, peeled,
cored and chopped
Zest and juice of 1 lemon
6 cloves
1 cinnamon stick
6 allspice berries
Caster sugar (450g sugar for
every 570ml juice)**

Simmer the rowan berries (or redcurrants), apples, lemon zest and juice and the spices in 850ml water until the berries (or currants) are just tender – no more than 15 minutes. Pour the mixture into a jelly bag or muslin bag to drip overnight, or until all the juice is extracted.

Measure the juice into a heavy-based saucepan and add 450g sugar for every 570ml of juice. Stir over a low heat until the sugar has completely dissolved and then bring to a rolling boil and continue to cook until the jelly reaches setting point. To test for setting point, remove the pan from the heat, put a teaspoonful of the jelly on to a cold saucer and put it into the fridge for a minute or two until cold. If you push the jelly with your finger and the surface wrinkles, it has reached setting point.

Remove any scum from the edge of the pan with a metal spoon and pour the jelly into warm screwtop jars that have been sterilised by being boiled in a pan of water for 10 minutes or run through the dishwasher. Cover with a disc of waxed paper and seal while hot. Label and date the jars.

This jelly will last at least a year. Once opened, keep it in the fridge.

Cranberry and orange compote

Cranberries – in some form or another – are the classic accompaniment to your Christmas turkey. This recipe makes a delicious orangey and chunky-textured compote. It is indeed lovely with turkey and very good with cold ham (see page 220), and I also use a good dollop in gravy to eat with game. You can make this at the last minute, but the flavours mix and deepen with a bit of storing, so try to make it at least two weeks before Christmas.

For 6:
  675g cranberries
  **Pared rind of 2 oranges, cut
    into strips**
  100ml fresh orange juice
  130ml red wine
  2 tablespoons redcurrant jelly
  1 cinnamon stick
  3 or 4 cloves
  120g granulated sugar
  100ml port

Put the cranberries, strips of orange rind, orange juice, red wine, redcurrant jelly, cinnamon stick, cloves and sugar into a medium-sized saucepan.

Dissolve the sugar and jelly by whisking over a low heat, and then bring to the boil. Simmer for about 5 minutes until the cranberries are tender. Add the port and test for sweetness; add more sugar if you wish.

If you are giving this as a present, ladle it into warm jars that have been sterilised by being boiled in a pan of water for 10 minutes or run through the dishwasher, and cover. Label and date the jars. If you're making it for yourself, pour it into a bowl and cover with cling film. Eat within 2 months. Once opened, keep it in the fridge.

Cranberry and juniper jelly

I first ate this in St Petersburg ten years ago and loved its clean and aromatic taste, so I try to make it when cranberries are around every Christmas. It's excellent served with any cold meat or cheese.

For 2 small pots:
  800g cranberries
  6 juniper berries
  250ml red wine
  150g granulated sugar

Rinse the cranberries and put them into a saucepan with 250ml water and the juniper berries. Simmer these for about 20 minutes until the fruit pops open and softens. Allow the fruit to drip through a jelly bag or muslin bag overnight.

Put the liquid into a medium-sized saucepan with the red wine and add the sugar. Place over a gentle heat to dissove the sugar, and then bring to a rolling boil until the jelly reaches setting point. To test for setting point, remove the pan from the heat, put a teaspoonful of the jelly on to a cold saucer and put it into the fridge for a minute or two until cold. If you push the jelly with your finger and the surface wrinkles, it has reached setting point.

Pour into warm jars that have been sterilised by being boiled in a pan of water for 10 minutes or run through the dishwasher. Cover with a disc of waxed paper and seal while hot. Label and date the jars.

This jelly will last at least a year. Once opened, keep it in the fridge.

Damson cheese

There's something good and old-fashioned about damson cheese. Have it on a cheeseboard, or eat it with any red meat or game. You'll need to make this in the early autumn when damsons are still around, or if you don't have time then, buy the fruit and freeze it.

For about 2.5kg:
  2.7kg damsons
  **Granulated sugar (for each
    570ml purée, add 450g sugar)**

Wash the damsons and put them into a heavy-based pan with 275ml water. Cover, bring to the boil and simmer gently until soft. Meanwhile put the packets or bowl of sugar in a very low oven (130°C/gas mark 1) to warm up for about half an hour.

Rub the fruit mixture through a sieve, rinse the pan and put the fruit purée back into it. Simmer over the heat until it is thick and has reduced by about a third. Measure the purée, and for every 570ml, add 450g granulated sugar. Cook this mixture, stirring continuously, until when you draw a wooden spoon across the bottom of the saucepan, it parts for a few seconds.

Damson cheese has a firm consistency (much thicker than jam), so rather than storing it in jars, it's best to pour it into a clean, oiled, warm shallow bowl or trays so that it can be turned out easily and cut into slices.

Ideally, allow it to mature for a couple of months before you eat it. You'll probably eat one slice at a time but the high sugar content of this solid fruit cheese makes it store very well. Just wrap the block up again in waxed paper and store somewhere cool.

Quince cheese

Another traditional fruit cheese – loved by the Spanish – which is again fantastic on a cheeseboard. You can also melt this in gravy with pork dishes or eat it with apple pies; and it is delicious served like Turkish delight, but rolled in caster sugar rather than icing sugar.

For about 2kg:
  2kg quinces (or quince and cooking apples if you are short of quince)
  Granulated sugar (for each 600ml purée, add 350g sugar)
  A little ground cinnamon, to taste
  Caster sugar, to dust (optional)

Roughly chop the unpeeled quinces and put into a pan with 300ml water. Cover and stew gently until the fruit is soft. Meanwhile put the packets or bowl of sugar in a very low oven (130°C/gas mark 1) to warm up for about half an hour.

Sieve or mouli the fruit and measure the purée. For each 600ml of purée, add 350g of sugar. Gently heat the mixture in a deep saucepan until the sugar has completely dissolved. Add the cinnamon, raise the heat and bring to the boil. Stirring almost continuously to prevent it catching, reduce by about two-thirds. As it reduces, it will spit and splatter, so cover your hand with a cloth.

After about 45 minutes, the quince mixture will have turned a lovely reddish brown and will begin to come away from the side of the pan as you stir. Pour it into baking trays lined with non-stick paper, or an oiled mould.

Leave uncovered at room temperature for 2–3 days. Cut into 15cm x 15cm squares. Wrap them in waxed paper and seal in an airtight tin. They will store for at least a year. You can cut some smaller cubes and roll them in caster sugar – delicious to eat as sweets or with cheese.

Apricot and almond compote

In summer you can't beat a breakfast of good white bread, unsalted creamy Normandy butter and jam made with fresh apricots. It reminds me of being on holiday abroad. In winter, this richer-tasting jam, made from dried apricots, is equally good. I also love it spooned over ice cream or some natural yoghurt.

For 4–5 jars:
  450g dried apricots (ideally undyed), stoned
  Zest and juice of 1 lemon
  700g granulated sugar
  100g blanched almonds, slivered
  3 tablespoons brandy
  Vanilla pod

Halve the apricots and just cover with water. Leave either overnight or until they are well soaked and plump.

Add the lemon zest and juice to the apricots (left in the water – most will have been absorbed) and simmer for approximately 20 minutes. Add the sugar and dissolve over a low heat before bringing to the boil again and simmering for about 40 minutes.

Remove from the heat and add the almonds. Stir in the brandy (this small amount prevents the jam from being too sweet, and it won't give the compote a strong taste that might make it a bit much for eating at breakfast). Divide the vanilla pod between four or five warm jars that have been sterilised by being boiled in a pan of water for 10 minutes or run through the dishwasher. Pour the compote into the jars, cover with a disc of waxed paper and seal while hot. Label and date the jars.

This compote keeps for about 6 months. Once opened, keep it in the fridge.

Apricot and apple chutney

This is rich, chunky and delicious, with lots of lovely flavours – apricots and apples and ginger and cardamom. It has a wonderful texture too, with coarsely chopped fruit and plenty of halved hazelnuts. The taste will improve as it matures, so make it a couple of months before Christmas.

Ideally, use cardamom seeds that have been taken fresh from their pods, as these have a much better flavour than the dried variety.

For about 10 x 350g jars:
700g cooking apples, peeled, cored and chopped
700g 'no-soak' dried apricots, stoned and chopped
400g onions, chopped
250g sultanas
250g toasted hazelnuts, halved
800g soft light brown sugar
40g mixed spice
2 teaspoons cardamom seeds
About 4cm piece of fresh root ginger, peeled and chopped
Salt, to taste
800ml cider vinegar

Put all the ingredients into a large pan. Stir and heat gently until the sugar has dissolved. Simmer gently for about 1½ hours, stirring from time to time and watching carefully to make sure that it doesn't catch on the bottom.

When the chutney thickens, but before all the excess liquid has evaporated, take it off the heat. (It will thicken a bit as it cools.)

Allow it to cool for about 10 minutes before spooning it into warm jars that have been sterilised by being boiled in a pan of water for 10 minutes or run through the dishwasher. Cover with waxed discs and seal. Label and date the jars.

Stored in a cool place, this should last for a year. Once opened, keep it in the fridge.

Prunes in Armagnac

Prunes in Armagnac are invaluable at Christmas. They are brilliant with savouries such as foie gras (see page 158) and puddings (see page 227). They are at their best after six weeks, so it's worth preparing them in advance. If you're going to stay with people for Christmas, they make an excellent present. Use a reasonable-quality Armagnac – it makes all the difference to the taste.

For 1 large (1.5 litres) jar:
Approximately 0.5 litres freshly made warm tea, such as Earl Grey
700g pitted prunes
100g caster sugar
3–4 strips of lemon peel
1 vanilla pod
Armagnac (enough to cover the prunes)

Pour the tea over the prunes and leave them to soak for about 12 hours or overnight. Drain the prunes and put into a large warm jar or two smaller ones that have been sterilised by being boiled in a pan of water for 10 minutes or run through the dishwasher.

Put the sugar, lemon peel and vanilla pod (split lengthways) into a small saucepan with 500ml water. Dissolve the sugar over a gentle heat and then bring to the boil and simmer for 2–3 minutes. Remove from the heat and strain the syrup over the prunes in the jar.

When it is quite cool, fill up the jar with Armagnac, making sure it completely covers the prunes, and seal securely. Label and date the jars.

Turn the jar several times to combine the Armagnac with the syrup, and leave it in a cool dark place for at least 6 weeks before serving. The longer you leave them, the punchier they will taste. You can store this for at least a year.

Homemade sweets

Candied peel, fruit or ginger dipped in chocolate

Candied peel – the sulphurous, mass-produced cheap, diced version that you buy in little pots – can be rather disgusting. That's not what you're after. What you want are large crystallised slices of identifiable fruit, such as orange, lemon and grapefruit. (You can make your own candied peel or slices of candied fruit, but it's a bit of a palaver.) Decent-sized chunks of crystallised ginger are also delicious dipped in chocolate in the same way.

These (and the peppermint creams, right) are dead easy and very good for children to make as presents, but the chocolate will start going cloudy after a couple of weeks unless you temper it (a complicated process that involves altering the texture and gloss of the chocolate by heating and cooling). This is a fiddle, so recommend to whoever you give them to that they eat them straight away.

For 30 sweets:
**150g dark chocolate
(70% cocoa solids)
30 slices of candied fruit or peel,
or 30 decent-sized chunks of
crystallised ginger**

Melt the chocolate in a bain-marie. Dip the fruit slices, peel or ginger halfway into the melted chocolate and then leave on a sheet of greaseproof paper to set.

Store in an airtight container until you want to portion them up into presents in boxes (such as Camembert boxes – see page 16).

Peppermint creams dipped in chocolate

This is a speciality of Margaret Rice, the eleven-year-old daughter of my friends Matthew and Emma. Margaret makes them every year for her grandparents and gives packets of them to her friends at school.

For about 30 creams:
**225g icing sugar, sifted
The white of 1 large egg
Peppermint oil
150g dark chocolate
(70% cocoa solids)**

Sift the icing sugar. Beat the egg white until frothy but not stiff, and gradually add the sifted icing sugar, mixing thoroughly with a wooden spoon until the paste becomes thick and smooth.

Shake some icing sugar on to your work surface and put the paste in the middle. Drop 4–5 drops of peppermint oil (the amount depending on how strong you want it) on to the paste and knead it into the paste until it is really smooth. Divide the paste into balls the size of hazelnuts and flatten each one with the back of a fork. Put these on to a sheet of greaseproof paper and allow to dry for a few hours or overnight.

Melt the chocolate in a bain-marie and dip the peppermint creams halfway into the melted chocolate. Then leave to set again on the greaseproof paper.

Store them in an airtight container until you have collected enough boxes (such as Camembert boxes – see page 16) to portion them into presents.

Fruit and nut chocolate cartwheel

In good Italian food shops you see lots of these chocolate circles studded with nuts in the build-up to Christmas, and they make ideal presents. They are another easy thing for children to make and to give away to family and friends; you can make some with chocolate and some with caramel (see right). If you want to make a cartwheel well before Christmas, use caramel, as the chocolate goes cloudy after a week or two.

Neither white nor milk chocolate works with these, as they don't have enough cocoa solids and go grainy in texture on heating, so use dark chocolate.

For a 20cm cartwheel:
> **200g hazelnuts, Brazils or**
> **almonds**
> **300g dark chocolate**
> **(70% cocoa solids)**
> **1 tablespoon butter**
> **1 tablespoon golden syrup**
> **75g sour cherries (optional)**
> **Vegetable oil, to grease tin**

If you're using Brazil nuts, coarsely chop them. Toast the nuts briefly in a medium oven (190°C/gas mark 5) and then place the chocolate, butter and golden syrup in a bain-marie over a low heat and melt very slowly. Add the nuts and cherries (if using). Stir gently to combine.

Rub a trace of vegetable oil around the ring of a 20cm loose-bottomed sandwich tin. Remove the base of the tin and stand the ring on greaseproof paper rubbed with a trace of sunflower oil, or a silicone mat. Pour the chocolate mixture into the circle and smooth the top. Once it has cooled a little, use a knife to score the surface with lines like the spokes of a wheel. Allow it to get quite cold.

Run a sharp knife round the edge and remove the ring. Wrap in cellophane or decorated paper.

Nut caramel cartwheel

Nuts and caramel make a delicious combination. As well as eaten straight, this is good broken up and scattered over ice cream or trifle (see page 200).

For a 20cm cartwheel:
> **200g hazelnuts, Brazils or**
> **almonds**
> **Vegetable oil, to grease tin**
> **230g granulated sugar**
> **½ teaspoon cream of tartar**
> **1 teaspoon vanilla extract**

If you're using Brazil nuts, coarsely chop them. Toast the nuts briefly in a medium oven (190°C/gas mark 5).

Rub a trace of vegetable oil around the ring of a 20cm loose-bottomed sandwich tin. Remove the base of the tin and stand the ring on greaseproof paper rubbed with a trace of sunflower oil, or a silicone mat. Fill the circle with the toasted nuts in a single layer. This takes time, but makes it easier later on.

Make the caramel by combining the sugar, cream of tartar, vanilla extract and 6 tablespoons of water together in a small saucepan. Heat gently to dissolve the sugar, and then raise the temperature and boil until light golden brown. Remove the caramel from the heat and pour it over the nuts. Once it has cooled a little, use a knife to score the surface with lines like the spokes of a wheel to indicate sections. It will set very quickly.

Allow the cartwheel to cool completely, run a sharp knife round the edge and remove the ring. Wrap in cellophane or decorated paper. This will keep for several months.

Strawberry or raspberry white chocolate truffles

These are an inspired invention of my twin sister, Jane, using fruit harvested and frozen from her Edinburgh allotment. Charbonnel & Walker's coarse drinking chocolate is ideal for the coating. I'd recommend Green and Black's for the white chocolate (theirs is made with vanilla).

For about 40 truffles:
> **150g strawberries or raspberries,**
> **fresh or frozen**
> **60g dried strawberries or**
> **raspberries (available from**
> **good delis/health food shops)**
> **400g white chocolate**
> **50g unsalted butter**
> **50g full-fat crème fraîche**
> **Milk chocolate flakes or**
> **drinking chocolate**

Put the fruit in a saucepan and cook over a gentle heat until reduced to about a tablespoon of intensely flavoured pulp; this will take about 30 minutes if they are frozen, fewer if fresh. (If using raspberries, push through a sieve to get rid of the pips.)

Meanwhile, chop the dried fruit into pieces as small as possible.

Melt the chocolate in a bain-marie over a low heat. Remove from the heat and add the butter, cut into chunks. Stir until it has melted. Then add the strawberry or raspberry pulp, dried fruit and crème fraîche, and stir again. Allow the mixture to cool and then put it in the fridge or freezer until it is hard enough to roll into balls.

Roll it into balls between the palms of both hands. Put the balls back in the fridge or freezer until hard and keep in the fridge until you want to serve them. (They will last for at least a couple of weeks if kept chilled.) Before serving, roll each ball around on a plate of chocolate flakes or drinking chocolate until coated.

Easy chocolate truffles

These are genuinely easy and very delicious. The mixture takes just a few minutes to make. They store well in the fridge for about ten days, so you can make them a little before Christmas – but coat them in the cocoa and pistachios just before you eat.

For about 20 truffles:
150g dark chocolate (70% cocoa solids)
150ml double cream
2 tablespoons brandy or rum (optional)
1 heaped tablespoon pistachio kernels
1 tablespoon good-quality cocoa powder

Break the chocolate into pieces. Place the cream in a small saucepan and bring to simmering point. Take off the heat, add the chocolate and brandy or rum (if you want it) and stir together until you have a smooth mixture. Transfer to a bowl, leave to cool, cover with cling film and put in the fridge overnight.

Next day remove the mixture from the fridge and roll it into little balls. Meanwhile toast the pistachios in a medium oven (190°C/gas mark 5) until they are just beginning to brown, and then chop them up quite finely.

Just before you eat them, roll half the chocolates in cocoa powder and half in the toasted chopped pistachios (see picture on page 17).

Rose Turkish delight

In my view, as well as tasting quite delicious, Turkish delight has a wonderful texture and looks beautiful; but to my children, it's a mouthful of rose-flavoured soap. If you know someone who appreciates it, this makes a lovely Christmas present.

For about 60 x 4cm squares:
Vegetable oil, to grease baking sheet
50g powdered gelatine
8 teaspoons rose water
900g caster sugar
50g whole pistachio nuts
4–6 drops of natural red food colouring
2 teaspoons cornflour
6 tablespoons icing sugar

Lightly oil a baking sheet measuring approximately 23cm x 30cm. Mix the gelatine, 310ml water and the rose water in a large saucepan and add the sugar. Warm this over a gentle heat and stir until the sugar and gelatine have completely dissolved. Bring to the boil without stirring and then simmer for approximately 20 minutes.

Remove from the heat, add the nuts and food colouring, stir and then leave the mixture to cool for a couple of minutes. Pour it on to the baking sheet and leave to set for 24 hours. Cut into squares.

Sift the cornflour (which helps to keep it dry) and icing sugar together and toss the squares of Turkish delight in it.

Stored in an airtight container, layered with greaseproof paper, this will last at least a year.

Homemade biscuits

Florentines

These Florentines are delicious eaten on their own, or broken up in vanilla ice cream (see page 172). I prefer them without the chocolate, but it does help to hold them together.

For about 30 small Florentines:
135g unsalted butter
2 tablespoons golden syrup
    or runny honey
150g caster sugar
50ml double cream
20g plain flour
100g flaked almonds
50g whole blanched almonds,
    chopped
30g pistachio nuts, toasted
    (see page 34) and chopped
65g candied peel (see page 31)
    and glacé cherries, chopped
100g sultanas
150g dark chocolate (optional)

Melt the butter, golden syrup or honey, sugar and cream in a small saucepan over a gentle heat and bring slowly to the boil. Remove from the heat, add the remaining ingredients (apart from the chocolate), stirring thoroughly, and leave to cool.

Preheat the oven to 180°C/gas mark 4.

Put small spoonfuls of the mixture on to greaseproof paper rubbed with a trace of sunflower oil, or a silicone mat on a baking tray, leaving plenty of space between each, and flatten them with the back of a spoon. Bake in the preheated oven until golden; this will take about 15 minutes. Re-shape them if necessary while they are still warm and allow to cool on the paper. When cold, remove them from the paper with a palette knife.

Melt the chocolate, if using, in a bain-marie. With a palette knife, smooth the chocolate over one side of the Florentines. Allow to set hard.

Put the Florentines in an airtight container. They will last for weeks.

Orange, cranberry and walnut biscuits

I'm not generally a biscuit person, but these are incredibly quick to put together – so they make an excellent, last-minute, homemade Christmas present. They're also good to eat with any ice cream.

For about 12 biscuits:
75g caster sugar
75g unsalted butter
1 egg
150g plain flour
50g candied orange peel,
    chopped (see page 31)
50g dried cranberries
50g walnut pieces
Zest of 1 orange
1 tablespoon orange juice

Combine all the ingredients and mix well. Put the soft dough into a piece of cling film. Then roll it into a sausage shape and chill for an hour or so.

Preheat the oven to 180°C/gas mark 4.

Unwrap the dough and slice it into 12 thick rounds. Place these well apart on a baking sheet – greased or lined with greaseproof paper rubbed with a trace of sunflower oil, or a silicone mat – and bake in the preheated oven for about 10 minutes. Leave to cool on the sheet for a few minutes before moving to a rack.

Store in an airtight container. They will keep for a couple of weeks.

Gingerbread house

Over Christmas in Scandinavia almost every home has one of these in their hall or porch. They range in size from modest gingerbread cottages to huge, lavishly decorated mansions that fill a whole table. You can buy kits with gingerbread building blocks already made for you to assemble, but if you have time, make your own one weekend before Christmas, either using your own paper pattern, or a bought one.

These houses make wonderful presents for children to build themselves. I love them simply iced, with a snowy dusting of icing sugar on the roof, but if you're making one with young children, just stud the whole thing with sweets. The ingredient quantities below make the middle-sized house shown opposite (with quite a bit left over for trees and reindeer for the garden, and some biscuit decorations for the tree). For a small house, use half the ingredients and for a large one, at least double.

You will need a piping bag and a cake board. The house opposite has a 30cm x 50cm board, leaving plenty of room for a garden.

For the gingerbread dough:
450g runny honey
4 eggs
350g caster sugar
1kg plain flour
Zest of 1 lemon and 1 orange
100g ground almonds
100g ground hazelnuts
8 teaspoons ground mixed spice
Pinch of salt
2 teaspoons bicarbonate of soda

For the toffee:
225g white caster sugar

For the royal icing:
2 egg whites, beaten until frothy
450g icing sugar
Juice of 1 lemon

Heat the honey gently. Beat the eggs and sugar until fluffy, add the warm honey, and then combine the wet mixture with the remaining dry ingredients. Fold them gently together and knead into a soft dough. Wrap the dough in cling film and leave it in the fridge for 24 hours.

Preheat the oven to 180°C/gas mark 4.

Roll out the dough thinly (approximately 5mm thick) and cut it into the shapes of your pattern.

Put the sections on greaseproof paper rubbed with a trace of sunflower oil, or a silicone mat. Bake each section in the preheated oven for about 10 minutes until golden brown and leave to cool on a wire rack. The gingerbread will cool to a crisp biscuit.

The dough will keep for up to 4 weeks in the fridge. If you have any left over, make biscuits and shapes to hang on your tree (see page 40).

When you're ready to construct the house, make the toffee to use as glue. Melt the sugar slowly in a saucepan until it starts to brown. Take care not to let it burn. Pour the toffee into a measuring jug, and from there into the piping bag. Take care not to touch the toffee as it will be exceptionally hot. (To be extra safe, use heat-proof gloves.) Pipe the toffee out of the bag, using it to stick one bit of the house to the next.

Next make the royal icing for the base and snow on the roof. Whisk the beaten egg whites until frothy but not stiff, and mix in 2 tablespoons of icing sugar and the lemon juice to make a paste. Gradually add the rest of the icing sugar until the icing is soft and white and holds its shape. If the mix is still sloppy, add more icing sugar.

First spread the icing all over the base board quite thickly – like snow – using it to hold the walls in place. Then pipe it on to the house. For the one opposite, I iced the tops of the windows and ridge of the roof and then dusted the whole thing with icing sugar.

If you let it, the gingerbread house will keep for months.

Gingerbread biscuits for your tree

In Germanic countries, people make lots of edible things to decorate their trees. The gingerbread recipe on page 39 is ideal for making these. You can make gingerbread men, stars, mini iced trees, reindeers and angels – whatever shapes you have cutters for.

For 25–30 decorations:
   **Half quantity of gingerbread
      dough (see page 39)**
   Ribbon, for tying to the tree

For the royal icing:
   1 egg white, beaten until frothy
   225 icing sugar
   Juice of ½ lemon

Preheat the oven to 180°C/gas mark 4.
   Roll the dough out thinly (approximately 5mm thick) and cut it into shapes, remembering to make holes in the tops for the ribbons.
   Place the shapes on lightly oiled greaseproof paper or a silicone mat and bake for 10 minutes in the preheated oven until golden brown. Leave to cool on a wire rack.
   Mix the icing ingredients as above and, using a piping bag, decorate each of your shapes. Thread some ribbon through the holes and store in an airtight container until you're ready to decorate your tree. Stored airtight, these will still be good to eat at least a month after making.

Chocolate and ginger crisps

A tower of these crisp, thin biscuits – wrapped in cellophane – is a wonderful present. They are quick and easy to make, and as good with a cup of tea as they are with simple fruit puddings such as poached pears (see page 168) or ice cream. Make a delicious variation by using chopped pecan nuts rather than hazelnuts and replacing the dark chocolate with white.

For about 20 crisps:
   90g plain flour
   ½ teaspoon baking powder
   ½ teaspoon bicarbonate of soda
   60g unsalted butter
   40g caster sugar
   ½ piece of stem ginger, chopped
   1 dessertspoon ginger syrup
   **25g good dark chocolate
      (70% cocoa solids) or white
      chocolate, broken into pieces**
   25g hazelnuts or pecans, chopped
   **Zest and juice of ½ lemon
      (optional)**

Sift the flour with the baking powder and bicarbonate of soda. Cream the butter with the sugar until pale and light, and add the flour, chopped ginger, ginger syrup, chocolate, hazelnuts or pecans and lemon zest and juice, if using. Cover and chill for an hour or so. Put the dough into a piece of cling film, roll it into a sausage shape and chill again for another 30 minutes.
   Preheat the oven to 200°C/gas mark 6.
   Unwrap the roll and slice it into 20 rounds. Place them well apart on a baking sheet – greased or lined with greaseproof paper rubbed with a trace of sunflower oil, or a silicone mat – and bake in the preheated oven for about 10 minutes. Leave to cool on the sheet for a few minutes before moving to a rack. Store in an airtight container. They will keep for a couple of weeks.

Drinks for the larder

Damson or sloe vodka or gin

This is ideal for drinking with Banbury cakes (see page 22) and Lancashire cheese, and it's excellent for adding flavour to your mincemeat (see page 22). For the final bottling, collect unusual-shaped, pretty bottles.

For a 750ml bottle:
450g damsons or sloes
710ml vodka or gin
250g caster sugar
Handful of roasted almonds

Make sure that the damsons or sloes are dry and remove any stems. Prick each fruit with a fork. If you're doing a large batch and can't face pricking every one, put the damsons in the freezer overnight and then you won't need to prick them. With sloes, a frost will have the same effect, so wait until it's been frosty before collecting them; this breaks the skins, but doesn't affect the flavour. Put the damsons or sloes into a large, clean jar. Add the vodka or gin, the sugar and the roasted almonds.

Seal the jar tightly and put in a dark place for 2–3 months, turning it as often as you remember – ideally every few days – until the sugar has completely dissolved.

Then strain the liquid and discard the almonds and sloes or damsons. (Discarded damsons are delicious eaten on top of ice cream or yoghurt.) Taste the vodka or gin and check that it's sweet enough. I prefer it not too sweet, so I use less sugar than you'll see in other recipes, but you can add a little more if you wish. When adding sugar, turn the jar vigorously until it dissolves. Pour the vodka or gin through a funnel into a dry, warm bottle (sterilised as above) and seal. Label and date the bottle. It will keep indefinitely.

Lemon vodka

This has a strong lemony taste and is slightly sweet. I like to drink it as a shot, and it's excellent as a 'sauce' poured over a glass of blood orange sorbet (see page 172). In fact, a topping of flavoured vodka with almost any sorbet makes a quick and delicious light pudding for when you fancy something sweet but not too filling.

Cranberry makes another good flavoured vodka, with a lovely bright red colour. Use this recipe, replacing the lemon zest with 100g fresh cranberries to 750ml vodka.

For 20 small glasses:
2 large or 3 small lemons
750ml bottle of vodka
1 tablespoon clear honey

Pare the rind from the lemons, aiming to get the yellow skin without too much of the white pith. Add this to the bottle of vodka and then the honey, and give it a good shake. Leave to infuse at room temperature for 2 weeks and then strain. If you leave the rind in much longer, it will give a bitter taste. Label and date the bottle. Store in the freezer and it will keep indefinitely.

Chilli vodka

My favourite of all flavoured vodkas. It has a clean, bright taste, but doesn't take your head off. It is perfect for drinking as shots with blinis and smoked fish – or caviar if you're lucky – on Christmas Eve.

For 20 small glasses:
3 small red chillies or 1 long red chilli
750ml bottle of vodka

Slice the chillies and remove the seeds. Add the chillies to the bottle of vodka. Leave to infuse at room temperature for 24 hours and then strain. If you want it hotter, use one long thin chilli, cut in half lengthways and deseeded. Submerge it in the vodka and leave it in for decoration, as I do. This means the vodka will get gradually hotter, so don't wait too long to drink it. (If it does get too hot, just dilute with pure vodka.)

Label and date each bottle. Once you've infused the flavours, store the vodka in the freezer before drinking. It will keep indefinitely.

Rosehip syrup

Rosehip syrup, made with hedgerow rosehips, is delicious, particularly with the additional spicy flavours of cinnamon, cloves and star anise. It is also famously full of vitamin C, and so excellent for drinking through the winter to keep colds and flu at bay. It tastes good as a cold or hot drink (diluted five parts to one with water), or drizzled over ice cream. Make plenty for yourself and some extra bottles to give away. Use small bottles, as the syrup will not keep for more than a week or two once it's been opened.

For 2 x 500ml bottles:
1kg rosehips
2 cinnamon sticks, broken up (optional)
6 cloves (optional)
3 star anise (optional)
450g granulated sugar

Crush the rosehips. Bring 1.7 litres water to the boil in a large saucepan. Tip the rosehips into it and bring back to the boil. Then remove from the heat and allow to stand for 30 minutes or so to infuse before straining through a jelly bag or muslin bag. Leave the liquid to stand. Bring a further 800ml water to the boil in another saucepan and add the pulp from the jelly bag. Bring back to the boil and infuse and strain as before. Mix the two extracts together in a clean pan. Add the spices if using and boil over a brisk heat until the volume has reduced by half.

Add 450g sugar to this and stir over a gentle heat until the sugar has completely dissolved before boiling hard for 5 minutes. Strain and pour into small, warm bottles that have been sterilised by being boiled in a pan of water for 10 minutes or run through the dishwasher. Seal, label and date the bottles.

Unopened, this will keep for months. Once open, store in the fridge and drink within a couple of weeks.

Pink grapefruit cordial

This cordial is a wonderful colour and not too sweet, with a clean, refreshing taste. It's a good winter alternative to elderflower. I like it best diluted about one part to four with fizzy water.

Its flavour goes well with mint and sage, so serve it with plenty of ice and a sprig of either herb. A splash of this cordial makes a great addition to gin or vodka and tonic.

For about 3 litres:
6 pink grapefruit
1.8 litres boiling water
1.7 kg white sugar (granulated or caster)
50g citric or tartaric acid

Scrub the skins of the grapefruit in hot water to remove any wax. With a swivel potato peeler, cut ribbons of rind from the fruit, leaving the white pith behind.

Put the rind into a heatproof bowl and pour over the boiling water. Stir in the sugar, keeping the water moving until the sugar has dissolved. Leave the mixture to cool and then add the juice from the grapefruit and the citric or tartaric acid, and steep overnight, covered.

Next day, strain off the rind. Pour the cordial through a funnel into small, warm bottles that have been sterilised by being boiled in a pan of water for 10 minutes or run through the dishwasher. Seal, label and date the bottles.

The cordial will store for about a month in the fridge, or you can pour it into clean plastic milk cartons and freeze.

Forced bulbs
for Christmas

A twinkly, colourful, fragrant house is all part of the Christmas ritual, and you can start preparations for this several months before. From September onwards, start forcing pots of bulbs to bloom all around your house. Hyacinths in particular take their time (see page 46). Most early-flowering narcissi and crocus (see page 50) won't flower for Christmas unless planted in September. You need to plant even the galloping-grower *Narcissus* 'Paper White' in November if you are to coach it into flower by December (see page 53).

Forced bulbs also make great presents. Plant amaryllis (see page 59), anemones (see page 56), freesias, tulips or more unusual spring-flowering bulbs such as miniature *Iris reticulata* (see page 54) and you'll have a fantastic range for anyone who loves scent and colour. These probably won't be in flower by Christmas, but will carry the promise of coming out soon.

Although I wouldn't feel particularly happy if someone gave me a mass-produced, imported bowl or basket of bulbs from a supermarket or garden centre, I'd love it if they'd chosen some spring bulbs and then planted up a bowl or painted wooden box themselves. These don't have to be expensive. A drift of narcissi, hyacinths and amaryllis growing in a wide, shallow bowl – picked up in a bric-a-brac or antique shop – is as good as it gets, and it doesn't matter two hoots if the bowl is chipped. If you're planting your bulbs in a container without holes, it's best to use bulb fibre. This contains charcoal which keeps the compost 'sweet' and prevents it from putrefying.

If you can't face the palaver of planting the bulbs yourself, buy them ready planted and then re-pot and doctor them so that they look good. Even before there's any sign of a flower, all these will provide weeks or months of pleasure, through the rest of winter and into spring.

Hyacinths

Bulbs to flower at Christmas

One hyacinth flower can fill a warm room with scent, so spread hyacinths all over the house. White hyacinths are wonderful, but the beetroot-purple 'Woodstock' and brilliant pink 'Jan Bos' win the day for me. I also love the dark blues, which are the quickest to force and have the strongest scents. 'Peter Stuyvesant' and 'Kronos' are my current favourites: deep and deliciously fragant, and ideal for forcing.

12 hyacinth bulbs
Container 40cm long x 30cm
    wide x 20cm deep
Several handfuls of crocks or grit
    (if your container has holes)
Planting medium – two-thirds
    soil-based compost, one-third
    grit, or bulb fibre (see below)
5 x 60cm silver birch twigs
2 handfuls of dried leaves
    or moss

You can buy prepared bulbs that have been pre-chilled and then released in time for flowering at Christmas, or you can buy ordinary garden hyacinths and prepare them yourself. To do this, you need to begin early. Put them in a paper bag in the bottom of the fridge in August for 4–6 weeks. Then plant them and start the forcing process.

To guarantee flowers, plant the hyacinths at least 12 weeks before Christmas. I wear gloves when handling the bulbs as they can cause a strong skin reaction.

If your container has drainage holes, lay 2.5cm of grit or crocks in the bottom, and then add a shallow layer of soil and grit mix. In a contained pot with no holes in the bottom, it's best to use bulb fibre.

Place the bulbs on the planting medium, 3–4cm apart. Backfill with the same planting medium, leaving the pointy bulb tip just protruding from the soil surface. After planting, keep the compost moist, but not dripping wet, as hyacinth bulbs are prone to rot.

Once planted, hyacinths need a spell in the cold and dark to flower well, at a temperature below 10°C for about 12 weeks. A cold cupboard, potting shed or garage is ideal. The cold fools them into thinking it's winter, and when they are brought into the warm it breaks the bulbs' dormancy, so they flower early. The darkness is also important, as it gives the root time to develop before the light pulls the flower and leaves from the bulb. (The problem with quick-to-market, bought hyacinths is that they haven't had a spell in darkness. They begin to bloom when brought inside, but the under-developed root can't quite push the flowers and leaves out of the bulb.)

Once they've had their cool, dark period, and each has a shoot at least 4cm tall, you can bring your hyacinths in somewhere warmer (above 15°C) and they will start to grow more quickly and bloom within 2–3 weeks. As they grow, the foliage and flower buds will need supporting. To stop them flopping about, make them a nest of twigs. Poke some sticks in – good and sturdy – all through the pot and scatter dried leaves or clumps of moss in any gaps.

When the hyacinths are in flower, water them frequently to maximise their shelf life. You may get two flowers from each bulb, with a smaller flower spike often following on as the first goes over. Once the first has browned, cut it down to soil level to make room for the next.

Once they've flowered, plant them out in the garden, leaves and all. Their food stores will be depleted by the forcing process and they may not flower well next year, but should do so for years after that.

Hyacinths in glass forcers

Hyacinths grow just as well with their roots in water as they do in soil. For the most beautiful effect, force lots of hyacinths, using different-coloured glass vases. When you bring them inside, backlight your collection to highlight the containers as well as the flowers and create a stained-glass effect. Spread them out all over a window ledge or down the centre of a brightly lit table. With low winter sun at Christmas, you'll have brilliant shafts of Venetian-coloured light radiating into the room.

By the way, although it's tempting to buy hyacinths already forced in compost and wash the roots before placing them on a hyacinth forcer, it doesn't really work. Without the roots growing in situ, they won't go deep enough to secure the top-heavy bulb firmly on to the top of the forcer and the bulb will fall all over the place and often end up on the floor.

Several hyacinth bulbs
A series of different-coloured glass hyacinth forcers (or any narrow bottle where you can jam a bulb in the neck)

Fill the forcing jars up with water so that the water is just below the basal plate of the bulb when you sit the bulb on top. As the roots begin to grow, they will touch the water and this will encourage them to grow faster. Keep the water topped up to the same level.

The process of forcing hyacinths in water is much the same as in soil (see page 46). They need a period in the dark as well as the cold (at a temperature below 10°C for 12 weeks). If you can't find anywhere dark, make mini-cone paper hats to cover the top of the bulb. This works almost as well as all-round proper dark. Once the shoots are up about 4cm, you can bring them into the light and warm.

Crocus

If you fancy growing some crocus inside, these should be next on your list after hyacinths. I force the more delicate varieties – *C. tommasinianus* and *C. vernus* – in time for Christmas or soon after. Once they're up and out, place them beside a bed or on a desk, where you can look down into the delicate flowers. The beauty of forcing crocus inside is that they remain pristine: with no birds, wind or rain to contend with, they will flourish for several weeks.

With crocus, you can use standard, untreated garden bulbs and they should produce a succession of 3–4 flowers from each. They work well in fine, shallow terracotta bulb trays and in mini glass forcers.

15 crocus bulbs
Shallow bulb tray 20cm diameter at top x 10cm deep
Bulb planting medium – two-thirds soil-based compost, one-third grit, or bulb fibre
Crocks or grit
Or:
One crocus bulb per mini glass forcer

If planting your crocus in a bulb tray, plant them up in August or early September. Put some crocks or grit in the bottom and cram them in with a couple of centimetres between each bulb, filling around them with a mix of grit and soil-based compost (or use bulb fibre). Then keep them somewhere cold and dark, at a temperature below 10°C, for 12 weeks, before bringing them into the warm. They should be in flower by Christmas, about 6 weeks earlier than they would outside.

Single crocus bulbs also work brilliantly in mini bulb forcers – a series of them looks good as a centrepiece running down the middle of a table. To do this, store the bulbs in a bag at the bottom of the fridge or somewhere cold and dark until 6 weeks before Christmas. Then place each bulb on the glass of the forcer and fill with water to just below the bulb. This leaves the basal plate dry, but the roots will quickly access the water as they grow. If the water level is too high, it will rot the basal plate. Put the crocus somewhere bright and warm and change the water at least once a week.

Whether grown in a pot or a glass forcer, once they've flowered plant your crocus out in the garden for another year.

Narcissus 'Paper White' table centre

This is the most successful, long-lived Christmas table centre I have ever made: a great tiered fountain of scented 'Paper White' narcissi. Kept cool in my greenhouse, it looked good for nearly a month.

Most narcissus varieties take 16–18 weeks from planting to flowering, but not 'Paper White'. These, I've found, need only 8–10 weeks in my frost-free but cold polytunnel (or 4–6 weeks somewhere a little warmer at about 10–15°C). Narcissi do not require a period in the dark to force them, and if you don't get round to planting them yourself, you can buy pots of them at the last minute. With buds already formed, they will come into flower reliably within a week or two in the warm.

There are several other 'Tazetta' varieties which, if you got on with planting them in late summer and bring them into the warm house about three weeks before Christmas, will be in flower by then too. I force 'Erlicheer', 'Avalanche' and 'Silver Chimes'. All these need a spell in the cold to flower well, at a temperature below 10°C.

If you don't have the room for a 'Paper White' arrangement like this, still make a few pots with seven or eight bulbs in each to scatter round the house. You can do these in glass containers full of pebbles and water, with no compost. This alternative looks modern and crisp.

3 pots of decreasing size (see below)
60 Narcissus 'Paper White' bulbs (see below)
Planting medium – two-thirds soil-based compost, one-third grit, or bulb fibre
Bunch of silver birch or hazel twigs, 1m long
Silver and clear-glass baubles, and candles, to decorate
Crocks and a very large platter

You will need as large a pot or bowl as you can fit in the middle of your table to form the base of the arrangement (mine is huge – 60cm wide at the top x 20cm deep), with a smaller one stacked on top and then a final one on top of that, small enough for the bulbs in the next layer down to encircle it. Narcissus bulbs are large, with an extensive root structure, so deep pots are ideal.

You can plant the bulbs in plastic pots, five to a pot (or buy them already planted), and then move them into your final table centre as they come into flower, or plant them straight into their final pots from the start.

Plant the bulbs just below the soil surface, about 2.5cm apart, into a soil-based compost lightened with some grit, with crocks at the bottom of the pot (or use bulb fibre). Store them somewhere cold, at a temperature below 10°C. Keep the compost moist, but not dripping wet.

Once the bulbs really start to shoot, with leaves up to 20–25cm, bring them into the warm. If they're still in plastic pots, transfer them into your three final pots. (Place a large platter underneath the largest pot.) Add the bulbs to the pots layer by layer, packing them in as thickly as you can with more of the planting medium.

If you've planted them straight into the final pots, then just assemble them at the table. Poke in a handful of silver birch or hazel twigs around the bulbs in every layer to support them. This looks lovely and staves off collapse. Water as and when the compost begins to dry out.

As a final touch, hang silver and clear glass baubles on the twigs and surround the whole thing with a halo of candles on the table. With this on your Christmas dining table, who needs a Christmas tree?

Once it's all over, bear in mind that Narcissus 'Paper White' are not hardy. But don't chuck them: store them. When they've finished flowering, leave them in their pots for the following year, or dry them off, leaving the leaves to shrivel on the bulb, and re-pot them again late next year. I've had the same 'Paper White' bulbs flowering every winter for the past 3 years.

Miniature iris

**Bulbs to give
as presents**

I love the mini *Iris reticulata*, with
its deep rich colour and magnificent
velvet texture. Unfortunately, thrushes
and blackbirds love it too, gobbling
whole flower heads. It's heartbreaking
– just as they come up, they go –
so now I only grow them in pots for
flowering inside. The golden yellow
I. danfordiae is another lovely
miniature variety, with the added
bonus of scent. I haven't yet managed
to have either of these in flower by
Christmas, but from a September
planting, they're not far off. All
wrapped up beautifully in clear
cellophane, a shallow bulb tray full
of silvery buds and grey-green leaves
makes a good present.

> **10 *Iris reticulata* bulbs**
> **Deep square bulb tray 20cm long**
>   **x 20cm wide x 10cm deep**
>   **(these bulbs are small)**
> **Bulb planting medium –**
>   **two-thirds soil-based compost,**
>   **one-third grit, or bulb fibre**
> **Moss, to carpet the surface**
> **A few twigs and dry leaves**
> **Crocks and a large plate**

Put crocks in the bottom of the tray
and plant the bulbs in a soil-based
compost, lightened with some grit
(or use bulb fibre), poking the small
bulbs in just below the soil surface.
    Like most bulbs, once planted
these iris need a spell in the cold and
dark (at a temperature below 10°C)
for 12–15 weeks to flower well. If the
compost is moist at the start, they will
need very little water, but check
occasionally that it has not dried out.
Once the shoots reach a couple of
centimetres, bring them into the warm
and put the pot on a plate. Cover the
surface with moss and scatter a
handful of leaves between the foliage.
As one flower collapses, others will
follow, giving them a flowering season
that will last about a month.

Instruct whoever is receiving
them that once the bulbs have
finished flowering, they can either
plant them out in the garden or force
them again next year. For the latter,
leave them against a wall or in a cold
frame in their pots undisturbed until
the early autumn. Then begin the
forcing process in the cold and dark
again, before bringing them in a week
or two before Christmas.

Anemone coronaria

The *Anemone coronaria* varieties are another fabulous group of bulbs for forcing. They have an exceptional texture, as well as beautiful colour, with the centre of the flower like a fleshy sea anemone in a rock pool. The single-flower single colours are the loveliest: 'Mr Fokker' (deep purple-blue), 'Hollandia' (bright red), 'Sylphide' (deep pink), 'The Bride' (pure white) and the brand-new 'Cristina' (crimson-purple – shown opposite). The more widely available mixed colour bags often include varieties in dull, muddy, greyish colours without the clarity and velvet texture of these more expensive named forms.

7 *Anemone coronaria* corms
Terracotta flowerpot, 20cm wide
    at the top x 20cm deep
Bulb planting medium –
    two-thirds soil-based compost,
    one-third grit
Crocks and a plate

Anemone coronaria varieties take 16–18 weeks from planting to flowering (including 6 weeks' chilling). Plant them in September and whoever you give them to will have flowers by mid-January.

Anemone corms look unlike any other bulb, like crinkly lumps of dry soil. Give the corms a squeeze: they should feel hard, almost like a stone. To get them off to a good start, soak them in water for a couple of hours before planting. Leave them in just long enough so that you can make a dent in the skin of the bulb with your fingernail.

A soil-based planting medium, lightened with some grit, is ideal. Put crocks in the bottom of the pot before the compost, and plant the bulbs about 4–5cm apart, 2.5cm deep, so that their tips are just below the compost surface.

After planting the corms, put the pot somewhere dark and cold for 6 weeks.

To flower best, after the 6 weeks have passed, they need bright light, a cool location and consistently moist (not wet) soil. Regular watering is key with anemones: don't let the compost dry out. Once the leaves are fully up and one or two flower buds are showing, bring them into the warm. You'll need a plate under the pot to protect your furniture.

Once in flower they should give you, or the person you are giving them to, a succession of blooms for well over a month.

When they've done their stuff, leave them where they are and they'll flower happily again next year, or dry them off and store for re-planting in a pot, greenhouse or sunny, sheltered spot in the garden next autumn.

Amaryllis

Amaryllis bulbs make a good Christmas present, but not all boxed up from the supermarket. Go a bit further and plant the bulbs yourself into a beautiful pot, bowl or urn. Just one statuesque single bulb looks good, but they're even better in a group of three or five. My sister was given a beautiful chipped bowl planted up with three huge amaryllis bulbs as a present twenty years ago and I remember it to this day.

The natural flowering time of this warm-climate, tender South African bulb is early spring. You can coax amaryllis into flower a bit earlier, but I've found it tricky to have them reliably in flower by Christmas. If you create a spectacular centrepiece, they will be lovely enough to look at with the flower bud still growing.

Try to get a pink and white, very early-flowering variety such as 'Apple Blossom' or a pure white, 'Mont Blanc' or 'Ludwig Dazzler'. I also love the latest glamorous varieties such as 'Royal Velvet', 'Bacchanal' or 'Tinto Nights' in deep velvet red. All these are several steps up from the more usual pillar-box 'Liberty' or brazen scarlet 'Red Lion'.

3 dry amaryllis bulbs
Ceramic bowl or similar
    container, or pot with crocks
    and plate (see below)
Bulb planting medium
    (see below)
Silver birch, alder, oak or hazel
    twigs, 60cm long

Amaryllis bulbs are huge (they can measure up to about 12cm across) and they like a tight fit in their pot, with about 2.5cm between the bulb and the side. If you're planting just one bulb, then use a container 15–20cm in diameter, and nearly twice that in depth. For 3–5 bulbs, the pot needs to be very big; mine is 50cm wide at the top and 20cm deep. Place the container on a plate.

Before planting, hydrate the desiccated bulb roots by soaking them in tepid tap water overnight: rest the base of the bulb on a jam jar, with all the roots, but not the bulb base, sitting in the water below.

Amaryllis are huge bulbs and have a tendency to rot, so drainage is vital. If planting in a pot, put a good handful of crocks in the bottom to help with drainage and then mix together equal parts of peat-free multi-purpose compost and horticultural grit or perlite and place the pot on a plate. If you're planting in a container without drainage holes, use bulb fibre. The shoulder of the bulb should sit one-third above the surface of the compost when you plant. This vulnerable part mustn't get wet on watering. Water from the top, using tepid tap water, and once the water has drained through into the plate, tip it away. If the container has no holes, water very conservatively.

To make the display look beautiful immediately, poke silver birch, alder, oak or hazel twigs between the bulbs. The twigs will give the amaryllis support as they grow – they'll need that or else they will flop about and break – and the burgeoning nest of twigs and soon-to-emerge shoots make a fantastic table centre even without the flowers.

Whichever way you plant them, these plants love warmth: 20°C is ideal in a light and well-ventilated place, free from draughts, such as a shelf above a radiator. Keep the compost moist until a shoot appears and then water more. If you, or the person you are giving them to, want to keep the bulb to grow again, this is also the time to start giving it a weak balanced liquid feed every month.

As soon as the flowers start to open, move the plant to a cooler place to prolong their life – 10–15°C is fine – with as much light as possible. Each flower stem should last about 3 weeks before it browns, but with a great big bulb, there should be at least 1–2 more flowering stems to come.

Even when the show is over for the year, all is not lost. To ensure the amaryllis bulbs flower next year, you need to encourage the foliage to photosynthesise as long as possible. As these are not hardy, don't plant them out in the garden. Cut the old flower spikes down but leave the foliage, keep them somewhere light and warm, and continue to feed and water. They also need a dry, dormant season, so once the leaves begin to die back in late summer, stop watering and allow the foliage to shrivel. Keep the bulbs completely dry in a garden shed or under a greenhouse bench until the autumn. When the temperature plummets to below 10°C, bring them into the warmth, begin gentle watering again and your bulbs will re-shoot.

Don't re-pot them for the first couple of years: they hate root disturbance and will thrive on being crowded.

Decorations

The Christmas tree

It's not every day that you have a tree inside, and Christmas is the time to go to town, so choose the biggest one possible. Of the widely available varieties, the Norway spruce is the cheapest. It is bright green with short needles, but these do start to drop after only a week. For this reason, avoid buying your Norway spruce too far in advance – it won't be looking good in three weeks' time – and purchase from a source that harvests the tree as close to the date of sale as possible.

Another popular variety is the Nordmann fir, a very dark green tree with short, soft needles. It is bushier and more generous, with a graceful shape and more space between branches than the Norway spruce. It has the advantage of being 'Hoover friendly'. Keep this one in a bucket of water and away from central heating. It will last inside for three or four weeks.

My favourite of the fir brigade is the blue spruce. It is a pale silvery blue with short, stiff, pointed needles, against which Christmas decorations look magical. It has a wonderful piney smell, which you notice as soon as you walk into the room. This tree is the longest lasting, looking good for a month, and is the best for making great swags and loops down your stairs and over the mantelpiece, being more heat and draught tolerant than the rest. However, it is the most expensive.

Of course, you do not have to have an evergreen at all; you could choose skeletal, elegant silver birch branches instead. Several of these arranged to make a mini copse or wood are perfect for a party (see page 120), and a single well-shaped branch makes an excellent alternative to a Christmas tree. This is a much greener option, as the birch will regenerate afterwards.

For me, there are two choices when decorating the tree. The first is to go for a peacock range of colours – turquoise, green, purple, deep red and a contrasting splash of magenta and orange. The alternative is to use deep red or purple with silver, as shown opposite. Silver has a brightness and sharpness to it, and is much more glamorous than gold. I use as much natural material as possible, and there is no better star for the top of your tree than an allium head sprayed silver (see page 65). I love making baubles from poppy seed heads, honesty, chillies and blown ducks' and quails' eggs (see pages 65–6). To these I add gingerbread shapes (see page 40), attaching them to the branches with purple ribbon. It mustn't get too perfectly tasteful, though – you need a bit of tinsel, some silver rain and fairy lights to give the tree depth and sparkle.

Tree decorations

Allium heads

Some of my favourite garden-harvested Christmas decorations are allium seed heads, of almost any size, sprayed either crimson or silver. Their structure is complex, with a ray of narrow stems, each one ending in a flower and then a seed head, the whole creating a dramatic silhouette. The football-sized *Allium schubertii* is the showiest (see page 177); the smaller varieties *A. cristophii* and *A.* 'Purple Sensation', as in the picture opposite, are more modest. Like the beans and artichoke buds on page 82, you can store these from one year to the next – the paint makes them less fragile. If your allium heads are already shot, agapanthus make an excellent alternative.

Seed heads of *Allium schubertii*, *A. cristophii* or *A.* 'Purple Sensation'
Silver or crimson spray paint
Ribbon (optional)

When spraying anything, it's a good idea to do so with adequate ventilation, gloves and acres of newspaper. (If you forget the gloves – as I have done before – and your fingers get covered in silver, clean your hands with a mixture of 2 tablespoons sugar, 1 tablespoon lemon juice and 1 tablespoon olive oil. This works brilliantly.)

Place your allium heads on the newspaper and spray with paint. Leave them to dry overnight, and then hang them on the tree with ribbon, or just throw them at it and they will attach!

Poppy seed head chains

Shaped liked bells, poppy seed heads are ideal for Christmas tree decorations. You can attach ribbon to them individually and hang them from the tree, or combine lots together into a chain. Honesty seed heads, sprayed silver or crimson in the same way and threaded together also work very well.

Poppy or honesty seed heads
Silver spray paint
Purple ribbon

When spraying anything, it's a good idea to do so with adequate ventilation, gloves and acres of newspaper. (If you forget the gloves – as I have done before – and your fingers get covered in silver, clean your hands with a mixture of 2 tablespoons sugar, 1 tablespoon lemon juice and 1 tablespoon olive oil. This works brilliantly.)

Place your poppy seed heads on the newspaper and spray with paint. Leave them to dry overnight.

Tie them so that they are evenly spaced down the length of 2–3m of purple ribbon. Lace these from the top to the bottom of the tree (or alternatively, down the length of your Christmas lunch table).

Chilli decorations

Chillis are very long lasting, and so make ideal Christmas decorations. Hanging from a tree, they will gradually dry, so you can store them away and use them from one year to the next. Fine silver bridal reel wire looks bright and clean against the red chilli shapes and – even if stored damp – won't rust.

Red chillies
Silver bridal reel wire

Use the silver bridal reel wire to attach the chillies to the tree. As the stems dry and shrink, they may come loose from their twist of wire, but this can just be tightened.

Duck eggs

I love ribbons studded with quails' eggs decorating a tree or table (see page 85) and the simplicity of single pale-blue and cream duck eggs hanging on a tree (see picture on page 63). If you make these and store them carefully, you'll have them for life.

Duck eggs
Bleach or vinegar, to rinse
Ribbon

To blow the eggs, make a little hole with a needle in the pointed end and an even smaller hole in the other. Hold the egg gently with your thumb and forefinger and carefully blow out – from the small hole end – the contents. If this doesn't happen easily, enlarge the hole in the pointed end and try again.

Once they're blown, if you want to keep the eggs, you must rinse them thoroughly in a bowl with bleach or vinegar to stop any smell, and then bake them in a cool oven for 15 minutes at about 150°C/gas mark 2. This hardens the eggs and dries them out thoroughly so that they won't go bad.

Thread a large darning needle with ribbon (ideally wired at the side so that you can bend it into shapes) and pull this through the small holes in each egg. Go up and through the egg once and then down again, leaving a good loop of ribbon from which you can hang the egg on to the tree.

Tie a knot in the ribbon, but leave a good section below the knot. Then with sharp scissors, split the bottom sections of ribbon into narrow strands and bend and twist them in all directions.

Kumquats

Kumquats – or any citrus – make excellent mini scented pomanders.

Kumquats
Cloves
Bright beaded wire

Stud the kumquats with cloves and then wrap a length of beaded wire around each one to hang it from the tree.

Flowers and foliage

It's hugely worth making a wreath – hanging one on your door tells visitors they're entering a house where Christmas is embraced and enjoyed. Limes, peppers, pomegranates, kumquats, mini Spartan apples and cranberries are perfect for wreaths and decorations, and all last well. If the spirit of Christmas has well and truly taken hold of you, and you can find lots of evergreens such as blue spruce and eucalyptus, use them to make delicious-scented swags to surround a door or run down the rail of a staircase (see page 80), which you can then decorate with fairy lights.

The first thing to do is go and have a look in your garden or a hedgerow. There may be things out there which you can pick: some crab apples or rosehips, a few branches of early alder or hazel catkins, pussy willow, or evergreens – ivy, eucalyptus, camellias and hebes. Do you grow any evergreen herbs – rosemary, sage, santolina, bay or lavender – particularly the pretty *Lavandula dentata*, which still looks bright and silvery at this time of year? *Prunus autumnalis*, *Viburnum bodnantense*, *V. tinus* and winter jasmine will all be in flower now, and these are perfect for light and delicate arrangements for mantelpieces, fireplaces and bedside tables (see page 90). It's worth growing these and winter ornamental shrubs such as spindle, callicarpa and *Viburnum tinus* 'French White', which has beautiful, gun-metal silver berries. Spindle berries can be linked together with Chinese lanterns in chains to hang in loops from a mantelpiece or to run down the middle of your Christmas table (see page 85). Only when you've exhausted your immediate surroundings should you go shopping.

The final thing, a day or two before Christmas, is to buy a few flowers for table decorations and arrangements around the house – see pages 86–91 and the flower arranging ideas on pages 104–21. Christmas is also the time for a few well-chosen houseplants (see pages 93–7). Unlike cut flowers, if you invest in a good houseplant to decorate your house at Christmas, it should still look good well into spring.

When buying cut flowers, concentrate on what's in season, or near its natural flowering time. Just as you wouldn't want to eat tasteless strawberries at Christmas, you don't want out-of-season flowers such as roses, tulips and peonies on your table either. They may have been shipped from the other side of the world or dragged into flower many months out of their season. This makes them last less well, and, anyway, there are some lovely things around naturally – or almost so – at Christmas. Nerines and chrysanthemums are just coming to the end of their season but still available, and there are plenty of others – the Christmas rose (*Helleborus niger*), freesias, hyacinths, narcissus, anemones and amaryllis – that are just beginning. Most will have to be forced a little to flower at Christmas, but not as much as a rose, tulip or peony.

To condition your cut flowers, it is important to bear in mind the following points:

Temperature

In a hot, bright, dry atmosphere, cut flowers go over quickly. If you can, put them outside the back door or in a cool porch when you go to bed. As long as there is no frost forecast, they'll last twice as long if they spend twelve hours in the cold.

Foliage

It's important to remove all foliage below the water level. Left on, it will draw in bacteria.

Flower food

You can buy flower food in sachets to sprinkle into the water in the vase, but this includes sugar which, although it feeds the flowers, feeds the bacteria too. It's best to make your own, containing a mixture of bleach and an acidifying agent, which help to reduce the proliferation of bacteria.

In a 30cm-tall vase, add 1 teaspoon of bleach and 1 tablespoon of clear, cheap malt vinegar to the water. The bleach is particularly important for flowers with big, rubbery stems such as hyacinths, which will collapse twice as quickly without it in their water.

I use bleach to clean my simple vases. Narrow-necked containers are best cleaned with Steradent and Magic Balls – little copper balls, designed to clean decanters, which you can swill around and clean even the tightest corner of a vase. I also put a drop of bleach in water with alliums and any brassicas (see 'Redbor' kale, page 89) to prevent their characteristic pong developing.

Searing

Searing works by increasing the surface area for water absorption by softening the tough, impermeable layer on the outside of the flower stem. Hammering the stem end has a similar effect, but it also causes the area of cell destruction to become a site for bacterial build-up. With the searing technique, the stem end is sterile.

Anything that begins to look floppy should have its stem ends seared in boiling water for 30 seconds. Give woody stems a bit longer and very soft stems less. Put 2.5–5cm of boiling water into a mug and plunge the stems in. The amount of stem you sear is to an extent proportionate to the length of stem you've cut. If it's 2m tall, sear 15cm. If it's 50cm, sear 3–5cm. Don't leave the stems in for too long, or else they'll cook and disintegrate. With short-stemmed plants, take care to keep the flower heads away from the steam.

Even if they have flopped already, many flowers will make a total recovery after searing. I always say: If in doubt, sear, as you will never do anything any harm by searing, and most things will benefit hugely.

Some flowers and foliage to sear at Christmas include herbs (sage, rosemary, lavender), all euphorbias, hellebores, blossom (such as *Prunus autumnalis*), and plants that drop their petals readily (such as *Viburnum bodnantense*).

Submerging

There are only a few plants I know of that benefit from submersion. Those you may come across at Christmas include hydrangeas and some shrubby foliage plants such as hebes and ivy. Because they can absorb water through their whole leaf or petal surface area, submersion under water gives them more of a chance to suck up enough fluid to sustain their complex structures than through a narrow stem alone.

Float the cut flowers, or foliage, in a sink or bath of tepid water, pushing them below water level – the flower as well as the stem. They'll float to the top again, but that doesn't matter. A few hours in the water will do, but if you can, leave them overnight.

Caring for amaryllis and lilies

Amaryllis and lilies have various specific requirements.

If you're going to transport amaryllis, always buy them in bud, as the petals bruise exceptionally easily once open. For this reason, when you're arranging amaryllis, it's best to hang them over the side of a table rather than laying the flowers out flat.

Another point to bear in mind is that the hollow stem will last much longer if you insert a cane inside it. Without it, the weight of the flower tends to break the stem as it ages and you lose the amaryllis's glorious height. Push a slender bamboo cane up the middle of the stem to just beneath the flower head. Cut the cane to the right length with florists' snippers. (If it is too thick, score it with the snippers and bend it over your knee to make a clean break.)

Ideally, the cane will jam just below the flower and will be held inside. However, some stems have a wider diameter and the cane slides out as you lift them into the vase. If you need to, you can keep it in place with a wad of cotton wool packed in behind it.

Lastly, twist a rubber band round the very bottom of the stem. Without this, the stem ends tend to split and curl like a pig's tail.

Lilies need their anthers removed as soon as the flower unfurls. Quite apart from the annoyance of having tablecloths and clothes stained by the pollen, if the anther is allowed to ripen, it will pollinate and fertilise the flower. Having done its job, it will die. If you remove it – in effect castrating the flower – it will keep going for longer.

Drying cut flowers and foliage

There are three ways of preserving what you've harvested from outside. Some plants – alliums, agapanthus, beans and globe artichokes – can be sprayed with paint. This makes them last for years (see pages 65 and 82). Others last well dried as they are. Some will keep their colour; this is true of spindle and callicarpa.

Something worth having up your sleeve is glycerine. If slowly sucked up by the flower or seed head's stem, this oily solution is absorbed into the plant cells and gives the plant tissue suppleness and strength. Wispy clematis seed pods of varieties like *C. tangutica* and *C. vitalba* look delicate and beautiful when you pick them, but once dry, they drop as soon as you touch them. I used to preserve these by spraying them with hair spray, but using glycerine (available from chemists) is a more lasting technique. It is also brilliant for long-term storing of hydrangeas, Chinese lanterns, agapanthus seed heads and pussy willow.

The stems you treat have to be mature, as they are in the autumn; new growth won't suck up the solution. Condition the stems well by searing in boiling water for 30 seconds and then leaving them overnight in deep water to drink. Then make up a small amount of 1 part glycerine to 2 parts hot tap water in a jug or jam jar so that you have only a few centimetres sitting in the bottom. Leave the stems of whatever you want to preserve in the mixture until it has all been absorbed or evaporated. This usually takes about a fortnight and will leave the heads soft and silky, lasting for years.

Equipment

You'll need to get a few bits of kit for your flower arranging. Those that you will come across in the following arrangements include florists' wire (thin wire on a spool available at florists and hardware shops), pin holders (heavy metal disks covered with small metal pins on one side, which can be stuck to the bottom of vases and used for holding flower stems in place), and glue tack/Florafix (a waterproof sticky-tape).

Forager's wreath

Wreaths and swags

Go on a forage and see what's still looking good outside, picking anything colourful and decorative, such as brilliant-pink spindle berries, orange physalis, still-plump rosehips, orange-berried *Iris foetidissima* seed pods or *Cyperus eragrostis* seed pods.

I add colour to the wreath in terms of 'zones'. Zone 1 is strong and dramatic, with 3–4 bright ingredients, repeated three times at around three, six and nine o'clock. Zone 2 is the intermediate area in between. This needs to have some colour, but without competing with zone 1.

This wreath takes about half an hour to make. Rehydrate the moss if it dries out by floating the wreath in a sink of water for half an hour every week or so. It will last at least a month, kept cool, hanging outside.

> **Double-ring wire frame with bridges between the rings (available in many sizes from florists and good garden centres) – I use a 35cm one**
> **6–7 handfuls of moss**
> **Florists' wire**
> **Silver birch twigs, sprigs of rosemary or bracken**
> **3–4 strong and dramatic ingredients for zone 1 (see below)**
> **A lighter mix of ingredients for zone 2 (see below)**

The first step is to pad out the frame. For this, the best material is moss. (You can buy this or forage your own.) Lay an even and generous layer over the frame, putting the same amount all round. I use 6–7 handfuls. Wire this padding on to the frame with florists' wire, binding it tightly. Aim for the padding to be about 7.5cm across. Add a loop of wire with which to hang up the finished wreath.

The second step is to cover the moss with silver birch twigs, some sprigs of rosemary – rich, dark-green and scented – or even bracken for a pretty, autumnal feel. You need only a few twigs or fronds to add to the moss base. They help create a more generous look and strengthen the frame. Push the stem ends in hard so that they jam into the moss and then, every so often, bind them in a curve on to the base with wire.

The third step is to add the colour. My zone 1 consists of Chinese lanterns, *Iris foetidissima* and spindle seed heads and borlotti bean pods. Zone 2 includes eragrostis, hydrangea and stipa seed pods and leaves.

Start with zone 1. If you've got decent stems on whatever you're adding, push them firmly into the moss and twig base. If they don't have good stems, poke wire through them and bend it round the base. Borlottis, for example, need wiring to attach them to the frame. You can buy different thicknesses of stub wire from a florists' supply shop, but any hardware shop will have wire you can cut into lengths yourself. Push the wire through the middle of a group of three beans and then back through again in a loop. Then poke the double section of wire through the base. Once it is out through the back, twist the two ends together to hold the beans in place.

Then fill in zone 2 with the lighter mix of seed pods and leaves. Keep going until you have covered your whole wreath base.

Finally, you may want to back the wreath with plastic. Cut up some black plastic dustbin bags into several strips about the width of your wreath. Attach the first strip to the back with lengths of wire bent into hoops, like large staples. Pleat the plastic, to and fro, pinning it on to the back of the moss as you go. Then add another strip, till you've covered the whole of the back of your wreath.

Fruit-studded wreath

If you don't have enough foraged items available to fill a wreath, your next stop is the greengrocer or supermarket. Buy small bright red Spartan or crab apples, chillies or mini peppers, cranberries and limes. All are easy to wire, last well and will look good on your door. If you can, share a box of chillies or limes with a friend from a vegetable wholesaler. You'll pay much less than in the supermarket and may even get them delivered to your door.

I add colour to the wreath in terms of 'zones' (see page 73). Here I have used limes, chillies, cranberries and crab apples as a colourful group for zone 1 with a few sprigs of eucalyptus, *Garrya elliptica* catkins and green hydrangea heads for the calmer zone 2.

With the extra time that is needed for wiring, this wreath takes longer to make than the Forager's wreath (see page 73) – about an hour. It looks good on a shiny, smart painted door. Rehydrate the moss if it dries out by floating the wreath in a sink of water for half an hour every week or so. It will last at least a month, kept cool, hanging outside.

Double-ring wire frame with bridges between the rings (available in many sizes from florists and good garden centres) – I use a 35cm one
6–7 handfuls of moss
Florists' wire
Silver birch twigs, sprigs of rosemary or bracken
3–4 strong and dramatic ingredients for zone 1 (see above)
A lighter mix of ingredients for zone 2 (see above)

The first step is to pad out the frame. For this, the best material is moss. (You can buy this or forage your own.)

Lay an even and generous layer over the frame, putting the same amount all round. I use 6–7 handfuls. Wire this padding on to the frame with florists' wire, binding it tightly. Aim for the padding to be about 7.5cm across. Add a loop of wire with which to hang up the finished wreath.

The second step is to cover the moss with silver birch twigs, some sprigs of rosemary – rich, dark-green and scented – or even bracken for a pretty, autumnal feel. You need only a few twigs or fronds to add to the moss base. They help create a more generous look and strengthen the frame. Push the stem ends in hard so that they jam into the moss and then, every so often, bind them in a curve on to the base with wire.

To wire your limes, poke a 30cm length of wire about a third of the way up and through the fruit. Taking care not to rip the lime's skin, bend both ends down and twist them together to make a false stem.

To wire the chillies, push a 30cm-long wire through the middle of a clump of three or five and then back through again in a loop.

If the fruit is smaller still, like crab apples or cranberries, thread them like beads on a chain. Leave plenty of bare wire at either end so that you can poke these into the base and secure them well on to the frame.

Add the zone 1 fruit first, poking the wires into the frame and bending them round to attach the fruit securely. Remember that the wreath will be hanging, so the heavy fruit, in particular, must be firmly attached. Then add your zone 2 ingredients.

Keep going until your whole wreath base is covered. Back your wreath with black plastic, as described on page 73, if you wish.

Pepper wreath

I like the simplicity of this wreath with multi-coloured chillies and peppers in different shapes and sizes. I add the colour in terms of 'zones' (see page 73). Large bell peppers are used for zone 1, and smaller bell peppers and chillies for zone 2. All members of the capsicum family (both chillies and peppers) are very long lasting if kept cool, so they're ideal for Christmas wreaths. But take care when wiring hot chillies: wear plastic or rubber gloves and be careful not to wipe your eyes.

This wreath takes about an hour to make, including the wiring, and, like the fruit-studded wreath, looks good on a shiny, smart painted door. Rehydrate the moss if it dries out by floating the wreath in a sink of water for half an hour every week or so. It will last at least a month, kept cool, hanging outside.

> **Double-ring wire frame with bridges between the rings (available in many sizes from florists and good garden centres) – I use a 35cm one**
> **6–7 handfuls of moss**
> **Florists' wire**
> **Silver birch twigs, sprigs of rosemary or bracken**
> **Large bell peppers for zone 1**
> **Small bell peppers and chillies for zone 2**

The first step is to pad out the frame. For this, the best material is moss. (You can buy this or forage your own.) Lay an even and generous layer over the frame, putting the same amount all round. I use 6–7 handfuls. Wire this padding on to the frame with florists' wire, binding it tightly. Aim for the padding to be about 7.5cm across. Add a loop of wire with which to hang up the finished wreath.

The second step is to cover the moss with silver birch twigs, some sprigs of rosemary – rich, dark-green and scented – or even bracken for a pretty, autumnal feel. You need only a few twigs or fronds to add to the moss base. They help create a more generous look and strengthen the frame. Push the stem ends in hard so that they jam into the moss and then, every so often, bind them in a curve on to the base with wire.

To wire peppers, choose which end of the pepper you want showing on the wreath and then push a 30cm length of stub wire straight through the other end of the fruit from side to side about one-third up. Now push another one in at the same height but at right angles to the first wire. Very carefully bend these wires down, making sure you don't tear the fruit, bringing all four wires together at one end of the pepper.

To wire mini bell peppers and chillies, do them individually or in groups of three. Push a 30cm length of wire through the middle of the single fruit or clump, and then back through again in a loop. Bind the two ends together into a false stem.

You can add the peppers to the wreath while it is hanging up or lying flat on a worktop. Starting with the large bell peppers, push the wires straight into the twiggy frame and bend them round to secure the fruit firmly.

Repeat this process all the way round, covering the base with the large bell peppers and then filling in the gaps with smaller bell peppers and chillies.

Back your wreath with black plastic, as described on page 73, if you wish.

Hydrangea wreath

As well as hanging a wreath on your door, why not fill the middle of your Christmas table with a beautiful, generous wreath of twigs and flowers? Hydrangeas are ideal for this purpose. With the long, mild, dry autumns we now have, they are still flourishing in December. Cut the best flowers, always looking for a good bud just below where you snip; then you're doing your harvesting and pruning all in one go. Bring them inside and float them – flower and all – in a bath or sink of water overnight (see page 70). This will prolong their life out of water, so they will not flop, but dry elegantly.

This wreath is very quick to make. Once you've made it, fill the hole in the middle with candles, or embellish the hydrangea heads with brilliant green beaded wire, quails' eggs and cranberry chains (see page 85).

> **Double-ring wire frame with bridges between the rings (available in many sizes from florists and good garden centres) – I use a 45–50cm one**
> **5 branches of silver birch**
> **Florists' wire**
> **20–30 hydrangea heads (depending on size)**

Cover the frame with a really generous amount of silver birch twigs, cut from the branches. You are aiming for a big messy nest. Wire the twigs securely on to the wreath, but for a good relaxed feel allow lots of whippy ends to escape.

Cut the stems on your hydrangea heads to about 20cm. If the stems are a bit short, you can create a false stem by pushing wire straight up the centre of the stem stump and then another wire across at a right angle, as near the flower as you can get it. Then bend both ends of the second wire down and twist round the first to hold everything securely and prevent the flower plopping off as you push it on to the wreath.

Attach the heads, two abreast, all the way round the wreath, saving the largest and best-coloured hydrangeas to add last on top of all the others. This gives the finished wreath plenty of depth. All you need do is push the strong hydrangea stems through the silver birch twigs.

Once you have achieved the look you want with the flowers, add extra silver birch twigs so that it feels as if twigs are coming out at you from all directions.

Silver birch swag

To give your sitting room a beautiful, skeletal, wintry look, surround your fireplace with silver birch. Then drape the branches with glass droplets, small silver balls and allium heads, sprayed silver (see page 65). Don't add any colour: just keep it simple and then light the whole thing with white fairy lights.

> **Nails or tacks**
> **1 bunch of silver birch branches**
> **(5 x 1m branches)**
> **Florists' wire or ribbon**
> **Silver Christmas decorations**
> **Clear-flex, white-bulbed**
> **fairy lights**

If you have a beam across a fireplace, you can knock in nails or tacks and then attach 1m lengths of silver birch to these, with wire, across the width, making it as dense as you like. If the birch branches are no thicker than your finger, they won't weigh much, so even thin wire will safely support the structure.

You can also run a silver birch swag all around a room – a dining room, for instance. Just like putting up a ribbon for Christmas cards, fix nails or tacks into the walls at the corners of the room and attach taut lines of wire or ribbon between each nail. Then attach the branches of silver birch, tying them securely on to the wire or ribbon.

Decorate your silver birch swag with lights and baubles.

Evergreen garland

It's extraordinary that in this lush and wooded country, we all too often bring the leaves with which we decorate our houses at Christmas from the other side of the world. There are plenty of wonderful home-grown evergreens, so let's all use more of them.

Mix the luxurious shiny leaves of elaeagnus or camellias with soft-textured *Ozothamnus* or aromatic eucalyptus, as in this garland. When you brush past it, the room will fill with sharp, bright scent, and all of these will look good as they dry, retaining their colour and leaves for weeks into the New Year.

Per 30cm of garland:
> **Florists' wire or twine**
> **5 branches of *Elaeagnus ebbingei***
> **12–15 branches of *Eucalyptus***
> ***gunnii*, *E. rubida* or *E. cinerea***
> **(one or a mix of all three)**
> **10 branches of *Ozothamnus***
> ***rosmarinifolius* 'Silver Jubilee'**
> **5 stems of orange chillies**
> **40cm length of sage-green**
> **ribbon (optional)**

If you can, do this with one other person to help.

Decide on the length of your garland and cut some florists' wire or twine to match. Create a loop at both ends from which you can hang it once completed. Fix the ends to firm points – a door handle, or the back of a chair – while you make the garland.

Cut the mix of leaves into approximately 15cm pieces and then make them into generous foliage bundles, tying them together with florists' wire or twine.

Bind the bundles on to the length of twine or wire. Add the first one and then place the second over the stems of the previous bundle, effectively working backwards

along its length until the garland is complete.

Wire – or just poke in – 20cm stems of orange chillies and loop a ribbon (if you want one) down the whole length of the finished swag.

Mist the garland with water lightly (do not drench), cover with moistened paper towels and store in a cool place until you're ready to hang it in its final place. Hang over a fireplace, down a staircase or, like a pelmet, above a main door or a window.

Table decorations

Silvered artichokes and runner beans

Tiffany's used to make a beautiful solid silver runner bean paperweight. Here's how to create your own version, for a fraction of the price. The silver coating highlights the bulge of the beans and the lovely curve to the tip of the pod.

The weightiness of globe artichokes makes them ideal Christmas decorations, too. The paint highlights every wrinkle and ridge and makes them look as if they've been cast in silver, enticing you to pick them up and weigh them in your hand to see if they're real.

It's best to arrange each vegetable, seed pod or fruit in its own group; avoid a hotchpotch of different things, which tends to look fussy and lacks style. Here I use beans and globe artichokes, but try adapting the principles to other seed heads such as agapanthus and alliums, as on page 65.

> **Borlotti or 'Rob Roy' or
> 'Rob Splash' beans
> Globe artichoke buds
> Silver spray paint
> Florists' wire or ribbon**

If you can, it's good to buy your artichokes when they're still around in the summer and autumn, or better still, pick them from your garden. (Spiky cardoon flower buds do just as well.) Harvest them before they get too blown apart by wind and rain. It doesn't matter if they're going brown – you'll cover the lot with spray – but they look better if they're not too ragged.

Cut them with a length of stem and a leaf or two – the leaves add a good twist, making a striking contrast with the chunky stem. Try to find artichokes of different shapes and sizes. This will give your final arrangement much more interesting forms.

Once picked, leave them somewhere airy and cool (not in a damp garden shed), so that they dry and don't go mouldy. Spray them, after a few days, along with the beans, and leave to dry. As the artichokes dry more and open up, you may need to spray the inner leaf scales again.

When spraying anything, it's a good idea to do so with adequate ventilation, gloves and acres of newspaper. (If you forget the gloves – as I have done before – and your fingers get covered in silver, clean your hands with a mixture of 2 tablespoons sugar, 1 tablespoon lemon juice and 1 tablespoon olive oil. This works brilliantly.)

Scatter the artichokes over your Christmas table or along the length of a mantelpiece or window ledge, or arrange them in a large bowl interspersed with brightly coloured Christmas baubles.

Scatter the silvered beans over any flat surface, or thread them on to ribbon or wire and stretch them across the room as an alternative to paper chains.

Chinese lantern and spindle table runners

Bright pink and orange has been a favourite colour combination of mine for years. The foraged seed pods of physalis – Chinese lanterns – and spindle work well together threaded in a chain.

> **Chinese lanterns**
> **Florists' wire**
> **Spindle berries**
> **Ribbon**
> *Allium schubertii* **seed heads,**
> **sprayed crimson (see page 65)**

Segment the Chinese lantern stems so that you have one lantern and a bit of stem on each. Then thread these sections on to a length of florists' wire – the stems are almost hollow, so this is easy to do – leaving a gap between each lantern and threading the spindle berries into these gaps as you go.

You can then brighten and tidy the whole thing up by winding ribbon all the way along the length of your chain.

Lay the chain across the table and, in each curve, scatter vast sparkler heads of *Allium schubertii*, sprayed not silver but crimson (see page 65).

Quails' eggs table runners

As with the duck eggs on page 66, if you make these and store them carefully, you'll have them for life.

> **Quails' eggs**
> **Narrow ribbon**
> **Green beaded wire**

To blow the eggs, make a little hole with a needle in the pointed end and an even smaller hole in the other. Hold the egg gently with your thumb and forefinger and carefully blow out – from the small hole end – the contents. If this doesn't happen easily, enlarge the hole in the pointed end and try again.

Once they're blown, if you want to keep the eggs, you must rinse them thoroughly in a bowl with bleach or vinegar to stop any smell, and then bake them in a cool oven for 15 minutes at about 150°C/gas mark 2. This hardens the eggs and dries them out thoroughly so that they won't go bad.

Thread a large darning needle with narrow ribbon and pull this through the small holes in each egg, linking them together in a chain. To add a bit of sparkle, twist brilliant green beaded wire down the length of the chain.

Cranberry table runners and cranberry candlestick

Deep crimson cranberry chains look elegant, and they last amazingly well. Marry them with a cranberry candlestick made from a clear glass vase filled to the brim with fruit.

> **Cranberries**
> **Florists' wire**
> **Tall, thin clear-glass vase,**
> **with a wide rim at the top**
> **Glue tack (Florafix)**
> **Candle, the same diameter as**
> **the rim of your vase**
> **Bright beaded wire or ribbon,**
> **to decorate**

To make the chains, aiming right for the middle of the berry, thread the cranberries like beads on to 45cm lengths of florists' wire. Leave a bit of spare wire at each end and then join as many lengths together as you need.

To make a cranberry candlestick, fill the vase with cranberries and then, with a strip of glue tack (Florafix), attach a candle to the top of the vase (it should rest on the rim). Decorate with bright beaded wire or ribbon.

Massed hyacinths

This table centre is incredibly easy and quick to make. It's also long lasting – a fortnight if kept cool – so you can enjoy it all through Christmas until New Year's Eve and beyond. A splash of bleach in the water increases the hyacinths' vase life (see page 69); it keeps bacteria at bay from their thick, juicy stems and prevents them from collapsing.

About 50 stems of hyacinths
8 rubber bands
Pin holder
1 brightly coloured, flat-bottomed
  salad bowl, 30cm in diameter
Waterproof glue tack (Florafix)

Cut the flowers short – to about 20cm – and collect about 7–8 stems together with a rubber band. The base of the bunch needs to be a good 4cm across to stand easily and not fall out over the edge of the vase. Once you've collected together 6–7 bunches, you'll have a critical mass.

Secure the pin holder in the middle of the bowl with a lump of waterproof glue tack. Make sure the bowl is really dry before you stick it – it won't hold strong if damp. Move the bowl to its final position and then half-fill with water. The pin holder will help keep the stems in place around the outside and hold the middle bunch upright. Stand the first bunch in the bowl, and then add the next beside it and the next and so on, finishing by sticking one in the middle in the pin holder. The whole bowl will be filled and the flowers will help each other stand up. You can then cut any rubber bands that you can see.

Hyacinth napkin rings

To complete your Christmas table, decorate your napkins. Paula Pryke, a wonderful florist, showed me this technique. Hyacinths are perfect for napkin rings, as the flowers last out of water without flopping for a couple of days.

Hyacinth stem
Florists' wire

Lace individual hyacinth flowers cut from the central stem on to a short length of florists' wire, and then bend the wire round a napkin and secure it at the back.

To make them last as long as possible, when they're not on the table put the rings in the salad drawer of the fridge.

Rosemary-covered vase

You can turn any old drinking glass or jam jar into a vase for a small table centre by covering it with strongly coloured or boldly shaped foliage. (Bonne Maman jars work particularly well.) I like to use leaves that I know last well out of water – rosemary, lavender or phormium will stay looking fresh for four or five days. Make a simple arrangement of winter flowers and twigs in your covered vase, and it will be fit to take pride of place in the middle of your dining-room table.

> **Slightly flared drinking glass or jam jar**
> **Waterproof glue tack (Florafix) or wide, double-sided sticky tape**
> **15 x 30cm stems of rosemary, cut in half**
> **Pin holder**
> **1 bunch Narcissus 'Paper White'**
> **10 stems of Helleborus niger**
> **A few twigs of silver birch**
> **Ribbon**

Wrap the glass or jam jar in two circular bands of waterproof glue tack, spaced 5cm apart. If you can't find glue tack, use wide, double-sided sticky tape. Stick the stems of rosemary on to the tape, adding them bit by bit, all the way round.

Attach the pin holder to the bottom of the vase with glue tack and arrange the flowers in the glass. Start with the 'Paper Whites' and then spread the hellebores evenly throughout. Add a few twigs of silver birch to make an interesting silhouette.

Wrap a ribbon around the glass to stop any stems from dropping off the sides.

Christmas chrysanthemums

There may be a room in your house where you have a large table calling out for a spectacular vase of flowers at Christmas: an armful of brilliantly coloured chrysanthemums works beautifully. Chrysanthemums can be hideous, uptight and plastic looking, but they can also be splendid. Choose rich and bright colours: acid-greens, tangerine and deep red-oranges, purples, magenta pinks and conker-brown crimsons. If you combine these colours with the wild and wayward Japanese Spider shape, you'll be on to a winner.

> **1 large-necked, clear-glass vase, 15cm wide at the top x 35cm tall**
> **2 tablespoons bleach or 5 tablespoons clear vinegar**
> **5 tall stems of kale 'Redbor' (or another similar, winter foliage)**
> **3 stems each of Chrysanthemum 'Froggy', 'Shamrock', 'Flyaway', Seaton's Galaxy', 'Orange Allouise' or similar**

Fill the vase with water and add the bleach or vinegar. This will help to keep the flower stems fresh and will prevent any cabbage pong developing from the kale as it ages (see page 69).

Create a base from the kale 'Redbor', making a balanced but not over-neat dome in the vase. Add the chrysanthemum stems in through this structure, aiming for a balanced but relaxed mix of colour and shape.

Keep the vase topped right up so that all the stems are in deep water. This arrangement will last 2–3 weeks if kept cool.

Winter scented blossom

As well as having one or two large arrangements in your house at Christmas, it's good to have lots of small vases scattered about in bedrooms, and on mantelpieces and window ledges – jugs filled with winter flowers and lines of single stems (see page 106).

One of my favourite containers for flowers at this time of year is a simple glass log nightlight holder. Its shape is ideal on a mantelpiece or window ledge. I like to fill it with *Chrysanthemum* 'Shamrock', highly scented deep red freesias, hellebores (with their stems seared – see page 69–70) or, as here, sprigs of winter scented blossom such as *Viburnum bodnantense* and *Prunus autumnalis*.

Waterproof glue tack (Florafix)
3 magenta-purple candles
Glass log nightlight holder
with 7 dimples
4 small pin holders
Small mixed bunch of *Viburnum bodnantense* and *Prunus autumnalis*

With a small lump of waterproof glue tack, secure the candles firmly into every other shallow dimple in the glass log. Attach a small pin holder in the dimples in between.

Fill these dimples with water and stick a few blossom branches into each pin holder.

Cyclamen

Houseplants for Christmas

There's one good general rule with winter houseplants: the more you get them looking as they would outside, the better. A pot of miniature cyclamen is perfectly all right as it comes, in its plastic container, but with a bit of doctoring can be made into something fabulous. The same applies to a potted azalea or hellebore, a bowl of hyacinths (see page 46), narcissi (see page 53), or a frame of jasmine (see page 94).

When buying cyclamen, I choose the small-flowered varieties – usually hybrids – in white, crimson or magenta, in preference to the large-flowered, large-leaved forms.

**Dried autumn leaves
  (see below)
Small bunch of branches
  (see below)
7 pots of deep-red miniature
  hybrid cyclamen
Planting medium – two-thirds
  soil-based compost,
  one-third grit
1 big salad bowl, 30cm in
  diameter**

Fill a carrier bag with some dried leaves. If they have good strong colour in them still – as will maple, cotinus and cherry trees – so much the better, and if not colour, a distinctive shape. Oak, the huge serrated, sweet chestnut and small yellow splashes of silver birch are all excellent. The leaves don't have to be bone dry: you can lay them out overnight somewhere warm and they'll be crisp and beautiful by the morning.

You'll also need a few branches. Silver birch, cornus, hazel and willow are good. Freshly cut, these will be bendy and you will be able to weave and knot their whippy ends like string.

Take your cyclamen out of their pots and plant them in the bowl.

Fill in around the cyclamen roots with compost, scatter dried leaves randomly over the surface and push in a few whippy twigs.

Cyclamen like bright, indirect light, so an east-facing window ledge is ideal, but they don't like it too hot, preferring a daytime temperature of 15–18°C and 10°C at night. Don't put them near a radiator. Keep them cool and moist, but not dripping wet. In my kitchen, which has an Aga, they struggle, yet in our chilly, quite dark bedroom, they do fine.

Jasmine globe

Last winter I bought a metre-tall pink jasmine, *J. polyanthum*, tied on to a frame of canes. Once transplanted into a nicer pot and trained on to a woven basket of silver birch rather than bamboo, it made a magnificent and long-lasting table centre right through Christmas and on into May. We had a continual succession of beautiful and fragrant flowers, filling the whole room with scent every evening.

Pink jasmine, 1m tall
**Pot 45cm wide at top x 20cm
    deep with a drainage hole**
Potting compost
Crocks
Tray full of pebbles
Twine
**A bunch of silver birch branches,
    75cm–1m long**

You can buy jasmine all over the place at Christmas. Look out for a tall one. Get it home and remove the canes. Spread the twining stems out on to a table and gradually separate out each stem. You'll need to be patient – it's like unknotting hair.

Put crocks in the bottom of your pot and re-pot the plant in potting compost. Depending on the pot size, poke 6–8 branches of silver birch into the compost around the edge of the pot. Bend the first one over into a dome, attaching it to the one straight opposite. Twist and bind these on to each other to make a hoop, doubling back when you get near the whippy ends and so tying off and securing each branch. This sounds difficult, but is in fact very easy to do. If there are any lower branches, turn them at right angles and bind them on to the next branch around. This makes a lower level to your plant basket and strengthens the frame. Then move on to the next pairing and do the same, until the twiggy dome is complete. Stem by stem, attach the jasmine to the globe with twine. Water the globe.

The jasmine will thrive if kept cool (not above 18°C) in a bright, very well-lit room (that's crucial – kept too hot and dark, the flowers will go brown and drop quickly). Jasmines also like high humidity, so put the pot on a tray full of pebbles in water. The water level must be kept below the top of the pebbles so that the compost doesn't get too wet, but the extra humidity the water provides will keep the flowers fresh for longer.

Tropical orchids

With orchids we've got stuck in our ways. The good old moth orchid, the phalaenopsis, is a staunch and reliable houseplant. Yes, it flowers for four or five months and yes, it suits our modern, centrally heated lifestyle. But aren't we all a bit bored of it? It's time to be brave.

There are other cool-growing, equally easy, more interesting orchids you can grow, and Christmas is the time for these. None are better than the zygopetalums: they are winter-flowering and have a lovely sweet scent. They can turn their scent on and off according to light levels, time of day and temperature, but on the whole it's strongest in the morning, at about 15°C in dappled light.

1 zygopetalum orchid
2 saucers
Pebbles
Terracotta pot
Several canes or sticks, for support
Orchid compost (for suppliers, see page 256)

Grow your orchids hard: that means watering only when the pots are properly dried out and giving them very little food. The water to use for all orchids is rainwater; tap water – in many areas – contains too many salts.

As far as temperature is concerned, it's more of a problem growing these orchids too hot than too cold – 14°C in the day and 10°C at night is ideal. If kept dry, they could be colder than this at night, but only for a short time. Most modern houses run at about 10 per cent humidity and 20°C-plus temperatures, and for orchids, that's like living in a desert. Their ideal growing conditions would be at 70–80 per cent humidity. This is not possible in a normal house, but to raise the humidity a little, grow your orchid on a saucer filled with

pebbles. Put an upturned saucer on the pebbles and stand the orchid pot on that. That way the orchid will be kept away from standing water, but you'll create a damper microclimate immediately around it.

If your orchid is in a plastic pot, re-pot it in a terracotta one (with a hole in the bottom), which will look much more attractive, using orchid compost. Support flopping stems with sticks or canes.

Zygopetalums and most other cool-climate orchids like dappled light, not bright sun. To keep them doing well from one year to the next, feed them regularly with orchid feed and avoid putting them by south-facing windows during the summer.

Cacti

For a modern Christmas table, cacti reign supreme. Backlit, or in bright light, they'll warrant repeated examination. They are easy to look after throughout the year, but at Christmas you can doctor them to make them centre stage. Arrange a collection in brightly coloured pots down the centre of your table. To jazz them up further, scatter matching coloured Christmas baubles in between.

Collection of cacti including the zebra plant, *Haworthia attenuata*
Very free-draining compost: use a standard houseplant potting compost and add 50 per cent extra grit
Ceramic pots (with drainage holes) and trays in mixed colours, 10cm deep x 9cm wide at top
Crocks and saucers

When you buy your cacti, re-pot them in your chosen pots, using free-draining compost with crocks in the bottom. Place the pots on saucers, in groups on trays.

The zebra plant, *Haworthia attenuata*, will be happy on a window ledge, or in a greenhouse, frost free and bright, or on the patio in summer.

In the winter the less you do to cacti the better, and they need minimal watering. During their summer growing period, they need more, but they should never be left standing in water, and shouldn't be watered again until the compost has completely dried out – typically every couple of weeks in the summer and less in the spring, autumn and winter.

To water, fill a sink with water, plunge the cactus pots into it for a few minutes and then leave them to drain.

A Christmas Party

A party timetable

Christmas is a time for parties. If you're having one, whether at home or at work, a written timetable can be very helpful.

About a week before the party, order the drink to be delivered, along with the ice and glasses. Try to buy all drink sale or return. (Alternatively, if you like me live a stone's throw from the Channel, it's an excellent idea to go to France for a weekend and bring the alcohol back – you can get so much more for your money.)

The week before your party is the time to start thinking about flowers. I find it's best to buy amaryllis and lilies in bud (see pages 119–20). They are easier to transport without bruising and you can put them somewhere cool but bright to open up in a few days' time. Now is also the moment to collect together all the useful bits of kit, including vases and anything you need in the way of linen or crockery, so that you're not haring around at the last minute trying to find them. If you don't have everything you need, borrow from friends, or check local directories or online for specialist catering hire companies. Most will deliver and collect and will take the hired items back dirty for a small washing fee.

A couple of days before the party, buy the rest of the flowers. Unwrap them, sear the ones that will benefit (see pages 69–70) and leave them in buckets of deep water somewhere cool and dark until the morning before. I'd recommend buying your Christmas tree and decorating it at this point (see pages 60–67).

The day before the party, make and distribute your flower arrangements (see pages 104–121). Try not to leave this to the eleventh hour – you'll have more than enough to do then. You may have nuts and biscuits already made and stored in tins, but take out anything you have frozen and do any last-minute food shopping.

On the morning of the party, start your food preparation. In the afternoon, all you'll have left to do is to put the finishing touches to the food and drink, and brief your helpers – and they are key.

For a party of thirty to forty people, you'll need three helpers for serving food and drinks and for clearing and washing up. For fifty guests, you'll need four helpers; for sixty guests, five helpers; for seventy guests, six helpers; for eighty guests, seven helpers; for ninety guests, eight helpers. Ask them to come at least an hour before everyone is due to arrive, and to stay until the washing up is done. For parties of over fifty people, it's useful to have one person in charge of making drinks and two people serving them, with at least one other person concentrating solely on the food that has to be heated or cooked at the last minute.

Party planning for fewer than thirty people

If you're having a few people round over Christmas, you'll probably cope yourself, with a bit of help from family, but choose recipes that can be made in advance and are ready to roll.

Flowers

Single hyacinth stems – will last into the New Year (page 106)
Flower grid – amaryllis will last two weeks if kept cool (page 111)
Nero ring – impressive and easy (page 115)
Large vase of amaryllis or lilies – can be made a day or two before; will last two weeks if kept cool (pages 119–20)

Food

For a 2–3-hour drinks party, choose 7–10 different canapés. Allow 8–10 canapés per person. If guests are likely to stay for longer than 2–3 hours, up this to 15. They can be served in this order:
Roasted almonds – fine stored airtight for weeks (page 126)
Spiced nuts – fine stored airtight for weeks (page 126)
Very cheesy biscuits – fine stored airtight for a week (page 125)
Pesto cheese straws – make up just before (page 125)
Smoked salmon on brown bread – make up just before
Sage and anchovy tempura – can be made earlier in the day and heated up in a hot oven (page 127)
Stuffed Peppadew peppers – make beforehand and reheat (page 130)
Bruschetta – make the toasts several days before and store in an airtight container; do the toppings a day or two before the party and combine them at the last minute (pages 133–4)
Bagna cauda – prepare the sauce the day before and the crudités earlier in the day, keeping them in bags in the fridge (page 157)
Sausages in honey and mustard – make up just before (page 132)
Mini mince pies – freeze and reheat (page 24)

Drinks

For a 2–3-hour drinks party, allow half a bottle of wine, Prosecco or champagne per person, or serve some Christmas drinks:
Danish glögg – assemble well beforehand and heat it up as people arrive (page 138)
Lemon cordial – make beforehand and refrigerate (page 139)
Rosemary lemonade – make the syrup beforehand and add lemon juice and water at the last minute (page 139)

Party planning for more than thirty people

If you're having lots of people over, don't do it all on your own. Start with an idea of how long things will take to do, and then double it. Everything takes longer than you think.

Flowers

Single hyacinth stems – will last into the New Year (page 106)
Floating flowers (page 109)
Submerged flowers (page 112)
Flower grid – amaryllis will last two weeks if kept cool (page 111)
Nero ring – impressive and easy (page 115)
Hanging globes (page 116)
Large vase of amaryllis or lilies – can be made a day or two before; will last two weeks if kept cool (pages 119–20)
Create a silver birch grove (page 120)

Food

For a 2–3-hour drinks party, choose 7–10 different canapés. Allow 8–10 canapés per person. If guests are likely to stay for longer than 2–3 hours, up this to 15. They can be served in this order:
Very cheesy biscuits – fine stored airtight for a week (page 125)
Spiced nuts – fine stored airtight for weeks (page 126)
Fennel chunks with Parma ham – make a few hours beforehand (page 126)
Light kale seaweed – make a few hours beforehand and reheat (page 127)
Sage and anchovy tempura – can be made earlier in the day and heated up in a hot oven (page 127)
Crispy cumin and caraway squid – make just before (page 129)
Turkish borek with fillings – freeze and reheat (page 132)
Mini blinis – freeze and reheat (page 133)
Bruschetta – make the toasts several days before and store in an airtight container; do the toppings a day or two before the party and combine them at the last minute (pages 133–4)
Mini mince pies – freeze and reheat (page 24)

Drinks

For a 2–3-hour drinks party, allow half a bottle of wine, Prosecco or champagne per person, or serve some Christmas drinks:
Sea breeze (page 137)
Asolanos (page 138)
Danish glögg – assemble well beforehand and heat it up as people arrive (page 138)
Mulled cider – make up just before (page 139)
Lemon cordial – make beforehand and refrigerate (page 139)

Christmas party flowers

Before your party kicks off, you'll need to transform a room. You may have a whole day to decorate your party space, or only an hour. Either is achievable if you've got an idea up your sleeve.

If you have plenty of decorating time, create a mini winter wood with silver birch trees and jam jars of scented narcissi (see page 120). If you want one or two flamboyant flower arrangements, create a hanging globe of winter flowers and evergreen leaves (see page 116). Even when the room is jam-packed, it will still be visible above everybody's heads. If time is short, go for a cheaper and quicker solution. Try out the easy Nero ring (see page 115), which has huge impact considering how few flowers it needs.

Whenever I'm making a mixed colour arrangement I use the same formula: choose six ingredients – three foliage plants and three flowering ones – and add them to the arrangement one by one.

The first ingredient is primary foliage. To qualify for this all-important role, it needs to have a robust, upstanding structure. You want something with interesting colour or shape, rather than dull privet picked from the hedge. Ideally, it will also have thin stems, but a generous horizontal top, so that it's easy to put into oasis or the neck of a vase, filling up lots of space in the air rather than at the base.

The second ingredient is a filler foliage plant. It's good if you choose foliage of a different colour and form to the primary foliage that can be slotted in, filling up any gaps and unevenness.

The third ingredient is what I call the upper storey, another foliage plant with an interesting architectural shape. Grasses, seed pods, branches with catkins and straight vertical flower spikes are ideal here. The aim is to get away from any uniformity and create a more relaxed arrangement. Making the display too neat and uptight is a common mistake – you need a bit of waywardness.

With flowers, I always choose three different varieties. The first is the bride, the dominant flower of the bunch. This is the one that you fall in love with in the garden or flower shop; it forms the centre, the pivot of the arrangement. Then choose a bridesmaid, the same colour or similar to the bride but a smaller, less glamorous flower that is not as dominant and won't compete. Finally, I pick what I call the gatecrasher – the contrast that brings the whole thing to life. This needs to be a colour that clashes with the two other flowers. After all, this sort of arrangement is not about self-effacing harmony but being centre stage.

Single stems

Instant party flowers

The simplest way of arranging flowers very quickly is as single stems in narrow-necked vases. You can buy the vases, or collect pretty liqueur and olive oil bottles. Different bottle shapes, sizes and colours look wonderful together.

If possible, arrange them where they will be backlit, so as to maximise the stained-glass effect. Many flowers – like the hyacinths here – look their best like this; you can really appreciate the shape, colour and texture of the flower and they are all the more noticeable in isolation, or grouped to run down the length of a table. On a mantelpiece use five or seven; along a window ledge, shelf or table go for more.

The most striking single-stem flowers are bold and architectural, with an interesting silhouette. At Christmas, sweet-smelling hyacinths are ideal.

9 stems of white hyacinth
9 narrow-necked bottles,
   20cm high
A little bleach or vinegar
Brightly coloured candles

Hyacinths last well – at least 10 days in water – without any special conditioning technique. Put a drop of bleach or clear vinegar in their water. This will keep bacterial build-up to a minimum and hence allow the stem to last as long as possible (see page 69).

Place the flowers in the bottles, with the stems cut to slightly different heights, and surround them with brightly coloured candles.

This is as good as it gets – beautiful, simple, scented, life enhancing, and done in less than 5 minutes.

Variations: Other ideal winter single-stem flowers are *Prunus autumnalis* and *Viburnum bodnantense* (see picture on page 91), spider chrysanthemums, which are just coming to the end of their natural season at this time of year (see picture on page 108) and gloriosa lilies (see picture on page 113).

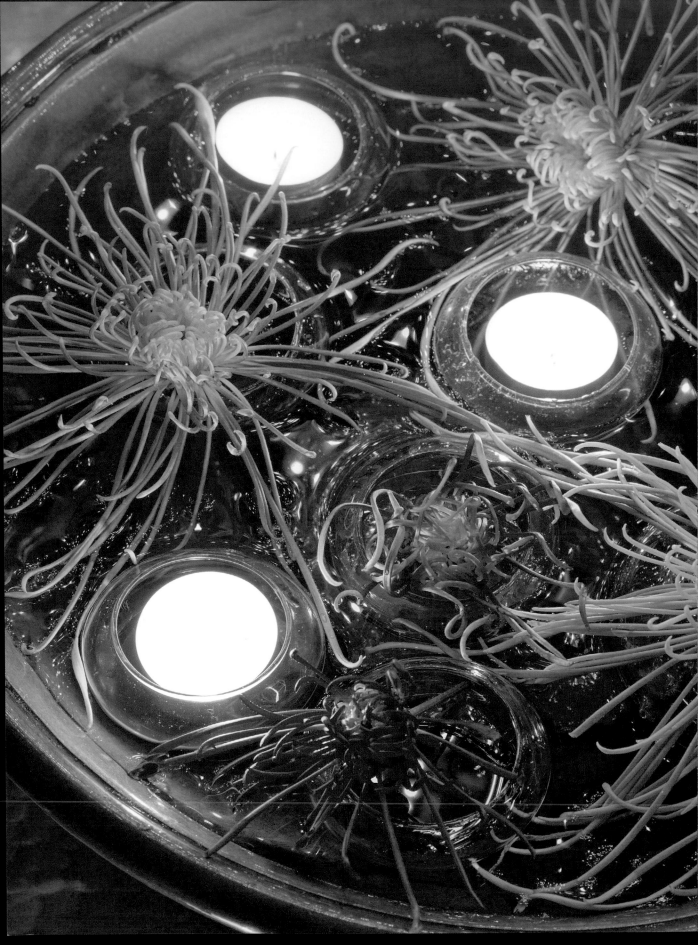

Floating flowers

One of the best ways to create instant flower arrangements at Christmas – or at any time of the year – is to float a few flowers in a shallow bowl. This works perfectly if you want something simple on the table that doesn't obstruct conversation.

An arrangement takes a minute to create, but the flowers will rot quickly if left wet all the time. This doesn't matter so much at a party, which is over before the flowers have time to age, but is not ideal if you want the flowers to last. To increase their life, use glass flower floats to keep the petals above the water (or if you can't find these, make your own wooden grid – see page 111).

There are two types of flower floats. One is a mini glass bowl, as shown in the picture opposite. You fill the bottom with water, and put in your flower. The stem sits in the water, with the petals resting on the rim, and you can then float several of these on the water surface of your overall container. The other kind – which is easier to balance and use – is like a glass version of a child's rubber ring: a circle of glass with a hole in the middle. You slot the stem through the hole and the petals then sit out of the water.

> 1 large bowl, 35cm wide x 15cm
>   deep
> 10–12 flower floats
> 5–7 stems of *Chrysanthemum*
>   'Fly Away'
> 5 long-burning (4–6 hour)
>   nightlights, to scatter
>   in between

Put the bowl where you want the arrangement to be, and fill it to the brim with water. (Don't fill the bowl first and then try to carry it.) Float your flower floats on the water, cut the flower stems quite short and drop them into the floats.

Put the nightlights in floats too. (If you drop them straight in the water, they will move around and the flames could burn the petals. With flower floats you avoid this.) The arrangement should last 3–4 days.

Variations: The best blooms to use have a large surface area – big and bold, and good for floating. At Christmas, other flowers I float are single-coloured florists' *Anemone coronaria*, any shaggy-flowered chrysanthemums like 'Shamrock', gerberas, gloriosa lilies and hellebores (sear their stem ends in boiling water for 30 seconds as soon as you pick them and then leave them in deep water for a couple of hours before arranging – see pages 69–70).

Grid of white amaryllis

The flower grid is my assistant Tam Lawson's speciality – an ingenious idea that she devised for botanical painting so that she could look down into the flower. It is also ideal for supporting delicate flower heads (like those of camellias with short woody stems) and keeping them just out of the water in your favourite shallow bowl as a table arrangement.

We have now made several grids in the school at Perch Hill – some small and some huge, like this one for amaryllis. The great thing about a grid is that you can choose any large bowl, such as one you normally use for salad or fruit. Just make a grid to hang about 3cm over the edge of the bowl.

10 straight branches of hazel, cornus or willow (see below)
1 large shallow bowl, 40cm wide x 15cm deep
Ball of string
9 stems of *Amaryllis* 'Mont Blanc' or 'Ludwig Dazzler'
9 elastic bands
10 stems of orange-berried *Ilex decidua* or *I. verticillata* (deciduous holly)
7 branches of silver birch

To make the grid, pick some straight hazel, cornus or willow branches, the thickness of your little finger. Cut them long enough so that they overhang the bowl you want to sit the grid on by about 3cm. Lay them in a noughts-and-crosses structure and, using the string, tie them in place with a succession of reef knots all tied in the same direction (this makes it possible to fold it away), tying the four corners first. Wrap an elastic band around each amaryllis stem end to stop them splitting and curling.

Put the bowl where you want the arrangement to be and fill it to the brim with water. (Don't fill the bowl first and then try to carry it.) Put your grid on the bowl and add your amaryllis – evenly spaced – through the whole huge bowl. Then add the ilex berried stems and the silver birch branches to fill it out and give it a more interesting silhouette.

The arrangement should last 2 weeks, so you can make it for a Christmas party and it'll still be looking good for New Year.

Variations: Other ideal flowers for floating on a grid at Christmas are deep velvet red amaryllis, such as 'Bacchanal' or 'Red Velvet', Oriental lilies, such as 'Casablanca', Christmas rose (*Helleborus niger*), and any spider chrysanthemum, such as 'Shamrock'. For a smaller grid, use polyanthus and primroses, or bunched snowdrops.

Submerged flowers

There are certain flowers – tropical orchids, gloriosa lilies (as here), and hydrangeas – which survive, petals and all, in water for several days. Cymbidium orchids will last at least a week. If you have a tall, narrow, handsome glass vase, or a round goldfish bowl, ring the changes by putting the whole flowers and stems in the water. With a tall, narrow vase, you may also be able to balance a candle on the top.

2 stems of gloriosa lily (with 5 flowers between the 2 stems)
Beaded wire or anodised florists' wire (see below)
Tulip vase, 25cm tall with top flaring to 30cm wide x 8cm deep
8cm-diameter crimson candle
20cm length of waterproof glue tack (Florafix)

Cut the gloriosa flowers off their stems, leaving at least 5–6cm of stem to make wiring them easier. With their large surface area, flowers float, so you need to secure them on to some wire to keep them submerged. I use lovely bright-beaded wire, which is magnified in the water. Cut a 1m length and bind it round the flower stem at intervals. If you're not sure that this thicker wire will hold the fine stems securely, add short sections of anodised florists' wire (this won't rust in water).

Fill the vase with water and feed the flowers and wire into it. If your container is narrow necked, use a stick to push the first end down right to the bottom of the vase.

Then rest the candle in the mouth of the vase where the flowers would normally stand. To ensure this is stable and secure, attach it to the vase with a circle of waterproof glue tack.

Variations: For submerging you want flowers with a waxy or leathery texture to their petals. Other flowers and seed heads that will sit in the water without rotting are gardenia, tuberose, cymbidium, phalaenopsis, lilies, large-flowered cyclamen, Chinese lanterns (*Physalis* seed heads), nigella seed heads and allium seed heads.

Nero ring

Showy party flowers

This is a brilliant arrangement for a party. It makes a fairly small number of flowers go a long way and look spectacular, but it is very easy. Use a standard oasis ring (usually 30cm, but this will depend on the size of your vase, which will need to be a bit narrower) and cover it with flowers, bearing in mind the rules for structure and colour combining (see page 104). Then, rather than leaving it sitting flat on the table, lift up the flower-studded ring and rest it on the shoulders of the vase.

> 30cm oasis ring
> Vase, 35cm tall x 20cm wide at the top, with shoulders or a decent lip
> Decorations to go inside the vase (optional)
> Primary foliage: 25 branches of drymis
> Filler foliage: 25 branches of pittisporum
> Upper storey: 25 branches of rosemary 'Miss Jessopp's Upright'
> Bride: 15 stems of *Nerine bowdenii*
> Bridesmaid: 25 stems of *Anemone coronaria* 'Sylphide'
> Gatecrasher: 15 stems of orange chillies
> Candle in a contrasting colour, 10cm tall, wide enough to fit tightly in the neck of the vase
> Waterproof glue tack (Florafix)

Soak the oasis ring in water for 5 minutes, leaving it floating to absorb the water naturally. Do this rather than pushing it into the water yourself, which will create air pockets in the oasis, and flowers in those will die.

If you're using a clear glass vase, you can fill it with whatever you fancy to add extra colour – Christmas decorations, walnuts, cranberries, Spartan apples, pine cones, lemons or limes (cut in half), kumquats or Quality Street chocolates in their multi-coloured wrappers. The lemons and limes will have the shortest life and look okay only for a couple of days, but the rest will last really well. With the citrus, pack them in from the bottom up, putting one whole fruit in the centre and then jamming in halves all the way around the edge; put in another whole lemon or lime in the middle and then another layer of halves around its edge, and so on until you reach the neck of the vase. The acid-green vase I've used opposite is opaque, so I have left it empty: its brilliant colour is enough to balance the flowers. If you are using a light vase, fill it with water so that the arrangement doesn't topple over.

Cover the oasis ring with the foliage and flowers in the numbers given. Start with the foliage, making sure that you leave no green plastic or oasis visible, even when you lift the ring on to the vase. Then add the flowers.

Put the ring on to the shoulders of the vase, where it should sit perfectly. Add the candle, securing it in the neck of the vase with glue tack to stop it wobbling about.

To keep the flowers fresh, remove the oasis ring of flowers at night and store them somewhere cool. To rehydrate, float the whole ring in water for 10 minutes every couple of days. This arrangement will look good for 4 or 5 days.

A hanging globe

A hanging globe is a great way of overcoming any sense of restriction. Flowers come at you from every direction, hovering above your head like a firework display. You can hang a row of globes along a room for a party, or use one on its own above a dining table or in an entrance hall. A globe always creates quite a stir and is easier to make than it looks.

When you're choosing what to use, don't pussyfoot around with anything too delicate: go out and find the most outrageously dramatic flowers you can, or choose something bold and simple. Globes also look good with fruit and glamorous vegetables (aubergines, peppers, grapes, lemons) wired in. Bear in mind the rules for structure and colour combining (see page 104).

> **Oasis globe, 20cm in diameter**
> **Cling film**
> **Chicken wire about 75cm long and wide, to wrap around the oasis globe**
> **Florists' wire**
> **Shackle (available from good ironmongers in various sizes) and stronger wire (or rope), to hang the globe**
> **Primary foliage: 30 branches of eucalyptus**
> **Filler foliage: 10 stems of green hydrangea**
> **Upper storey: 20 branches of silver birch**
> **Bride: 20 stems of Chrysanthemum 'Shamrock'**
> **Bridesmaid: 20 stems of Chrysanthemum 'Froggy'**
> **Gatecrasher: 15 stems of Chrysanthemum 'Bagley Tang Red'**
> **Extra splash: 7 seed heads of Allium schubertii and 10 seed heads of Allium cristophii, sprayed silver**
> **Ribbon**

Soak the oasis globe for a few minutes in the bath. It will absorb enough water to keep your flowers alive for 4–5 days and will end up weighing about 4kg. Bear that in mind when you are hanging it. It's a good idea to wrap the globe in plastic or cling film to prevent evaporation and dripping of water. In a hot centrally heated room this is crucial if you want the flowers to last as long as possible.

Wrap the chicken wire around the globe as if you are wrapping a present. At each end, fold in the flaps of wire neatly. Don't use too much chicken wire, as when it is doubled over it is difficult to insert the stems. Then sew the whole thing together, using florists' wire, making sure it's secure. At the top attach a shackle, or a loop of strong wire. You'll use this to hang the globe. Attach a good length of rope or strong wire to the shackle or loop and hoist the globe up. Attach the end of the wire to something out of the way, but again make sure the knot is secure. At the end, you can hide all this engineering with a length of ribbon.

Hang your globe at a comfortable working height, in situ, and start adding your foliage and flowers. When poking stems into the globe, always aim for the centre of the sphere. Begin with the foliage. Cut it all to about the same length – about 30cm long – or else your globe won't be round. Use primary first, then filler and upper storey. To help poke stems through the cling film and into the globe, cut the stem ends of firm, woody plants at an angle to make them sharp. For softer stems, you may need to use a knitting needle or skewer to make holes first.

The final touch is to add the flowers. Cut the stems to 30–35cm, with a few shorter stems, so that some hide in the foliage and some stand out a bit. Scatter them in a balanced but not totally symmetrical way. Pick the biggest and most beautiful for the middle zone. Few people will stand under the globe and look straight up at the flowers and you'll hardly see those at the top.

Now is the moment to lift the globe to its final position. Hoist it up high above people's heads, but not so high that people won't notice it.

Amaryllis with silver birch

My very favourite arrangement for Christmas is a vase full of amaryllis. This makes an impressive entrance arrangement for a party and lasts over Christmas and right through to the New Year without any fuss.

You can force amaryllis, growing it in a pot (see page 59), but it's even more luxurious to have them as a great velvet swathe in a vase. The white varieties like 'Ludwig Dazzler' and 'Mont Blanc' look lovely in the winter, but particularly at Christmas go for deep, rich crimson ones, such as 'Royal Velvet' or 'Bacchanal'.

Amaryllis – in whichever colour – are magnificent but expensive, so condition them well (see pages 70–71).

**7 amaryllis, e.g. 'Royal Velvet'
    or 'Bacchanal'
7 bamboo canes
7 red postman's rubber bands
1 large-necked vase 15cm wide
    at the top x 35cm tall
20 branches of pussy willow or
    10 branches of silver birch
Selection of fairy lights, coloured
    balls, baubles and candles,
    to decorate**

When I make a large arrangement, I usually put my foliage in place first – for structure – before I add the flowers, but amaryllis arrangements are an exception. Amaryllis stems damage easily and if you add them into an already full vase, their soft fleshy ends split as you push them in around other stems. It's best to put the amaryllis in at the beginning and then add the foliage carefully around them.

So start with your amaryllis, using a minimum of five stems or, in a really small vase, three. If I want my arrangement on a large table with lots of space around, I use seven. Whatever the number, it should be odd, not even; you don't want to create straight lines in your arrangement and that's what you'll get with small even numbers.

Push a bamboo cane up the hollow stem of each amaryllis to give it support (see pages 70–71). Then twist a rubber band round the very bottom of each stem to stop the ends curling (see page 71).

Place the stems in the vase in a relatively balanced but not perfectly symmetrical way.

Once the amaryllis are all in, add the branches to form a halo just above the flowers. I often use lovely early pussy willow, if I can find it, but silver birch twigs work well too. Either helps to support the heavy stems and fills out the vase, without adding much to the cost.

Deep red amaryllis on their own can look a bit sombre, so add some brightness into your vase at Christmas with fairy lights and lots of coloured balls and baubles. Pick up on the red of the amaryllis with matching or contractingly coloured candles on the table below.

Oriental lilies with pussy willow

There is one kind of out-of-season flower that is fantastic in the winter: a huge vase of pure white Oriental lilies like 'Casablanca'. Conditioned properly and kept as cool as possible, these will last at least two weeks and fill a whole room with the most delicious scent every evening and through the night. They work well with a structure of silver birch or pussy willow, with fairy lights threaded through the branches (see picture on page 105).

9 Oriental lilies (ideally order a named variety such as 'Casablanca' from good florists)
20 branches of pussy willow
1 large-necked vase, 35cm tall x 15cm wide at the top
Large pin holder
Waterproof glue tack (Florafix)
Fairy lights, candles or a selection of glass Christmas decorations

Ensure your vase is clean and dry. Attach a large pin holder to the base of the vase with glue tack (Florafix). Add the lily stems, one by one, with the first few pushed on to the spikes of the pin holder, creating an overall structure that is at least twice the height of the vase.

Add the pussy willow branches, cutting some down short – to create a heart to the vase – and leaving others long to make an interesting silhouette.

Finally hang lots of small decorations on twigs to mirror the shape of the pussy willow buds, and cover the whole thing with white fairy lights or candles in nightlight frames.

Remember to remove the anthers from the lilies as soon as they unfurl (see page 71).

Silver birch grove with jam jars of narcissus

This is a decoration for a special party: transforming a room into a twinkly winter party space by creating a wood from deciduous trees. You'll need to space the trees about 3m apart, so the suggestions below work for a room measuring about 7m by 10m. We had a room decorated like this at our wedding.

Cover the whole floor with a deep layer of dried leaves and scatter jam jars of scented flowers all the way through and round the room. To add an extra twinkle, spray a few of the boldest, biggest leaves – such as sweet chestnut – with silver spray. Collect these leaves in the weeks and months before making the grove, bring them in and leave them in a pile in a garage or shed to dry out.

6 silver birch saplings or branches, secured in pots
White fairy lights
Christmas decorations – silver (including sprayed allium heads, see page 65) and clear glass only
10–15 dustbin bags of dried leaves (see above)
Silver spray paint
200 stems of 'Paper White' or 'Avalanche' narcissus in jam jars or 30–40 hyacinths

First you need to find your trees, and the more of these the merrier. Silver birch is ideal. This is a weed in forestry woods – one of the first plants to encroach on scrubland – and therefore it is okay to remove mini saplings. A good florist should be able to get them for you. If you can't find mini sapling trees, use branches, but make sure they have a good and relatively even shape. You can secure these in pots (with gravel and stones) so that they look like trees.

Next decorate your trees. Keep it simple, with white lights, silver decorations and perhaps just one colour, deep red or purple. The more natural decorations you can use on your trees the better (see page 68): they'll look more in keeping than snazzy, shiny balls. I use lots of allium heads, and clear and silver shapes and balls.

Pick out some of the largest, perfect leaves from those you have collected and spray them silver.

Once your trees are in place, spread the leaves over the floor. Dot the silver ones about and scatter jam jars of scented 'Paper White' or 'Avalanche' narcissi all around the room. Lots of hyacinths are another (more expensive) alternative. Both will fill the room with a delicious perfume; the warmer the room gets, the headier their scent will be.

When the party's over, bag up the unsprayed leaves in black bin liners. Douse them a bit with water and leave them to rot down into perfect leaf mould. You can use the silver birch for a swag (see page 80) or firewood.

Christmas party food

If you have a Christmas party – with plenty of good drinks – you need to provide lots of small but gutsy things to eat. This is not the moment to be subtle and refined: one wants robust, alcohol-absorbing food. Serve food that is easy to eat – just one or two bites – or else you will find it is left untouched.

Choose a theme and a good sequence, almost imagining starter, main course and pudding. I've found the mezzes of the Mediterranean a great source of inspiration – canapés such as stuffed mini Peppadew peppers (see page 130) and Turkish borek (see page 132) work well. There are also some Northern European dishes that make more substantial party food. My husband, Adam, loves a mini blini at a party (see page 133), slightly sour from the buckwheat flour, served with a dollop of crème fraîche and smoked fish or salted roe. And you've got to have some British classics, like intensely cheesy biscuits (see page 125) and really good honey and mustard chipolatas (see page 132). Finish off with mini mince pies, topped with a piped ball of brandy butter (see pages 24 and 199).

With drinks you want those that quickly create a party mood without being too alcoholic. Cocktails such as pisco sours and Asolanos (see pages 137 and 138) are perfect in relatively small quantities. For the slightly more alcohol wary, provide something warming: the not-too-sickly Danish glögg or mulled cider (see pages 138 and 139) are great. Be kind to those who have to drive, and to any children, by being inventive with non-alcoholic drinks as well. Make rosehip syrup, vodka-free sea breeze and rosemary lemonade (see pages 43, 137 and 139). All these feel good on a cold winter night.

Small party food

Very cheesy biscuits

These delicious biscuits are ideal for a Christmas party – quick, easy and intensely cheesy. You can use any type of hard or semi-hard cheese; they're a good way of using up your leftovers – Stilton, Cheddar, even old dry bits of Parmesan or goats' cheese. The stronger the cheese, the better. The cayenne pepper gives the biscuits a bit of punch and the fennel seeds are a delicious addition. Also try making some topped with flaked almonds, poppy and sesame seeds.

For about 45 biscuits:
100g butter
50g strong Cheddar (or other strong cheese to hand)
50g Parmesan
100g plain flour
Pinch of cayenne pepper
2 tablespoons fennel seeds or sesame seeds

Have the butter at room temperature and cut it into chunks.

Put all the ingredients except for the seeds into a food processor and pulse until it forms a ball, or rub in and combine the mixture by hand. Roll the mixture into a sausage shape approximately 3cm in diameter and wrap in cling film. Chill thoroughly for a good hour to harden and then remove from the fridge, unwrap and cut into pound-coin-thick discs.

Preheat the oven to 180°C/gas mark 4.

Sprinkle the fennel or sesame seeds over the biscuits. Place them on a greased baking sheet or a silicone mat and cook in the preheated oven for approximately 10 minutes until pale gold. Remove from the baking sheet as soon as they come out of the oven to stop them cooking and put them on a biscuit rack to cool.

You can store these in an airtight container for about a week.

Pesto cheese straws

Another way of using the cheese biscuit recipe, left, is in these pesto cheese straws. The cheese, ham and pesto make a great combination of flavours and the contrast in texture is good too.

For 50 cheese straws:
1 quantity of cheese biscuit mixture, chilled (see left)
2 tablespoons pesto
25 slices prosciutto, cut into halves

Preheat the oven to 180°C/gas mark 4.

Roll out the chilled cheese biscuit mixture and cut into straws 5–6cm long. Place on a greased baking sheet or a silicone mat and bake them in the preheated oven for 8–10 minutes until they are golden.

Let them cool, and then spread a little pesto down one side of each straw and wrap in half a slice of prosciutto.

Roasted almonds

These salted almonds are lovely at a party and simple to prepare. It is worth skinning the almonds yourself, as they will have a much better flavour. You can also simply roast them on a bed of rosemary.

For a large bowl:
4 good handfuls of shelled almonds
1 teaspoon almond (or other light) oil
A good sprinkling of Maldon salt

Preheat the oven to 150ºC/gas mark 2.

Skin the almonds by pouring boiling water over them before taking off the skins. Toss them in the oil on a baking tray. You only want a tiny bit of oil; otherwise they will end up too greasy.

Put into the preheated oven and cook for 20–25 minutes, turning regularly so that they don't go too brown on one side. A slow cook is essential, otherwise the nuts will overcook and become bitter. Take them out when they are pale brown, and add a little salt.

Spiced nuts

These are excellent party nuts with extra punch.

For a large bowl:
20g butter
1 tablespoon groundnut oil
450g mixed nuts: Brazils, almonds, hazelnuts, walnuts, pecans, peanuts and pine nuts
½–1 teaspoon chilli powder, to taste, or cayenne pepper if you don't want them too hot
2 teaspoons dark brown sugar
¼ teaspoon ground cumin
1 teaspoon Worcestershire sauce
Salt

Preheat the oven to 190°C/gas mark 5.

Heat the butter and the oil in a heavy-bottomed pan and add the nuts, half the chilli powder or cayenne, the dark brown sugar, the cumin and the Worcestershire sauce. Cook over a moderate heat for a minute or so, and then tip everything into a baking tray and bake in the preheated oven for about 7 minutes, until just beginning to brown.

Drain on a thick layer of kitchen paper and toss in the remaining chilli powder or cayenne and salt to taste. Allow to cool.

Stored in a Kilner jar, these last for several weeks.

Fennel chunks with Parma ham

This is a recipe from my sister Jane. It's light, crunchy and fresh, and doesn't fill you up. It's also good with a glass of wine before dinner.

For 20 rolls:
2 medium-sized Florence fennel bulbs
Approximately 10 slices Serrano or Parma dry cured ham or prosciutto

Discard the outer layer of the fennel bulb if it's too fibrous to eat raw. Slice the bulb downwards, not across, into 1cm-thick fan slices. Then cut these into strips and cut the ham into strips a little wider than the fennel. Wrap the fennel in the ham.

Light kale seaweed

One of my favourite snacks for a winter party: a big plate of kale seaweed, to which everyone helps themselves. You can eat this with your fingers, like a handful of nuts.

You'll find kale seaweed deep-fried at Chinese restaurants, but this version, cooked in the oven, is lighter, less oily and less fattening.

'Redbor' or green 'Curly Kale' are the best varieties to use, but any kale will do. You can cook this in advance and then bung it back in a hot oven (230°C/gas mark 8) for a couple of minutes to heat it through and restore the crunch: it's far nicer eaten hot.

For each person:
1 kale leaf per person, with the midrib removed and sliced into ribbons
Oil (groundnut, olive or sunflower), for drizzling
1 dessertspoon Maldon sea salt per 100g kale
1 dessertspoon soft brown sugar, or to taste, per 100g kale
1–2 tablespoons chopped toasted cashew nuts per 100g kale (optional)

Preheat the oven to 200°C/gas mark 6.

Wash and dry the kale thoroughly in a lettuce spinner. Slice and put on to a baking tray. Drizzle with a little oil and toss to distribute the oil well. The easiest way to do this is to shake it in a plastic bag. Add salt to taste and place in the oven for 10 minutes until crisp. Kale burns easily, so keep an eye on it.

Drain on kitchen paper and sprinkle soft brown sugar and more salt to taste over it, and some chopped toasted cashew nuts if you want.

Sage and anchovy tempura

I love sage leaves dipped in tempura batter and shallow fried, but Rose Gray showed me how to make these and they are even better. The smokiness of the sage is perfect beside the sharp saltiness of the anchovy. They are ideal for a party because you can make them in advance and then heat them through in a very hot oven (250°C/gas mark 9) for a couple of minutes. If you don't like anchovies, use prosciutto instead.

For 50 canapés:
50 anchovy fillets in oil, or 8 slices prosciutto
100 large sage leaves
Sunflower oil, for frying

For the batter:
150g plain flour
1–2 tablespoons extra virgin olive oil
Warm water
3 egg whites

To make the batter, sift the flour into a medium-sized bowl and make a well in the centre. Pour in the olive oil and stir slowly, combining the flour with the oil. Slowly add warm water to loosen this paste, stirring all the time, until you have a batter the consistency of double cream. Leave for a minimum of 45 minutes.

Just before cooking, beat the egg whites until stiff and fold gently into the batter.

Place each anchovy fillet (or a small piece of prosciutto) between 2 sage leaves and press to hold together. Then dip in the batter.

In a high-sided pan heat a little sunflower oil until very hot. Shallow fry the leaves in small batches until golden brown and crisp. Drain on kitchen paper before serving.

Crispy cumin and caraway squid

This is a jazzed-up version of classic calamari. The fragrant tastes of cumin and caraway are delicious with squid. This is best eaten hot, so for a party have everything ready beforehand and fry the calamari at the last minute.

For 12–15:
> **1 tablespoon cumin seeds or caraway seeds**
> **Sunflower oil, for frying**
> **1kg calamari, cut into rings and tentacles divided into 2 or 3**
> **Salt and black pepper**
> **3 lemons, cut into chunks**
> **Chilli dipping sauce, to serve**

For the batter:
> **150g plain flour**
> **1–2 tablespoons extra virgin olive oil**
> **Warm water**
> **3 egg whites**

Toast the seeds for a couple of minutes in a dry frying pan and then crush them a little, using a pestle and mortar, to release their flavour.

To make the batter, sift the flour into a medium-sized bowl, add the seeds and make a well in the centre. Pour in the olive oil and stir slowly, combining the flour with the oil. Slowly add warm water to loosen this paste, stirring all the time until you have a batter the consistency of double cream. Leave in the fridge for a minimum of 45 minutes.

Just before cooking, beat the egg whites until stiff and fold gently into the batter.

Pour the sunflower oil into a high-sided pan, up to a third of the way up the side. Heat the oil until very hot (180°C). If you don't have an oil thermometer, it's easy to test. Drop a cube of bread into the oil. It should turn golden brown in less than a minute.

Dip the squid rings into the batter and fry them in small batches until golden brown and crisp. This is likely to spit a lot, so make sure you stand back well as you put the squid in, or better still, use a spit guard.

Drain on kitchen paper and sprinkle with salt and pepper. Serve straight away with chunks of lemon and the chilli dipping sauce.

Stuffed Peppadew peppers

I had this version of stuffed peppers on a boat in Turkey. It's light and fresh, with a mild punch from the chilli, and absolutely delicious. I use sweet mini Peppadew peppers – they are widely available in a bottle and come mild or hot. (If you use both types of Peppadew, label the plates hot or sweet, so that people know what they're getting.) The list of ingredients looks long, but I promise these are easy to do.

These can easily be made a day or two before, refrigerated and reheated at 180°C/gas mark 4 for 10 minutes, or until warmed through.

For about 60 mini peppers:
- **1 onion**
- **A little olive oil**
- **75g short-grain rice**
- **2 large tomatoes, skinned and deseeded**
- **½ mild to medium chilli, deseeded (or ½ teaspoon chilli flakes)**
- **2 tablespoons pine nuts, toasted**
- **1 teaspoon dried mint**
- **Small bunch fresh mint, finely chopped**
- **Small bunch fresh dill, finely chopped**
- **Salt and black pepper**
- **½ organic bouillon cube or ½ teaspoon bouillon powder, dissolved in 150ml water**
- **2 x 375g jars of Peppadew peppers**

For the sauce:
- **2 tomatoes**
- **1 tablespoon olive oil**
- **½ teaspoon mild chilli flakes**
- **Plenty of salt and black pepper**
- **A little more mint and dill, finely chopped**

Preheat the oven to 180°C/gas mark 4. Peel and coarsely grate the onion and fry gently in a little olive oil.

Wash the rice, add to the onion and fry, while stirring, for 2–3 minutes. Chop the tomatoes and chilli. Add to the rice with the toasted pine nuts, dried and fresh mint, dill, salt and pepper to taste and stock, and cook for another 10 minutes until the rice is almost but not quite cooked.

Slightly over half fill the peppers with the rice mixture, using a piping bag if you find it easier than a teaspoon. Put the peppers into an ovenproof dish. Mix the sauce ingredients together and pour around the peppers. Add a little water to the sauce so that it covers the base of the dish. Cover and bake in the preheated oven for 20–25 minutes and serve.

Turkish borek

Borek – stuffed filo pastry rolls – make brilliant party food. They are quick and easy to make in large numbers and they freeze perfectly. You can take them out and heat them through in the oven straight from the freezer (they take about 15 minutes at 180°C/gas mark 4). I love them with cream cheese and mint, and they're also delicious with pumpkin or squash, sweet red peppers and feta cheese. Try all these variations.

For 24 small mini cigar-sized rolls:
A little olive oil, for frying
Salt and black pepper
270g filo pastry
Melted butter, for brushing
1 egg, beaten

For the cream cheese and mint filling:
100g cream cheese
100g feta cheese, finely crumbled
Bunch of mint, finely chopped
1 tablespoon olive oil
10g pine nuts, toasted

For the pumpkin or red pepper filling:
½ medium-sized pumpkin or squash, or 2 red peppers
100g feta or cream cheese
Salt, black pepper and fresh mint or basil, to taste

Preheat the oven to 180°C/gas mark 4.
For the cream cheese and mint filling, mix the cream cheese with the feta and mint and the olive oil to loosen the mix. Add the pine nuts and salt and pepper to taste.

For the pumpkin filling, slice the pumpkins in half and remove the seeds. Bake these (or the peppers, whole) in the preheated oven – the pumpkins for 1 hour or the peppers for 20–30 minutes – and then peel them. (Keep the oven on afterwards, as you'll need it to cook the filled pastry rolls.) Mash the pumpkin or peppers with a fork, or in a food processor, and mix with the feta or cream cheese, and salt, pepper, and fresh mint or basil to taste.

You can either make mini individual cigars or stuff one whole sheet of filo pastry, roll and bake or fry as for mini cigars, and then cut it up.

For mini cigar shapes, lay or roll out the pastry and cut it into 12cm x 26cm rectangles, tapering in by about 3cm on either side, so that one of the 12cm ends narrows to 6cm. Brush each rectangle with melted butter and put a little mound of the cheese and mint mixture (about a teaspoonful) at the 12cm end of the pastry. Then roll over twice, turn in both edges and roll again until you reach the end. Brush this with egg and seal.

Bake in the preheated oven – or fry over a gentle heat in a little olive oil – until golden brown on both sides.

Sausages in honey and mustard

We get fantastic sausages from Wealden Farmers' Network, who make them from our pigs. They are so good that when we have a party, I just twist each sausage into two or three small chipolatas and cook them straight. But, particularly if you've got children at the party, chipolatas roasted with honey and mustard are also deservedly popular.

For 40 sausages:
40 chipolatas
150ml runny honey
2 tablespoons Dijon mustard
1 tablespoon grainy mustard

Preheat the oven to 180°C/gas mark 4.
Put the sausages on a baking tray and bake in the preheated oven for 15 minutes. Meanwhile mix together the honey and mustards. Brush the honey/mustard mix on the sausages and return them to the oven for another 15–20 minutes, basting occasionally with the mixture. (If the honey/mustard mix goes on from the start, it tends to burn.) Serve hot.

Mini blinis with smoked salmon and fish roe

This is my husband Adam's favourite party food, with the perfect mix of texture and taste. Don't buy your blinis: bought ones don't begin to compare with homemade and these are easy to make. Using buckwheat flour mixed with plain sharpens the flavour. You can also make larger pancakes. Either way, the blinis must be served warm.

For about 80 blinis:
225g plain flour
225g buckwheat flour, sifted
4 teaspoons dried yeast
2 tablespoons caster sugar
½ tablespoon salt
650ml milk
110g butter
4 eggs, lightly beaten
Sunflower oil, mixed with a little butter, for frying

For the topping:
200ml crème fraîche
1kg roe, gravadlax (see page 159) or any smoked fish
Bunch of fresh dill

Combine the flours, yeast, sugar and salt in a large bowl. In a small saucepan heat the milk and butter to blood heat, making sure that the butter melts completely. Stir this mixture into the flours and mix well. Stir in the beaten eggs. Using a hand mixer, beat at low speed for about a minute until smooth. (You can also do this by hand with a whisk.) Cover the bowl and leave the mixture to rise in a warm place for 1–1½ hours, until it is light and bubbly.

Brush a griddle, heavy-based frying pan or blini or pancake pan (or silicone mat on the simmering plate of an Aga) with oil and when it is really hot, drop half a tablespoon of the mixture on to it (or a whole level tablespoon for a large blini). When small holes begin to appear in the surface, turn the blini and lightly cook the other side. Cook a few at a time and keep the cooked blinis warm in a napkin in an oven at the lowest setting.

If you are pre-preparing (or freezing) the pancakes, you'll need to warm them up before serving. To do this, dampen a napkin, wrap the blinis in it and put them in a medium oven (190°C/gas mark 5) for about 10 minutes.

Top the blinis with the crème fraîche and roe, gravadlax or smoked fish and put a sprig of dill on each.

Bruschetta

A mixed plate of bruschetta is perfect party food. You can top the toasted bread – or even better, bread roasted over coals – with almost anything, but at this time of year, kale, squash and chicory are all in season. Make some of the delicious toppings described on page 134. You can use baguettes for your bruschetta, but sour dough bread or Pugliese (Italian simple, crusty bread) has a better texture and taste. Use a really good extra virgin olive oil for drizzling over the top. Serve with napkins.

For about 30 bruschetta:
1 stick of French white bread or about 1 loaf of sour dough or Pugliese bread (depending on size)
Extra virgin olive oil
2 garlic cloves, peeled and whole
Salt

Preheat the oven to 180°C/gas mark 4.

Cut the bread into finger-thick slices – at an angle if using French bread – and drizzle a little olive oil over one side. Grill, griddle or roast the bread slices in the preheated oven for 10 minutes. Keep an eye on them, as if left too long, the bread will go as hard as rock.

Lightly scrape one side of the bread slices with the garlic cloves and sprinkle salt over them. Then add the toppings and another little drizzle of olive oil.

Kale, capers and goats' cheese

With plenty of lemon juice, olive oil and parsley, this recipe is akin to a robust winter salsa verde. It's good spread on bruschetta. The softer-textured kale varieties – 'Cavalo Nero' or 'Red Russian' – are best for this dish.

For about 20 bruschetta:
  200g kale
  Salt and black pepper
  2 garlic cloves, peeled and whole
  Zest and juice of 1 lemon
  3 tablespoons chopped capers
  3 tablespoons chopped gherkins
  3 tablespoons chopped shallots
  3 tablespoons chopped black or green olives
  Large bunch of parsley, chopped
  150g fresh goats' cheese
  Bruschetta (see page 133)
  Olive oil, to serve

Prepare the kale by discarding the outer leaves and removing the stalks.

Bring 2 litres water to the boil and add some salt. Add the kale and the whole garlic cloves. Cook for 5 minutes, until the kale is tender, and drain, squeezing out as much water as you can from the leaves with the back of a spoon in a colander or sieve, or twist in a tea towel. Chop the kale and garlic (ideally by hand, so that you have a coarse-textured mix).

Add the lemon zest and juice, capers, gherkins, shallots, black or green olives and parsley, stir well and check the seasoning.

Spread a little goats' cheese on the bruschetta and add the kale topping. Drizzle a little olive oil over them and serve.

Squash caponata

In the summer, caponata made with aubergines is an excellent topping for bruschetta. In the winter, long-storing winter squash such as the rich, chestnut-tasting 'Red Kuri' (also called onion squash because of its shape) and sweet 'Butternut' make another ideal caponata base. If you can find 'Red Kuri', its flesh makes this caponata a brilliant colour.

For about 30 bruschetta:
  700g squash
  A little olive oil, for roasting and frying
  1 onion, finely chopped
  2 garlic cloves
  75ml red wine vinegar
  400g tin of chopped tomatoes
  Handful of raisins
  Handful of black olives, roughly chopped
  2 tablespoons capers, rinsed
  Bunch of winter herbs, e.g. parsley and chervil, coarsely chopped
  Salt and black pepper
  Bruschetta (see page 133)

Preheat the oven to 180°C/gas mark 4.

Peel and dice the squash and roast it in the preheated oven with a little olive oil for 30–40 minutes until the flesh is soft and the edges start to char.

In a saucepan, sweat the onion and garlic in oil until soft and then increase the heat a little and add the vinegar. Reduce until the vinegar has almost bubbled away and add the tomatoes, raisins, olives and capers. Cook for 10 minutes until the mixture has become thick and rich.

Add the squash and cook for a further few minutes. Remove from the heat and when the mixture has cooled a little, add the coarsely chopped herbs, give a good stir and season to taste. Spread the mixture on the bruschetta and serve.

Caramelised chicory with blue cheese

Based on a recipe of Sophie Grigson's, this is a wonderful winter vegetable dish on its own, and it is very good on bruschetta.

For about 15 bruschetta:
  4 heads of chicory (I divide large heads into 4 and smaller into 3)
  20g butter
  2 teaspoons runny honey
  Juice of ½ orange
  Salt and black pepper
  50g Dolcelatte cheese
  Bruschetta (see page 133)
  Salad leaves, to decorate

Preheat the oven to 180°C/gas mark 4.

Trim the chicory and cut in half lengthways. Rub half the butter thickly over the bottom of an ovenproof dish, and pack the chicory chunks, in a single layer, into the dish. Drizzle over the honey and orange juice and season with salt and pepper. Dot the remaining butter over the top.

Roast, uncovered, in the preheated oven for about 1 hour, turning and basting the chicory every 15 minutes. Keep a close eye on it towards the end of the cooking time, and take the dish out of the oven when the juices have reduced to a few spoonfuls of thick syrup and the chicory is looking well caramelised. (You don't want the honey to burn.)

Spread a little Dolcelatte on the bruschetta. This adds a wonderful flavour and helps the whole thing stick together. Then add a few salad leaves and the chicory and serve.

Drinks for a Christmas party

Sea breeze

The American Christmas classic. It's delicious and a wonderful colour, with the added bonus of not being too sweet.

To make a non-alcoholic version, mix together 500ml each of cranberry, orange, pineapple and grapefruit juice, along with lime juice to taste and a dash of grenadine.

For 6:
300ml vodka
1 litre cranberry juice
350ml freshly squeezed pink grapefruit juice
1 slice of lime, or 1 slice per glass
Ice

You can make this in a jug, by putting all the ingredients in it and mixing together, but it's even better to make it in six individual glasses. Put a few cubes of ice in each. Divide the vodka between the glasses, and then divide the juices between the glasses, pouring the grapefruit juice in first, before the cranberry. The two layers will then gradually bleed together and it will look marvellous. Add a slice of lime to each glass.

Pisco sours

For those who fancy something unusual, this is like a South American White Lady; it is drunk in large quantities at Christmas in Chile and Peru. The base is pisco, a powerful and narcotic grape distillate which, if unavailable in your local off-licence, you can buy online (see page 257).

For 1 glass:
3 parts lemon juice
1 part pisco
Crushed ice
1 tablespoon egg white (optional)

For the sugar syrup (makes 800ml):
450g sugar

Prepare the sugar syrup in advance. Dissolve the sugar in 600ml water and bring to the boil. Boil for 2–3 minutes and allow it to cool. Store in the fridge until needed. (The recipe makes 800ml, which will give you enough for several rounds of drinks.)

Place a cocktail shaker and glasses in the freezer and chill the lemon juice and pisco.

When all parts of the mixture are cold, half fill the shaker with crushed ice, pour in the lemon juice, pisco, sugar syrup to taste and, if you wish, the egg white – this gives the cocktail a bit of body. Give it a good shake and serve immediately.

Sloe gin and champagne cocktail

This is a delicious champagne cocktail, with a shot of sloe gin. For a party, frost the rims of the glasses by dipping them in egg white and then caster sugar.

Sloe gin, bought or homemade (see page 41)
Champagne

Put a small splash of sloe gin into champagne glasses and top them up with champagne.

Asolano

A drink served in the Café Centrale in Asolo, a lovely walled town in the foothills of the Dolomites. In its purest form, it's a shot of Campari topped up by about three times the amount of Prosecco. In my experience, it renders you speechless quite quickly, so I dilute it with a splash of freshly squeezed orange juice (use blood oranges if you can get them) and sometimes also add fizzy water.

For 8 small glasses:
100ml Campari
Plenty of ice
200ml orange juice
600ml Prosecco

Pour the Campari into a jug of ice and add and mix in the orange juice. Add the Prosecco and stir to combine.

Danish glögg

This is the best of all spicy hot red wine recipes, and knocks the socks off the usual over-sweet mulled wine or Glühwein. It's an ideal winter party drink.

For about 12 glasses:
1 orange studded with 10 cloves
100g raisins
4–5 shot glasses of aquavit (if you can't find aquavit, brandy, Madeira or rum will do)
2 x 750ml bottles red wine
2 cinnamon sticks
1–2 tablespoons sugar (or more, to taste)
Pared rind of ½ lemon
100g whole, peeled almonds

Overnight marinate the orange, studded with cloves, and the raisins, in a bowl with the aquavit (or brandy, Madeira or rum).

Pour 200ml of the red wine into a large saucepan and add the cinnamon, sugar and lemon rind. Heat it up, but don't allow it to boil. Then take the saucepan off the heat, add the marinated fruit and the almonds and leave to steep for at least half an hour. Then add the rest of the red wine and heat up before serving, again taking care not to let it get near boiling point.

Serve in mugs or glasses with a spoon in each for the nuts and fruit.

Mulled cider

Mulled cider is delicious, either warm or cold, and its relatively low alcohol content makes it ideal for a winter lunch party (see also the Bullshot recipe on page 229).

For 12–15 glasses:
- **2.5 litres dry cider, still or sparkling**
- **2 apples, washed, cored and sliced**
- **3 oranges, washed and sliced**
- **Zest and juice of 1 lemon**
- **2 teaspoons ground mixed spice**
- **10 cloves**
- **3 cinnamon sticks, snapped in half**
- **6 tablespoons soft brown sugar**

Put all the ingredients in a pan and gradually heat, simmering gently for about 1 hour. Do not let it boil. Strain and serve in heatproof glasses.

Lemon cordial

This recipe is perfect for a party, stores well and is easy to make in a big batch for lots of people. We often serve it at our garden openings. You can substitute other winter citrus fruits such as lime and grapefruit.

For 2 x 750ml bottles:
- **6 unwaxed lemons**
- **1.8 litres boiling water**
- **1.7kg white sugar (granulated or caster)**
- **50g citric or tartaric acid**
- **Coarsely chopped mint, to serve**
- **Ice, to serve**

With a swivel potato peeler, cut thick ribbons of rind from the fruit, leaving the white pith behind. Put the rind into a heatproof bowl and pour over the boiling water. Stir in the sugar, keeping the water moving until the sugar has all dissolved. Let the mixture cool, and then add the juice from the lemons and the citric acid, and leave everything to steep overnight.

Next day (don't leave the rind in any longer or else it will become bitter), strain the rind away and bottle the cordial.

Serve the cordial – just a little in the bottom of a glass – diluted with water; I love it diluted with fizzy water. If you're making up a jug, follow a certain order: first, throw in a small handful of coarsely chopped mint, then almost fill the jug with ice, and then pour in the cordial and finally the fizzy water.

The cordial will store for about a month in the fridge, or you can pour it into plastic milk cartons and freeze it.

Rosemary lemonade

A last-minute version of lemonade, with a lovely flavour of rosemary. The recipe comes from Darina Allen, who demonstrated it at our school at Perch Hill. Particularly at Christmas, it's worth keeping some of the 'stock syrup' in the fridge for making cocktails (such as pisco sours, page 137) and straight-up lemonade; if you're making a batch, add rosemary to a small jar of it and then you can rustle this up in minutes. There's no citric acid in this lemonade, so use it within a few hours.

For 4–6 glasses:
- **Freshly squeezed juice of 3 lemons**
- **4–5 sprigs rosemary**
- **Fizzy water, to taste**

For the sugar syrup (makes 800ml):
- **450g sugar**

To make a sugar syrup without rosemary, dissolve the sugar in 600ml water and bring to the boil. Boil for 2–3 minutes and allow it to cool. Store in the fridge until needed.

To make rosemary syrup, add the sprigs of rosemary to the above recipe before you bring it to the boil. Leave it to cool and steep overnight, and strain. The recipe makes 800ml, which will give you enough for several batches.

To make the rosemary lemonade, mix the lemon juice with 225ml rosemary syrup and fizzy water to taste.

Christmas Eve

Christmas Eve is often the best day of the whole celebration. People start arriving, any tensions haven't yet emerged and it feels like time for a party. There's a general desire to push the boat out and, once in a while, that's a marvellous thing. As a host, it's too late to panic about what you haven't done. Now you should just go with the flow.

With flowers and decorations, you can do a few last-minute tweaks, but the arranging should have been done by now. With drinks, it's time for a bottle or two of champagne. If you have someone around who likes making drinks, go for a cocktail to get everyone in the mood. After one or two of these, even the grumpiest relation will cheer up.

You may have people staying, so I've given some ideas here for breakfast over the next few days. If you like the idea of something bright and fresh, try the crunchy homemade granola with natural yoghurt or fruit (see page 147), or the blood orange granita (see page149) – both do the trick for anyone with a hangover.

For people arriving in dribs and drabs, make a light lunch. I love kedgeree and have included two different recipes (see pages 150–2). Baked eggs and potted shrimps are also classics, or go for a delicious fish soup topped with rouille (see page 154).

In the early evening, you may have extra people over for drinks. I've already given lots of ideas for party canapés (see pages 125–135), but if you feel like something more substantial, try making one big communal dish, such as the classic Italian party dish bagna cauda (see page 157), or a cheese fondue (see page 158).

At dinner, most people won't want to gorge. (That's all to come.) You could stick to drinks and snacks, and then a delicious pudding such as chocolate cake with kumquats (see page 171). If you want a more formal meal, this is a good moment for a few slivers of beef carpaccio with Gruyère crisps (see page 164), or try tagliata, a seared fillet of beef with lots of peppery winter salad leaves (see page 160). Fish is also perfect, as well as small but punchy-flavoured plates of game; there's a long and good tradition of eating these for dinner on Christmas Eve. For those who eat neither meat nor fish, there's the most delicious winter risotto or gnocchi with Treviso chicory (see page 167).

Small bowls of sorbets are an ideal end to the meal and you can make these a few days beforehand – although the fresher they are, the better the texture. There'll be more time for preparing elaborate puddings in the build-up to a New Year's Eve party, so save the more complicated recipes for then.

Mrs Titley's sticky buns

Mrs Titley helped my mother with the cooking when we were children. She was a truly amazing woman – resourceful, intelligent, hard-working and funny – and she died recently aged 105. She was one of the people who taught me my first recipes.

These are her sticky buns, which she would make for us on special occasions. You must also try her wonderfully easy and reliable recipe for chocolate and coffee éclairs (see page 246).

For 12 buns:
450g strong flour
½ teaspoon salt
1 heaped teaspoon dried yeast
300ml tepid water
50g caster sugar
Large handful of sultanas

For the sugar glaze:
125g caster sugar

Sift the flour with the salt and stir in the yeast, tepid water, caster sugar and sultanas. Bring them all together to form a dough and turn it out on to a floured work surface. Knead the dough for a few minutes and put it into a clean, dry bowl, covered with a tea towel or cling film, in a warm place to rise. The mixture should treble its size before you begin the next step (this could take 2–3 hours).

Knock the dough back and knead it again for a minute or two. Cut it into 12 pieces and shape into balls. Press them down slightly with the palm of your hand to flatten and put them on to a floured baking sheet. Leave them for 20 minutes or so to rise again. Meanwhile, preheat the oven to 200°C/gas mark 6.

Put the buns in the preheated oven and bake for 10–15 minutes. When they have risen well and turned pale gold on top, take them out of the oven and cool them on a wire rack.

To make the sugar glaze, put the sugar and 150ml water into a small saucepan and dissolve over a gentle heat. Bring to the boil and simmer for 2–3 minutes. This glaze keeps well in a jam jar in the fridge and is very useful for sweet breads and rolls.

Brush the buns with the sugar glaze a few minutes after they come out of the oven, and then again while they are still warm. These can also be frozen.

Cornmeal rolls

Light, fluffy, yellow rolls are ideal for breakfast or lunch, and they can be made beforehand and frozen. Eat them with plenty of unsalted butter and apricot and almond compote (see page 28).

For 12 rolls:
50g butter
275ml milk
275g strong white bread flour
175g medium-grade yellow cornmeal or maize meal
1 teaspoon dried yeast
Pinch of salt

Put the butter in a saucepan and melt it over a gentle heat. Add the milk and warm through, but take it off the heat before it gets too hot.

Sift the flour with the cornmeal or maize meal and stir in the yeast and salt. Gradually mix in the lukewarm milk-and-butter mixture. (You may not need all the liquid to make your smooth dough, as different flours vary in their absorbency.)

Turn the mixture on to a floured surface and knead for 5 minutes until you have an elastic dough that is no longer sticky. Then put it into a dry, clean bowl and cover with a damp cloth. Leave in a warm place and allow to double in volume (this could take 2–3 hours).

Knock it back and with a sharp knife divide it into 12 pieces. On a floured surface lightly shape these into rolls and place them on a floured baking sheet. Sprinkle the rolls with a light dusting of cornmeal or maize meal and allow them to rise again for about 15–20 minutes. Meanwhile, preheat the oven to 200°C/gas mark 6.

Bake the rolls in the preheated oven for approximately 15 minutes. Check that they're done, as you would a loaf of bread: knocked on the bottom, they should sound hollow.

Christmas muffins

These are halfway between muffins and scones, deliciously orangey and perfect for a breakfast or tea over Christmas. They're easy to make, so get the children involved. They are at their best eaten with a tart raspberry jam or redcurrant jelly (see page 25).

For 10 muffins:
75g caster sugar
250g self-raising flour
25g ground almonds
½ teaspoon bicarbonate of soda
1 teaspoon baking powder
50g dried apricots (ideally undyed), stoned, soaked and chopped
Zest of 1 orange
75g unsalted butter
4 cloves
100ml freshly squeezed orange juice (2 oranges)
100ml milk
1 egg, beaten

Preheat the oven to 180°C/gas mark 4.

Put all the dry ingredients and the zest into a bowl. Melt the butter over a gentle heat, add the cloves and let them infuse and cool a bit. Then remove the cloves and mix the melted butter, orange juice, milk and egg in another bowl.

Now combine the wet and dry ingredients. The mixture will look quite doughy at this stage. Divide it into 10 and put the portions into paper cases in a muffin tray.

Bake for 20 minutes in the preheated oven. Take the muffins out and let them cool slightly. These are best eaten while they're still warm, but they can be frozen.

Crispy bacon, apple and black pudding stack

A fantastic breakfast served at the lovely Claire Macdonald's Kinloch Lodge Hotel on Skye. Eat this on its own, or with bread.

For 4:
3 dessert apples
450g black pudding
350g green streaky bacon
50g unsalted butter
1 teaspoon sugar
Freshly ground black pepper, to serve

Core the apples, leaving the skin on, and divide into eighths. Cut the black pudding into 1cm slices. Fry or grill the bacon rashers until really crisp and put to one side.

Melt the butter with the sugar in a frying pan. Fry the apple slices in it until golden but still firm, and then the slices of black pudding for a minute or two each side.

On each plate make a pile of apple slices. On top of that put 2–3 slices of black pudding and top with the crispy bacon. Season with freshly ground black pepper.

Zanzibar breakfast

This is my sister Jane's interpretation of something that she had in a fantastic hotel off the coast of Zanzibar, where shrimps were in abundance. It's ideal when you have lots of people around who fancy a cooked breakfast. If you can't get shrimps, small tasty shelled prawns will do instead.

This is excellent eaten with thin crispy toast and some grilled or fried tomatoes.

For 2:
3 eggs
2 stems parsley
100g cooked and shelled
**   shrimps or small prawns,**
**   fresh or frozen**
Knob of butter
Salt and black pepper
Thin slices of toast, to serve

Hard-boil the eggs. Shell them and put into the small bowl of a Magimix, if you have one, add the parsley and pulse until both are chopped into small pieces. If you don't have a Magimix, chop finely by hand.

Put this mixture into a saucepan with the shrimps or prawns and add a knob of butter. Warm through and season with salt and pepper. Serve with thin slices of toast.

Homemade granola

Toasted homemade granola is good for you and tastes fantastic at any time of year, but I think it is particularly good when you feel you're on the verge of over-indulging. It's delicious with frozen raspberries or stewed plums and natural yoghurt.

For 2 medium Kilner jars:
100ml runny honey
100ml olive oil
100ml warm water
500g oats
200g millet
200g rye
200g barley
100g sunflower seeds
50g linseeds
100g pumpkin seeds
100g sesame seeds
Handful of nuts, chopped,
**   e.g. Brazil nuts, hazelnuts**
**   or pecans**
Handful of dried fruit, e.g. raisins
**   or chopped apricots**

Preheat the oven to 180°C/gas mark 4.

Make the dressing by mixing the honey and olive oil in the warm water. Then mix this thoroughly with the grains and seeds.

Spread the mixture out on to baking trays and roast in the preheated oven, turning it constantly until golden and tasty. Beware: this burns easily, so keep checking it.

Once it has cooled, break it up into small pieces with a fork, and add the nuts and dried fruit. Stored in a sealed jar, the granola will keep for a good fortnight.

Blood orange granita

Cold, fresh and tangy, granita is a delicious winter breakfast. Blood oranges are in season, but if you can't find them, use ordinary oranges. A few segments of pink grapefruit, also in season at this time of year, look and taste good with it.

For 10:

2 tablespoons caster sugar
1.5 litres freshly squeezed
   blood orange juice

Put the sugar and 500ml water in a saucepan and heat until the sugar is dissolved. Strain the orange juice into the pan to remove any seeds or pulp.

Pour the mixture into a shallow container. This is crucial: don't use an ice-cream maker, as you want some crystals to form. Place the container in the freezer.

Freeze for 2–3 hours, stirring the mixture with a fork every 20 minutes or so. Break up the film that forms on the surface and crush any lumps; this will give the granita its texture. Ideally, you would serve this immediately, but that would mean an early rise, so make it a bit beforehand. You won't get quite the perfect texture, but it's still delicious. If you are not using the granita straight away, keep it covered in the freezer.

Take the granita out of the freezer for 20–30 minutes before you want to eat it, and either chop it up in a food processor or with a fork, and serve in bowls or glasses.

Christmas smoothie

We have a smoothie for breakfast almost every morning, changing what goes into it from season to season. I avoid bananas, which I find are too sweet, but usually add yoghurt as the filler to stave off hunger before lunch. You can also add a handful of oats soaked in apple or orange juice overnight to make your smoothie more substantial.

For 4:

Juice of 2 pomegranates
   (seeds and flesh pulsed in
   a food processor and then
   sieved) or 200ml bought
   pomegranate juice
Juice of 2 oranges
Juice of 1 lemon
350g frozen raspberries
300ml natural live yoghurt (runny
   or drinking yoghurt – not Greek
   – is best)
1 tablespoon honey (optional)

Combine all the ingredients together in a liquidiser or food processor. Pour into wide-necked tumblers and serve with a spoon.

Spiced kedgeree

**A light lunch for
Christmas Eve**

This is at its best served straight away, but it will be okay made the day before and stored in the fridge. You can heat it up gently in the oven at 160°C/gas mark 2½ for 15 minutes, piled into a dish (or on to a greased baking tray) with a knob of butter and a little water and covered in foil.

For 8–10:

**900g smoked haddock
570ml whole milk
2 bay leaves
A few parsley sprigs, leaves
    chopped and stalks reserved
Thinly pared rind of 1 lemon
6 black peppercorns
2 onions, chopped
120g unsalted butter
Splash of olive oil
2 teaspoons ground coriander
2 teaspoons ground cumin
1 teaspoon freshly grated nutmeg
550g long-grain rice
Large handful of raisins
Salt and black pepper
12 quails' eggs, hard-boiled
    and halved
Bunch of parsley, chopped
Lemon juice, to taste
Greek yoghurt, to serve
Bunch of coriander, chopped,
    to serve**

Cut the fish into large pieces, place in a saucepan and cover with the milk, 570ml water, bay leaves, parsley stalks, lemon rind and peppercorns. Bring this to a simmer on the top of the stove. Cover, remove from the heat and let the fish cool in the liquid. Carefully lift the fish out into a dish and strain the liquid into a jug.

In a large pan, sweat the chopped onions in 25g of the butter with a splash of olive oil until translucent, and add the spices. Cook over a gentle heat for a couple of minutes and then stir in the rice, coating it well. Bring the reserved liquid to the boil in a separate pan and add it to the rice. Stir well, cover and simmer for approximately 15 minutes until the rice is just tender and almost all the liquid has been absorbed.

Remove from the heat and add the remaining butter and the raisins. Season well. Fold in the flaked fish. Place the mixture on a large, shallow plate and add the halved quails' eggs, most of the chopped parsley and lemon juice to taste.

Serve with Greek yoghurt mixed with the chopped coriander and the chopped parsley leaves. Either stir it gently into the kedgeree or serve it separately in a bowl.

Salmon kedgeree

The perfect comfort food, excellent with the addition of lots of fresh coriander as well as the traditional parsley. Take care not to over-cook it, and ideally use organic or sustainably raised salmon.

For 8:
   400g white long-grain rice
   50g butter, plus a little knob of
      butter for cooking the salmon
   500g good salmon
   4 eggs (or 12 quails' eggs)
   1 large bunch of coriander
   1 small bunch of parsley
   Plenty of salt and black pepper

Wash and cook the rice in salted water and drain. Add the butter, carefully forking it through, but not stirring (as this will make the rice mushy).

Meanwhile cook the salmon in enough water to cover the bottom of the pan, and add a little knob of butter to the water. As soon as the water comes to the boil, take the pan off the heat, put a lid on and allow the salmon to steam for 5 minutes. If you like your salmon only just cooked, it will be perfectly done. Alternatively you could steam the salmon in a steamer layer on top of the rice, again steaming for about 5 minutes.

Boil the eggs for 5 minutes, so that the yolk is still slightly runny (or 3 minutes if using quails' eggs). Once the eggs have cooled a bit, peel and roughly chop them.

Coarsely chop the coriander and parsley and then combine everything: mix the rice with the eggs and herbs and carefully fold in the cooked salmon. Season to taste before serving.

Devilled kidneys

These make a lovely, old-fashioned breakfast, brunch or lunch over Christmas. Serve them on toast with plenty of chopped parsley or, for lunch, with rice or mashed potato and a green salad.

For 4:
   8 lambs' kidneys
   1 tablespoon French mustard
   1 teaspoon dry English mustard
   2 teaspoons Worcestershire
      sauce
   1 tablespoon tomato purée
   50g unsalted butter, melted
   1 tablespoon sunflower oil
   50g mushrooms, thinly sliced
   Small pinch of cayenne pepper
   Salt and black pepper
   Dash of sherry
   Plenty of chopped parsley

Clean and halve the lambs' kidneys lengthways, removing the membrane on the outside. Snip away the white core with sharp scissors. Slice each half kidney into 3 or 4.

Mix together the two mustards, Worcestershire sauce and tomato purée and half the melted butter.

Put the remaining butter in a pan with the sunflower oil and toss the mushrooms in it over a medium heat. When they have softened slightly, remove from the pan with a slotted spoon and put to one side.

Put the sliced kidneys into the pan, with a little more butter if necessary. Sauté them with the cayenne pepper for no more than 3 minutes; they will go rubbery if over-cooked.

Season with salt and pepper. Pour in a dash of sherry and add the sliced mushrooms. Bubble the whole thing up together, add the parsley and take off the heat. Eat immediately.

Potted shrimps

We almost always have potted shrimps for lunch on Christmas Eve. You can buy them, but they're incredibly quick and easy to make. You can do this several days beforehand. They last in the fridge for at least a week, or you can put them in the freezer. Eat them with a bitter leaf winter salad and walnut bread (see right) or toasted fennel seed bread (see page 154).

For 4:
   200g fresh brown shrimps,
      cooked and peeled
   Zest and juice of 2 lemons
   2 teaspoons ground mace
   Salt and black pepper
   150g unsalted butter

In a small bowl combine the shrimps, lemon zest and juice, mace, salt and pepper. Put into four small ramekins (150ml).

Melt the butter in a saucepan over a low heat and skim off the froth (so that you are left with clarified butter). Pour over the shrimps in the ramekins.

Chill in the fridge. When set, turn out on to plates and serve.

Walnut bread

This is Sally Clarke's recipe, but I've upped the amount of walnuts and walnut oil. The extra oil makes this bread store well for a few days so, again, you can make this a day or two before Christmas and store it in the fridge or freezer.

For 2 loaves:
- **250g wholemeal flour**
- **250g strong white flour**
- **200g walnut halves, very roughly chopped**
- **1 teaspoon salt**
- **Heaped teaspoon dried yeast or 15g fresh yeast**
- **250ml warm water**
- **75ml walnut oil, plus extra for brushing**

In a food processor mixing bowl, mix the flours with the walnuts and salt.

In a small bowl mix the yeast with half the warm water, and pour this into the mixing bowl, whilst using the dough-hook attachment of the food processor on the slowest speed.

Add the walnut oil and then most of the remaining warm water to produce a soft dough. Continue to mix for approximately 5–8 minutes, until the dough becomes smooth. Add the remaining water if necessary.

Alternatively you can do the mixing by hand in a medium-sized bowl and then turn it out on to a clean table and knead for 5–10 minutes until smooth.

Place the dough in a clean bowl that has a light coating of walnut oil. Cover with cling film and leave in a warm place to rise to double its size. This may take up to an hour or more, depending on the temperature of the room and the weather.

Sprinkle a little wholemeal flour on a baking sheet. Place the dough on a table lightly dusted with white flour. Gently knead, expelling the air in the dough.

Cut the dough in two and shape into round balls or long sausage shapes and place on the baking sheet. Brush with a little walnut oil, cover with cling film and allow to rise in a warm place to half the size again. Meanwhile, preheat the oven to 180°C/gas mark 4.

Place the dough on the middle shelf of the preheated oven and turn up the temperature to 200°C/gas mark 6. Bake until crisp and dark golden brown; this may take up to 40–50 minutes, by which time the bread will sound hollow when you knock the base.

Cool and use within a couple of days, or freeze.

Sorrel egg pots

I love baked eggs. This version, with the sharp taste of sorrel, is one of my favourites. Sorrel is well worth growing: in a sheltered spot it keeps cropping lightly right through the winter, and is fantastic for sauces, soups and salad over this lean time. If you can't find sorrel, use a sliver or two of truffle, some truffle oil or a bit of crumbled Stilton and a dash of Tabasco to add flavour instead.

To make this more of a meal, up the eggs to two per person and cook for 15–20 minutes, and serve it with toast made with fennel seed bread (see page 154).

For 4:
- **Warm water**
- **250g de-stemmed sorrel leaves**
- **Unsalted butter**
- **4 eggs**
- **Salt and black pepper**
- **4 dessertspoons double cream**
- **Freshly grated nutmeg**

Fill a deep baking tray with warm water to a third of the way up the side. Preheat the oven to 170°C/gas mark 3, and place the tray in the oven while it heats up (about 10 minutes).

Wash the sorrel and dry it thoroughly. Then chop it and melt it in a little butter in a pan over a low heat so that the leaves just wilt.

Butter 4 ramekins, and into each put a knob of butter in the bottom and a good dollop of sorrel on top. Break an egg or two on to the sorrel, season with salt and pepper and pour a dessertspoon of cream over the lot. Add a good sprinkling of grated nutmeg.

Place the ramekins in the water-filled baking tray and cook for about 12–15 minutes, until the white is cooked but the yolk is still a little soft.

Quick fennel seed bread

An easy bread which you can prepare in five minutes. It is fabulous with potted shrimps, baked eggs, foie gras and Armagnac prunes (see page 158), or almost anything with a strong flavour. It also makes the best-ever cheese on toast.

For 1 loaf:
250g strong white bread flour
250g 100 per cent wholemeal, stoneground bread flour
1 heaped teaspoon salt
1 heaped tablespoon fennel seeds
1 teaspoon dried yeast
450–500ml tepid water

Oil a 500g loaf tin. Mix the two flours together with the salt, fennel seeds and yeast. Add 450ml of the water and mix together until you have a firm mixture with the texture of cold porridge. (Add the extra 50ml water, if needed, to achieve this consistency.) It's not necessary to knead. Put the mixture into the loaf tin and leave to rise in a warm place for about an hour until it has roughly doubled in size.

Preheat the oven to 220°C/gas mark 7.

Bake in the preheated oven for about 40 minutes or until the bread sounds hollow when you knock the top. If you don't want it too brown, lay a piece of foil over the top for the last 20 minutes of the cooking time. (It is also ideal cooked on the floor of the roasting oven of a four-door Aga with the cold plate slotted in two rungs above.)

Allow the loaf to cool for about 10 minutes before you run a knife around the edge of the tin and turn it out on to a wire rack to cool.

French fish soup with rouille

This is a delicious soup made with all parts of the fish – bones, shells, heads and flesh. Use a mixture of small whole fish, such as dabs, with whiting, monkfish, John Dory, red or grey mullet, a crab, some lobster shells and extra fish heads from your fishmonger. Serve the soup in the traditional French way with rouille spread on slices of toasted baguette – croûtes – floating on top.

For 6:
2kg mixed fish and shellfish
50g unsalted butter
Olive oil
2 onions, chopped
2 garlic cloves, finely chopped
2 bay leaves
2 tablespoons dill
1 tablespoon fresh thyme
900g tomatoes, skinned and coarsely chopped
Sea salt and black pepper
Fish stock (optional)
1 teaspoon saffron strands, soaked in 1 teaspoon boiling water
Slices of French bread, to serve
75g Gruyère, grated, to serve

For the rouille:
1 egg yolk
Pinch of salt
1 large garlic clove, crushed and puréed
1 teaspoon Dijon mustard
3 tablespoons sunflower oil
3 tablespoons olive oil
8 saffron strands, soaked in 1 teaspoon boiling water
Paprika, to taste
Lemon juice, to taste

Remove the gills from the fish and gut any large fish over about 15cm long. Chop everything into large pieces – bones, shells, heads, etc.

Melt the butter and a good glug of olive oil in a large saucepan and sweat the onions gently until they are translucent. Add the chunks of fish and cook for about 5 minutes, allowing the fish to brown slightly. Add the garlic, herbs and tomatoes and season lightly. Add just enough water or fish stock to cover and simmer, covered, for 15 minutes. Then remove the cover and cook for a further 25 minutes, topping up the liquid if necessary.

Remove from the heat and add the soaked saffron. Push it all through a mouli and put to one side while you make the rouille. If you're doing this for lots of people and a mouli feels inadequate for the job, or if you haven't got a mouli, you can liquidise this soup, but you will then need to sieve it several times, starting with a coarse conical sieve and moving down to a fine grade.

To make the rouille, put the egg yolk, salt, garlic and mustard into a mixing bowl. Whiz with a wand mixer or hand blender, or whisk until frothy. Keep the blender moving while adding the two oils in a thin stream until the mixture thickens. Add more oil if necessary. Stir in the saffron and add paprika and lemon juice to taste. Put into a bowl for serving.

Grill or bake slices of French bread until crisp and grate some Gruyère into a bowl.

Reheat the soup. Let everyone help themselves to the croûtes, which they can spread with the rouille, sprinkle with grated Gruyère and float on the soup. That's one of the great things about this soup – the business of assembling and eating it.

Christmas bagna cauda

The lovely Antonio Carluccio introduced me to this, and it's one of my very favourite party dishes. Everyone sits or stands around, dipping the crunchy vegetables into the strong, delicious anchovy and garlic sauce. To make this more of a meal, serve it with plenty of good robust bread, or better still make a bowlful of bruschetta or croutons to soak up the sauce. In case you want to make it in advance, the bagna cauda freezes perfectly.

Use any or all of the following ingredients listed below, adjusting the quantities accordingly.

For 8–10:
- 1 **Treviso chicory, stripped into leaves**
- 1 **Belgian chicory, stripped into leaves**
- ½ **celeriac, peeled and cut into matchsticks (and then doused in lemon juice to stop them discolouring)**
- 3 **Jerusalem artichokes, sliced**
- ½ **cauliflower, broken into small florets**
- 2 **carrots, cut into batons**
- 2 **Florence fennel bulbs, cut into chunks**
- 1 **celery head, broken into sticks and sliced**
- **Selection of crunchy-stemmed salad leaves, such as 'Red Giant' mustard, rocket or mizuna**
- 1 **large bowl of baked or fresh bread bruschetta (see page 133) or croutons**

For the bagna cauda:
- **200g anchovies**
- **Milk, to soak the anchovies and to cover the garlic**
- **16 garlic cloves**
- **100ml extra virgin olive oil**
- **100g butter, cubed**
- **60ml double cream**

First make the bagna cauda. Rinse the anchovies if they are in salt. Leave them soaking in a little cold milk for half an hour. (This recipe makes a relatively mild sauce. If you like punchy, strong food, you may want to up the anchovy count a bit.)

Preheat the oven to 150°C/gas mark 2.

Put a little milk in a saucepan and bring it to the boil. Peel the garlic cloves, slice them in half and put them into a small ovenproof dish or ramekin. Pour over just enough of the hot milk to cover. Cover this with aluminium foil and put into the preheated oven for about 25 minutes or until the garlic is soft. Mash the garlic cloves into the milk.

Retrieve the anchovies from the milk, put them into a bain-marie over a very low heat and, using the back of a wooden spoon, mash them to a paste. Add the garlic milk to the bowl.

Gradually add the oil, the cubed butter and, lastly, the cream. Keep stirring until it's all smooth. Pour this into a small dish over a nightlight, if possible, and put it in the centre of the table. Serve with the vegetables and the croutons or bruschetta.

Cheese fondue

This is the alpine alternative to bagna cauda and it is delicious once or twice a year, especially at Christmas. A little goes a long way and you need a good peppery rocket and mustard salad alongside. I also love it with raw winter vegetables dipped in. It is best for lunch or an early evening dinner after a long walk.

For 4:
2 garlic cloves
350ml dry white wine
300g Emmenthal cheese
300g Gruyère cheese
1 dessertspoon cornflour,
**   dissolved in a splash of kirsch**
Freshly grated nutmeg
Salt and black pepper
1 teaspoon lemon juice
Fresh crusty bread, to serve
Raw fresh vegetables such as
**   crunchy lettuce and salad**
**   leaves, celery and chicory,**
**   to serve**

Rub a fondue pot with the garlic cloves and pour in the white wine. Over a gentle heat, warm the wine and gradually add the two cheeses, stirring constantly until you have a smooth mixture. Bring to a simmer and add the cornflour/kirsch solution. Add a good grinding of nutmeg, and season with salt and pepper and lemon juice to taste.

Put the fondue pot in the centre of the table over a nightlight to keep it warm (don't let it boil or cook too fast). To serve, hand around two baskets: one with chunks of crusty bread and the other a mixture of lovely fresh vegetables, both for dipping into the cheese.

Foie gras with Armagnac prunes and pear salad

An intense, delicious dish which can be eaten as a first course, or made into a main course with a pear and watercress salad and some toasted brioches or thinly sliced, toasted fennel seed bread (see page 154). It's rich and filling – perfect winter party food. This dish is at its most delicious made with prunes that have been long-soaked in Armagnac, but you can prepare them the night before. To do this, soak 25 dried, stoned prunes (approximately 500g) in Earl Grey tea overnight, drain, and then soak in Armagnac (enough to cover them) for 3–4 hours before you start cooking.

For 8:
8 slices foie gras
Maldon salt and black pepper
Extra virgin olive oil
A little dessert wine or ginger
**   wine**
25 prunes in Armagnac
**   (see page 29)**

For the pear salad:
4 ripe but firm Comice pears, cut
**   into thin slices**
Large bunch of watercress,
**   large stems removed, rinsed**
**   and dried**
Salt and black pepper
Handful of pine nuts, toasted

For the salad dressing:
50ml balsamic vinegar
1 teaspoon caster sugar
Black pepper
3 tablespoons extra virgin
**   olive oil**

Heat a heavy-based frying pan and season the slices of foie gras. Sauté each slice in olive oil for no more than a minute on each side. Put to one side and keep warm. Add a little dessert wine or ginger wine to the pan and scrape up any juices.

To make the dressing, put the balsamic vinegar into a small heavy-based saucepan and add the caster sugar. Gently dissolve the sugar over a low heat and then simmer for 5 minutes. Season with black pepper and add more sugar to taste if you prefer a sweeter dressing. Once cooled, add the olive oil and whisk together.

Next make the salad. Combine the sliced pears with the watercress, season and drizzle over a very little of the dressing, adding the toasted pine nuts at the last minute.

Put a slice of the foie gras on each plate with a little of the pan juices and two or three of the prunes. Serve with the salad and slices of toasted brioche or thinly sliced toasted fennel seed bread.

Pickled herrings

I could eat pickled herrings almost daily, as they do in Scandinavia. Rye crispbread or black bread, beetroot, a bunch of dill and sour cream are classic accompaniments. Pickled herrings are also wonderful with blinis, smoked eel and gravadlax (see pages 133 and right). This recipe makes a sweet, dill-flavoured pickled fish.

For 3 jars:
6 herrings, boned and sliced into single fillets
50g salt
570ml white wine vinegar
20g pickling spice
1 tablespoon mustard seeds (in addition to those in the pickling spice)
50g onions, very thinly sliced
50g sugar
Large bunch dill, finely chopped
2 bay leaves

Soak the boned, filleted herrings in 570ml water and the salt for at least 2 hours to soften. Put the vinegar, spice, mustard seeds, onions, sugar, dill and bay leaves into a saucepan, bring to the boil and simmer for 2–3 minutes. Put to one side to infuse for half an hour.

Rinse the herring fillets and roll them up with the skin side outwards. Place in jam or Kilner jars that have been sterilised by being boiled in a pan of water for 10 minutes or run through the dishwasher. Make sure that the herrings are tightly packed. Pour over the liquid and cover the jars.

This will keep for several days in the fridge, and the flavour improves with storing.

Gravadlax

You can always buy gravadlax, but as long as you think about it well ahead, it's easy to make and homemade is a fraction of the price of ready-prepared. Buy good salmon – it's crucial to the excellent flavour of this dish. Serve it scattered with some coarsely chopped dill, and a bowl of dill and mustard sauce (see right).

For 6–8 (or more if serving with a selection of other fish):
1kg tailpiece of salmon in 2 pieces, scaled, boned and filleted, with the skin on
Large bunch of dill

For the marinade:
1 heaped tablespoon sea salt
1 heaped tablespoon caster sugar
1 teaspoon black or white peppercorns, coarsely crushed
3 tablespoons Calvados or brandy
Plenty of chopped dill
Zest of 2 lemons

Prepare the marinade by mixing all the ingredients together in a small bowl. Line a shallow dish with cling film and put a quarter of the marinade into the bottom of the dish. Lay the first piece of salmon, skin side down, on the marinade. Scatter half the dill over it.

Cover the salmon with half the remaining marinade and rub it into the flesh. Then lay the second piece of salmon (with some marinade rubbed in) on it, with the skin side uppermost.

Cover with the remaining dill and marinade, rubbing the marinade well into the skin. Lay some cling film over the dish and cover with a board weighted down with a heavy weight – this step is crucial. Chill for at least 12 hours; 24 is even better.

Drain the marinade off the salmon and slice it thinly with a very sharp knife.

Dill and mustard sauce

The classic accompaniment to gravadlax or pickled and smoked fish and blinis (see page 133).

For a decent-sized bowl:
1 egg yolk
2 tablespoons Dijon mustard
½ teaspoon sugar
1 tablespoon white wine or white wine vinegar
6 tablespoons vegetable oil
Salt and black pepper
Small bunch of dill, chopped

Beat the egg yolk with the mustard and sugar, and stir in the wine or vinegar. Slowly beat in the oil until the sauce emulsifies. Add salt, pepper and chopped dill. Chill before serving.

Tagliata

Tagliata is one of my very favourite winter dishes – a warm beef fillet salad with lots of excellent, peppery winter salad leaves. You can either stick with the original Italian flavours, marinating the beef in chopped rosemary, lemon, garlic and olive oil, or give it an oriental twist, with plenty of ginger and chilli, as here. I like both. You can use sirloin steaks, which are less expensive than fillet – cut them into strips after very brief cooking.

For 8:
About 1.3kg beef fillet, trimmed
5 or 6 large handfuls of mixed peppery winter leaves, e.g. rocket, mustards 'Golden Streaks' and 'Osaka Purple', Treviso chicory, chicory 'Variegata del Castelfranco', all refreshed in cold water and dried

For the marinade:
200ml soy sauce (or juice of 2 lemons)
1 red chilli, deseeded and chopped
3 garlic cloves, chopped
100ml sunflower oil

For the oriental dressing:
6 tablespoons soy sauce
1 heaped tablespoon chopped fresh ginger
1 red chilli, deseeded and chopped
Lemon juice, to taste
1 small tablespoon Thai fish sauce
1 small tablespoon light brown sugar
2 garlic cloves
Good handful of fresh coriander
Sunflower oil
Maldon salt and black pepper

For the marinade, put the soy sauce, chilli, garlic and sunflower oil in a blender and process until smooth.

Spread over the beef fillet and leave for several hours (or overnight) in the fridge, turning from time to time.

Bring the fillet to room temperature and preheat the oven to 220°C/gas mark 7.

Brown the fillet quickly on a griddle or in a frying pan over a high heat, and then on a griddle or in a roasting pan roast it for 15–20 minutes (depending whether you like rare or medium) in the preheated oven. Allow to cool a little. Combine all the dressing ingredients with half of the coriander.

Thinly slice the fillet and arrange the slices on a bed of salad leaves. Drizzle the dressing and scatter the rest of the coriander over the top, adding Maldon salt and freshly ground black pepper to taste.

Whole fish baked in salt with winter salsa verde

I first had this with sea bass in a café in the harbour of Palma in Majorca. Using all that salt may seem a scary prospect, but it seals in the moisture, protects the flesh and makes any already good fish absolutely delicious.

Serve the fish warm with potatoes, slow-roasted bulb fennel and this winter salsa verde, a herb dressing that is wonderful with almost anything – beef or lamb, vegetables, chicken and fish.

For 6–8:
**3.6kg coarse preserving salt
(or half-and-half Maldon
and fine table salt if you
can't find it)
Salt and black pepper,
for seasoning
1 x 2kg organic salmon or bass,
scaled and cleaned but
not filleted
1 lemon, sliced
Small handful of fresh fennel
stalks**

For the salsa verde:
**1 large bunch of parsley
1 large bunch of mixed winter
herbs (e.g. chervil, coriander,
sorrel and one or two sprigs
of thyme or winter savory, the
leaves stripped from the stem)
4 gherkins, rinsed
20–30 small capers, rinsed
250ml olive oil
Juice of ½ lemon
Salt and black pepper**

Preheat the oven to 200°C/gas mark 6.

In a large mixing bowl, mix the salt with about 500ml cold water to give a sand-castle consistency.

Season the cavity of the fish with salt and pepper and put the lemon and fennel stalks inside. Cover the bottom of a baking dish with half the salt and lay the fish on top. Cover the fish completely with the remaining salt and pat it down with your hands to form a smooth surface.

Bake the fish in the preheated oven. After 20 minutes, insert a skewer into the fish. If the tip of the skewer is hot to your lip, the fish is ready.

Crack open the salt crust by knocking in a large carving knife with a rolling pin and remove the hard salt pieces, taking care to brush away any loose salt from the flesh of the fish. This is easier to do if you leave the fish skin intact. Carefully lift the fish and place it on a platter. Remove the skin.

To make the salsa verde, chop the parsley and other herbs coarsely. Add the gherkins and capers with the olive oil and lemon juice. Blitz in a food processor just briefly, or chop by hand, so that you have a coarse-textured sauce. Season with salt and pepper to taste.

Fritto misto

Make this classic Venetian dish with a mixture of fish: small scampi, prawns, sprats, smelts, hake, small cuttlefish, a dab or two and some calamari. Serve with very fine straw chips and a green salad or wilted, buttered spinach.

As it is cooked in small batches and served immediately, it's best to make this dish for small numbers only.

For 4:
**1kg assorted fish
150g plain flour
1–2 tablespoons extra virgin
olive oil
Warm water
3 egg whites
Sunflower oil, for frying**

Leaving the heads on the smaller ones, scale and gut the fish and wash and dry thoroughly. Fillet the larger fish and cut into pieces. Leave the shells and heads on the prawns.

Sift the flour into a medium-sized bowl and make a well in the centre. Pour in the olive oil and stir slowly, combining the flour with the oil. Slowly add warm water to loosen this paste, stirring all the time, until you have a batter the consistency of double cream. Leave for a minimum of 45 minutes.

Just before cooking, beat the egg whites until stiff and fold gently into the batter.

Pour the sunflower oil to a third of the way up a high-sided pan. Heat the oil until very hot (180°C). If you don't have an oil thermometer, it's easy to test. Drop a cube of white bread into the oil. It should turn golden brown in less than a minute. Any quicker than 30 seconds, though, means the oil is dangerously hot.

Dip the fish into the batter and deep-fry – not too many at once. Stand well back as you put them in and cover your hand with a cloth, or use a spit guard. Serve immediately.

Beef carpaccio with Gruyère crisps

This is the perfect light, yet satisfying, celebratory meal: straightforward raw beef fillet, with a savoury, cheese version of brandy snaps. You can eat a small plate of this as a starter, or give everyone a larger plate, with peppery salad and good robust bread.

For 8:
800g beef fillet as a first course or 1.2kg as a main course, unsliced
175g Gruyère, grated
4 tablespoons extra virgin olive oil
Salt and coarsely crushed black pepper
A few coriander seeds, coarsely ground
6 handfuls of rocket (wild or salad)
Olive oil, to serve

Put the fillet into the freezer for 2 hours. This makes it easier to cut into very thin slices.

Slice the beef into slivers and put each slice in between two layers of greaseproof paper or cling film. Beat out with a rolling pin as thinly as you can without breaking the flesh.

To make the Gruyère crisps, preheat the oven to 180°C/gas mark 4. Sprinkle 8cm-diameter mounds of grated Gruyère on to greaseproof paper rubbed with a trace of sunflower oil, or a silicone mat, and bake in the preheated oven for 5 minutes or so until golden; they burn easily and then taste bitter, so keep checking them. Allow them to cool for 3–4 minutes and lift off carefully with a spatula on to a wire rack. These store well in an airtight container if you are not using them straight away.

To serve the dish, lay the beef slices out on a flat plate, drizzle some of the olive oil over them and scatter over the coarsely crushed black pepper and just a few crushed coriander seeds. Mix the rocket with a little olive oil, salt and more pepper and put a mound of rocket leaves in the middle of the beef. Place one or two Gruyère crisps on the side of each plate.

Roast partridge with cobnut stuffing

Partridge has a great flavour. The key when cooking it is to keep the flesh moist. Do this by covering the breast with streaky bacon and stuffing the cavity with this delicious nutty mix. This is another recipe that Peter Weeden (head chef of Paternoster Chop House) devised for using the great Kentish cobnut. Lay each bird on a slice of bread to catch all the gamey juice.

For 4:
4 partridges: reds or stronger-flavoured native greys, dry plucked, preferably not plastic-wrapped
8 rashers streaky bacon
4 half slices of crusty white bread, buttered

For the stuffing:
1 onion, chopped
25g butter
75g cobnuts
150g breadcrumbs
1 apple, diced
1 egg, beaten
Salt and black pepper
A little milk

Preheat the oven to 175°C/gas mark 3–4.

To make the stuffing, sweat the onion in the butter for 10 minutes over a gentle heat. Roughly chop the cobnuts and mix them into the breadcrumbs with the apple and beaten egg, salt and pepper and softened onion. If the mixture is too dry, add a little milk.

Stuff the birds with this mixture, cover the breasts with the bacon and sit them on a half slice of crusty white bread, butter side up, in a baking tray. This will fry and soak up the juices as it cooks. Roast in the preheated oven for 30 minutes. After roasting, allow the birds to rest for at least 10 minutes before serving.

Gnocchi with Treviso chicory

The Due More, one of the many restaurants in the beautiful hill town of Asolo in the Veneto, usually has this on its winter menu. It's one of the most delicious ways of eating Treviso chicory, with the gnocchi quite small, about the size of the base of my thumb. Don't be put off by the idea of gnocchi being stodgy: I promise these aren't.

If you're not cooking for vegetarians, you could also add some crunchy slices of roast pancetta or prosciutto, which both go well with Treviso chicory.

For 6:
2 onions, sliced
5 tablespoons extra virgin olive oil, plus a little more for the dish
3 garlic cloves, chopped
Salt and black pepper
Pinch of freshly grated nutmeg
200ml double cream or crème fraîche
150g grated Parmesan cheese, and some to serve
900g Treviso chicory or radicchio, sliced
A few knobs of butter

For the gnocchi:
1kg floury potatoes
200g potato flour
(or Italian 00 grade flour)
Pinch of salt

To make the gnocchi, steam the potatoes in their skins. (This may take up to 40 minutes.) When they are tender, leave them until they're cool enough to handle and remove the skins. Mash them and mix, with a wooden spoon or your hands, into a smooth paste with the flour and a pinch of salt.

Roll the paste into sticks as thick as your finger. Then cut the sticks into lengths of about 2cm and slightly flatten them against the back of a fork.

Cook in a saucepan of boiling salted water for about 3 minutes – the gnocchi will be cooked when they rise to the surface. Remove from the water immediately with a slotted spoon. Keep them warm.

To make the sauce, sweat the onions in the olive oil over a gentle heat with the chopped garlic. Add the salt, pepper, grated nutmeg and cream or crème fraîche and allow to thicken slightly. Add the Parmesan.

In another pan, just wilt (don't cook till fully tender – it's good for it to have a bit of a bite) the sliced Treviso in a little butter and a little olive oil. Combine this with the sauce and pour over the gnocchi. Serve immediately with plenty of Parmesan and scatter flakes of butter over the top.

Treviso chicory risotto

The bitter/sweet combination of the Treviso chicory with the Parmesan makes this one of the best winter risottos you can eat. Leave some of the chicory chunky so that it keeps a firm texture. Serve it topped with plenty of parsley, quite coarsely chopped, or try it with a scattering of light kale seaweed (see page 127).

For 4:
300g Treviso chicory
(or radicchio if you can't find it)
800ml good vegetable stock
1 onion, finely cubed
20g butter, plus extra for sautéing
2 tablespoons olive oil
300g Vialone – round risotto rice
½ glass of red wine
150g Parmesan cheese, grated
Salt and black pepper
Plenty of chopped parsley

Peel the Treviso chicory, leaving the hearts. Cut these into slices lengthways, and put to one side. Cut the outer leaves widthways into 1–2cm strips.

Bring the stock to the boil and keep on a low simmer. Gently fry the onion in the butter and olive oil. Add the rice, the outer chicory leaves and the wine. Allow it to bubble up until the wine evaporates. Add a ladleful of the boiling broth and stir constantly until the rice has absorbed the liquid. Repeat this, adding the broth a ladleful at a time and stirring constantly, until all the liquid has been absorbed.

Just before the rice reaches the al dente stage (after about 15 minutes), sauté the chicory hearts in a little butter until they soften but still have a bite. Add them to the pan and continue cooking for a further 2–3 minutes until the rice is al dente.

Take off the heat, and add the Parmesan, salt and pepper. Allow the risotto to rest, covered, for 5 minutes or so. Serve with chopped parsley.

Poached pears with bitter chocolate mousse

If you've had a bagna cauda (see page 157) or tray of blinis, this is the perfect pudding to follow. The sweetness of the pears is an excellent contrast to the soft fluffiness of the bitter chocolate. The key to this marvellous mousse – which is a pudding in its own right – is using good chocolate and not adding extra sugar. You'd think it wouldn't be very child-friendly, but my children love it. Note that it includes raw egg.

The mousse serves 8 if it accompanies the pears, or makes 4–6 pots if served on its own.

For 8:
650ml dessert wine
225g caster sugar
2 large pieces of thinly pared lemon rind
Juice of ½ lemon
A few allspice berries
A few star anise
1 cinnamon stick
8 firm Conference pears

For the mousse:
175g dark chocolate (70% cocoa solids), broken into pieces
10g unsalted butter
3 eggs, separated
Dash of brandy

Put the wine, sugar, lemon rind and juice, allspice berries, star anise and cinnamon with 650ml water into a heavy-bottomed pan with a lid that will snugly fit the pears standing upright. Stir over a moderate heat to dissolve the sugar.

Peel the pears, leaving on the stalks and cutting a little off the bottom so that they will stand upright. Put them in the pan. Make sure that they are covered with liquid and add a little more wine, if necessary. Bring to the boil and then lower the heat, cover, and then either simmer or transfer to the oven (preheated to 180°C/gas mark 4) for about 20 minutes.

The pears should be just tender but not soft. Lift them out and put into a dish. Reduce the liquid over a high heat for a few minutes until it has thickened slightly. Strain the liquid over the pears and allow to cool. These are best eaten chilled.

To make the mousse, put the chocolate and 75ml water into a bain-marie and dissolve over a pan of simmering water. Take off the heat and beat in the butter. Stir in the egg yolks one by one, followed by a splash of brandy.

Whisk the egg whites until stiff and fold into the chocolate mixture.

Pour into a dish or small pots and chill overnight before serving with the pears.

Tam's coffee meringue ice-cream cake

In my *Garden Cookbook* I suggested serving this delicious pudding with pomegranate sauce; try it, as here, with frozen raspberries or rosehip syrup.

For 8–10:

2 tablespoons strong instant coffee powder or granules
1 tablespoon boiling water
750ml double cream
1 tablespoon caster sugar
1 tablespoon coffee liqueur
3 pieces of stem ginger, thinly sliced, plus 1 tablespoon of the ginger syrup
Frozen raspberries or rosehip syrup (see page 43), to serve

For the meringues:

6 egg whites
180g granulated sugar
180g caster sugar
Sunflower oil

Preheat the oven to 110°C/gas mark ¼.

To make the meringues, whisk the egg whites until very stiff and dry, and slowly add the granulated sugar, whisking until the egg white regains its former stiffness. Fold in the caster sugar with a large metal spoon. In serving-spoon-sized dollops, spoon on to greaseproof paper rubbed with a trace of sunflower oil, or a silicone mat, and bake in the oven for about 3 hours until crisp. Remove from the oven and break into pieces.

Mix the instant coffee with the boiling water, and chill it well. Whip the cream to the soft-peak stage and mix in the sugar, liqueur and half the coffee. Fold the sliced ginger, ginger syrup and meringue pieces into the mixture. Spoon into a deep (8cm) straight-sided round cake tin, 22cm in diameter, or a loaf tin, lined with non-stick paper, and marble the top with the remaining coffee. Freeze for at least 24 hours. Serve straight from the freezer with the raspberries or rosehip syrup.

Chocolate cake with kumquat compote

This is a superb rich chocolate cake with a sharp citrus compote of kumquats. It's best served warm.

For 8:

50g self-raising flour
150g caster sugar
3 eggs
75g dark chocolate (70% cocoa solids), broken into pieces
25g cocoa powder
100g unsalted butter
50g toasted hazelnuts, roughly chopped

For the glaze:

100g dark chocolate (70% cocoa solids), broken into pieces
25g unsalted butter
2 tablespoons milk

For the compote:

350g kumquats
225g caster sugar
300ml orange juice

Preheat the oven to 150°C/gas mark 2.

Grease a 20cm shallow, round cake tin and line with greaseproof paper rubbed with a trace of sunflower oil, or a silicone mat. Beat the flour, sugar and eggs until the mixture is very thick. Melt the chocolate, cocoa powder and butter in a double saucepan over boiling water and add to the egg mixture, whisking for another few minutes. Fold in the chopped hazelnuts. Pour into the tin and bake in the preheated oven for 25 minutes. The middle should be still quite soft.

Remove the cake from the oven and leave in the tin for at least 10 minutes before turning out on to a rack.

Melt the glaze ingredients together and pour over the cake while it is still warm.

To make the compote, wash the kumquats and halve lengthways, removing the pips. Put the sugar and orange juice into a pan with 150ml water. Dissolve the sugar over a gentle heat and then bring to the boil. Reduce the heat and simmer for about 5 minutes. Add the kumquats and continue to simmer until the fruit is tender; this will take about 40 minutes, depending on the fruits' age and size. Remove from the heat and allow to cool a little.

Serve the cake with the warm poached kumquats.

Blood orange sorbet with lemon vodka

You may think winter is not the time for ice cream and sorbets, but I'd say the opposite is the case. If you've had a great dinner, there's nothing better than finishing with a few mouthfuls of something sharp and sweet. Blood oranges make a perfect light, tangy sorbet that's brilliant with a hit of lemon vodka.

For 4:
  8–10 blood oranges
    (depending on size)
  150g sugar
  1 tablespoon fresh lemon juice
  Lemon vodka (see page 41),
    to serve

Scrub and dry the fruit and, using a zester, remove the zest of four of the oranges. Dissolve the sugar in 200ml water in a small saucepan over a low heat. Add half the orange zest and bring to the boil for 2–3 minutes. Allow to cool and strain.

Squeeze the juice from all the oranges and combine it with the cold syrup, lemon juice and reserved, uncooked zest.

Pour into an ice-cream maker. Freeze/churn for 20–25 minutes and pack into a plastic container. Freeze for at least an hour before serving. If you haven't got a machine, pour into a Tupperware container and freeze for 2 hours. Take out of the freezer and stir with a fork. Return to the freezer and repeat this process twice, stirring at two-hourly intervals. Allow the sorbet 20–25 minutes in the fridge to soften slightly before serving.

To serve, put 2 scoops per person into a glass and pour a little lemon vodka over each one.

Apple sorbet with Calvados

Another sorbet with spirit, and equally good. You could serve everyone two little glasses, one containing this sorbet and the other the blood orange sorbet (see left).

For 6–8:
  8 eating apples, peeled, cored
    and sliced (Granny Smiths
    are perfect)
  3 teaspoons lemon juice
  175g granulated sugar
  Calvados, to serve

Put the sliced apples on to a tray and squeeze over the lemon juice. Put the tray into the freezer while you heat the sugar and 175ml water in a small saucepan over a low heat. Once the sugar has dissolved, increase the heat and boil for about 2 minutes. Remove from the heat and allow to cool, and then refrigerate.

Once the apples have partially frozen, put them into a food processor or hand blender with the cold syrup and process to a purée. Push this mixture through a sieve to extract as much juice as possible. You should end up with approximately 800ml juice.

Pour into an ice-cream maker. Freeze/churn for 20–25 minutes and pack into a plastic container. Freeze for at least an hour before serving. If you haven't got a machine, pour into a Tupperware container and freeze for 2 hours. Take out of the freezer and stir with a fork. Return to the freezer and repeat this process twice, stirring at two-hourly intervals. Allow the sorbet 20–25 minutes in the fridge to soften slightly before serving.

Serve with a tot of Calvados poured over it at the last minute.

Florentine ice cream with cranberry sauce

This ice cream is lovely eaten on its own and excellent with quickly cooked cranberries, poached pears (see page 168) or kumquat compote (see page 171). It's a wonderful use of those Florentine scraps which you inevitably get when you make a batch of the biscuits.

For 8–10:
  570ml milk
  100g caster sugar
  A few drops of good vanilla
    extract
  220g sweetened condensed milk
  Pinch of salt
  475ml whipping or double cream
  18 broken Florentines (see
    page 36)

For the sauce:
  1 good handful of cranberries
  Zest and juice of 1 orange
  1 tablespoon caster sugar
    (or add sugar to taste)

Heat the milk with the sugar and vanilla, and bring to boiling point. Remove from the heat and cool. Add the condensed milk, salt and cream.

Put in an ice-cream maker and freeze/churn the mixture for 15–20 minutes. Fold in the broken Florentines at the last minute before putting in a plastic container and freezing. If you haven't got a machine, pour into a Tupperware container and freeze for 2 hours. Take out of the freezer and stir with a fork. Return to the freezer and repeat this process twice, stirring at two-hourly intervals. Transfer the ice cream to the fridge 20–25 minutes before serving.

Meanwhile, heat through the cranberries in the orange juice and sugar. Allow to cool a little before serving with the ice cream.

Christmas Day

It's like when your friends get married: many of those who you'd think would baulk at a white wedding go for exactly that – they enjoy its certainty and predictability. It's the same with Christmas Day. By all means spread your culinary wings before and after, but on the day itself, stick with family tradition.

I come from a family who never, as far as I can remember, had turkey on Christmas Day. There was always goose, or game – a partridge each or wild duck. My husband's family never had anything but turkey. This was a source of friction for a while, but nowadays you can find really good free-range and organic turkeys, and a bird that's reared slowly, spending its life foraging in a field, will taste quite gamey and delicious. If you're feeding large numbers, a turkey is brilliant and will give you lots of useful leftovers. For a smaller gathering, I'd still say that goose has the edge.

Whether it's turkey or goose, you've got to have stuffing. Without it some people will feel cheated. My five stuffings (see pages 180 and 185–187) are all delicious and simple to make. Then there's the bread sauce (see page 182), gravy (see page 184) and cranberry and orange compote (see page 26). Don't forget the vegetarians amongst you. They may be happy with the non-meat stuffings (see page 185), but a warm Christmas salad with squash, peppers, nuts and fresh herbs (see page 188) or a fennel and Gorgonzola soufflé tart (see page 190) will make them feel you've gone the extra mile.

As far as vegetables go, plan three veg plus potatoes, and then everyone will be happy. It would be a shame not to have a crunchy roast potato or two on Christmas Day (see page 192), but the rest of the vegetables are a more movable feast. For colour and flavour, I'd vote for Brussels sprouts with chestnuts or puréed with nutmeg (see page 196). Red cabbage with blackberries (see page 196) goes particularly well with game or goose. Last Christmas, we had Parmesan parsnips with our turkey, and this year I used the same recipe for salsify (see page 193), and I always love slow-roasted carrots tossed in cumin butter (see page 195).

As well as Christmas pudding, you may want to have something else up your sleeve for those who don't like it, such as trifle (see page 200). Candied fruit dipped in chocolate (see page 31) and homemade truffles (see page 34) are a good end to any Christmas meal, and have some nuts and cheese on the table, as well as a plate of frosted grapes. To make these, dip individual grapes in quickly forked egg white, and then roll them in caster sugar. They'll look sparkly and beautiful for days.

Roast goose

The bird, stuffing and gravy

I love goose and would choose this over turkey any day if I had only a few people to feed. Buy a farmyard goose (a Toulouse/Embden cross), not one of the wild geese that are sometimes available from game dealers. These are usually too small and can be very tough and strong in flavour.

The standard 4.5kg goose will serve 6–7 people. You want the giblets too: you can save the liver for chopping into the stuffing (see page 180) or to add to a chicken liver pâté (see page 218) and use the rest of the giblets to make stock for the gravy (see page 180).

Goose
Apple and black pudding stuffing
   (see page 180)
Salt and black pepper

Preheat the oven to 220°C/gas mark 7.

Remove the lumps of fat from the cavity of the bird and season the whole bird with salt and pepper. Fill the cavity loosely – about three-quarters full – with stuffing, prick the skin but not the flesh, and rub the skin with salt and pepper.

Weigh the bird after stuffing and allow 15 minutes' cooking time for each 450g, plus 20 minutes' resting time after cooking.

Put the bird on a roasting tray, cover with aluminium foil and place on the bottom shelf of the preheated oven. After 20 minutes' cooking, lower the oven temperature to 180°C/gas mark 4. After an hour's cooking drain the fat from the tray.

For the last 30 minutes' cooking time raise the temperature again to 220°C/gas mark 7 and remove the foil to crisp the skin and allow it to turn golden.

Test by inserting a skewer into the thickest part of the thigh. If the juices run clear, the goose is ready.

Remove it from the oven and, keeping it warm under foil and tea towels, allow it to rest for 20 minutes before you carve.

Goose gravy

You can make the stock for this gravy before Christmas Day and store it in the fridge or freezer.

For 6–7:
1 tablespoon plain flour
Salt and black pepper
1 small glass of port,
    or 1 small glass of red wine with
    1 tablespoon redcurrant jelly

For the stock:
Goose giblets
1 onion, unpeeled and quartered
1 celery stick
1 carrot, scrubbed

To make the stock, put the giblets into a pan with the onion, celery and carrot. Cover them with water and a lid and simmer gently for an hour. Cool and strain, and once cool store in the fridge for reheating when you're ready to make the gravy. Skim off any fat.

To make the gravy, remove the goose from the roasting pan. Spoon off most of the fat in the pan and scrape up the bits into the remaining juices. Put the pan over a medium heat and add a tablespoon of plain flour. Allow it to cook for a minute or two while stirring it into the juices with a small balloon whisk.

Add some warm, strained giblet stock to the pan, little by little, stirring all the time, until you have made a smooth gravy.

Check the seasoning and add the port or red wine and redcurrant jelly. Allow the gravy to bubble up and simmer for 5 minutes.

Apple and black pudding stuffing

Black pudding is a delicious main component for stuffing with dark poultry – goose or duck – but you need to find a good supplier. You can make this beforehand and freeze it.

For a 4.5kg goose to feed 6–7:
300g onions
50g butter
200g fresh breadcrumbs
40g sage, chopped
30g parsley, chopped with stalks
2 garlic cloves, finely chopped
6 pickled walnuts, roughly
    chopped (optional)
Zest and juice of 1 orange
2 Bramley apples, peeled, cored
    and chopped
500g good black pudding,
    skinned and coarsely chopped
The goose liver, sautéed or
    poached and chopped
Salt and black pepper
1 egg, beaten

Chop the onions and melt the butter in a pan. Add the onions and sweat them for 10 minutes over a low heat until soft. Set aside to cool.

In a large mixing bowl, combine the breadcrumbs, herbs, garlic, walnuts (if using), orange zest and juice, chopped apples and cooled onions.

Carefully fold in the black pudding and chopped goose liver and season well. Bind together with the beaten egg. Stuff this mixture into the cavity of the goose.

Roast turkey

It's always worth buying the best turkey you can get your hands on, fresh rather than frozen, and free range or organic. Such turkeys are always more expensive, but definitely worth it. A Bronze or Norfolk Black, properly and humanely reared, and hung for two weeks, should have plenty of taste. When ordering your turkey, allow approximately 350g oven-ready weight (once drawn and trussed) per person.

The turkey will keep perfectly well in a cold place if you collect it a day or two before Christmas. To get ahead, it's a good idea to make your giblet stock for the gravy in advance. You can keep this in the fridge or freeze it.

Try using two contrasting stuffings with the turkey – one in the body cavity and one in the neck end; or if you prefer, stuff the neck end only and fill the body cavity with a large knob of butter, some quartered onions and a couple of rough-cut lemons. Serve it with bread sauce (see right), gravy (see page 184), sausages with bacon (see page 187), and cranberry and orange compote (see page 26).

Turkey
Stuffing (see pages 185–7)
1 tablespoon plain flour
Softened butter
Salt and black pepper
Streaky bacon, to cover the
    turkey breast and thighs

After stuffing, weigh the bird in order to calculate the cooking time. Put a tablespoon of flour in a roasting tray and sit the turkey on top. Rub the bird all over with softened butter, season with salt and pepper and cover the breast and thighs with streaky bacon to protect the flesh while it is roasting. Alternatively, you can protect it very efficiently with a double thickness of muslin and then a double piece of aluminium foil.

Preheat the oven to 220°C/gas mark 7 and roast for 30 minutes at this temperature. Reduce the heat to 180°C/gas mark 4 for a small turkey (up to 5.5kg) or to 160°C/gas mark 2–3 for turkeys over 5.5kg.

Roasting times (including the first 30 minutes):

3.5–4.5kg	3–3½ hours
4.5–6.4kg	3½–4 hours
6.4–8.2kg	4–4½ hours
8.2–9.1kg	4½–5 hours

Remove the foil for the last 30 minutes to brown the bacon.

Test to see if the bird is cooked by inserting a skewer into the thickest part of the thigh. If the juices run clear, the turkey is ready.

Remove it from the oven, cover with foil and several tea cloths to keep it warm and allow it to rest for at least half an hour before you carve.

Bread sauce

This is a traditional bread sauce with that wonderful flavour of cloves and bay. You could also add a good handful of halved toasted hazelnuts in with the breadcrumbs.

For 8–10:
    6 cloves
    1 large onion, peeled and halved
    1.2 litres whole milk
    2 bay leaves
    6 peppercorns
    2 sprigs of parsley
    200–250g good fresh white
        breadcrumbs
    Handful of hazelnuts, toasted
        (optional)
    Salt and black pepper
    Plenty of freshly grated nutmeg,
        to taste
    50g butter
    45ml single cream

Stick the cloves into the onion halves and put them into a saucepan with the milk, bay leaves, peppercorns and parsley sprigs, and bring slowly to the boil. Take off the heat. Cover and leave for 30 minutes or so for the flavours to infuse.

Strain and pour into a clean saucepan, and add 200g breadcrumbs, plus the extra 50g if you prefer a thicker bread sauce. Add the hazelnuts (if you want them), salt, pepper and nutmeg, and simmer on a very low heat for 5 minutes.

Remove from the heat and stir in the butter and cream.

Serve immediately or cool, cover and keep in the fridge until needed. It will also freeze.

Turkey gravy

Christmas Day really is the moment for lashings of gravy, so don't throw away any of the extra turkey bits. Use them to make stock, your base for delicious gravy. Don't include the liver if you want to use it for pâté (see page 218); or you can add it, chopped, to the chestnut stuffing (see right).

For 10–12:
1 tablespoon plain flour
1 large glass of red wine
Salt and pepper

For the stock:
1 onion, unpeeled
Turkey giblets and neck
1 carrot, scrubbed and halved
1 leek, cut into 3–4 pieces
Parsley stalks
5 peppercorns
1 garlic clove, unpeeled
3 bay leaves

To make the stock, cut the onion into quarters and put it into a large saucepan with the giblets, carrot, leek, parsley stalks, peppercorns, garlic and bay leaves, and pour over 2 litres water. Bring to the boil and skim off any scum after about 5 minutes. Cover tightly and simmer for at least an hour.

Take it off the heat and allow it to cool a little, before pouring through a sieve. Then leave it to cool completely. Keep in the fridge, or even freeze, until needed. Skim off the fat before using.

To make the gravy, remove the turkey from the roasting pan. Spoon off most of the fat and scrape up the bits into the remaining juices. Put the pan over a medium heat and add the flour. Allow it to cook for a minute or two while stirring with a small balloon whisk.

Add warm strained giblet stock, little by little and stirring all the time,
until smooth. Add the red wine and check the seasoning.

Let the mixture bubble up and simmer for 5 minutes. Add more stock if the gravy is too thick. To serve, pour it into a gravy boat so everyone can help themselves.

Chestnut stuffing

You can use fresh, vacuum-packed or tinned chestnuts for this recipe. The mixture of puréed and coarsely chopped chestnuts gives an excellent flavour and texture.

To make sure that the heat penetrates the turkey thoroughly during cooking, don't over-stuff it.

This stuffing can be made in advance. Pack into a plastic box and freeze.

For a medium-sized bird:
450g fresh, vacuum-packed or tinned chestnuts
Milk (optional)
2 onions, chopped
50g butter
150g streaky bacon, chopped
Turkey liver, chopped (optional)
2 tablespoons crushed juniper berries
2 garlic cloves, finely chopped
1 x 200g tin of chestnut purée, unsweetened
100g fresh breadcrumbs
Freshly grated nutmeg
Zest of 1 lemon
1 large egg, beaten
Salt and black pepper
Bunch of parsley, chopped

If you are using fresh chestnuts, make a slit on the flat side of each chestnut and put under a hot grill until the outer shell peels easily.

Put the chestnuts into a saucepan and cover with milk or water and simmer for 40 minutes. Cool and peel off the skins.

Roughly chop the chestnuts. Sweat the onion in the butter and add the chopped bacon and liver (if using). Cook for 2–3 minutes, add the juniper berries and garlic, and cook for a further minute or two. Mix the chestnut purée with the breadcrumbs, nutmeg and lemon zest, and add the onion mixture and beaten egg. Season well and when the mixture has cooled, add the parsley and roughly chopped chestnuts.

Use this to stuff the neck end of the turkey. Don't forget to weigh the turkey after you have stuffed it. You need to include the stuffing weight in your overall cooking time.

If you have some extra stuffing left over, make it into stuffing balls and bake in a preheated oven at 180°C/gas mark 4 for 25 minutes on an oiled baking sheet until crisp.

Sage and onion stuffing

The classic Christmas stuffing with the characteristic fragrant flavour of sage. It's easy and quick to make, but if you want to get it done well before, it's also fine frozen.

To make sure that the heat penetrates the turkey thoroughly during cooking, don't over-stuff it.

This stuffing can be made in advance. Pack into a plastic box and freeze.

For a medium-sized bird:
40g unsalted butter
4 large onions, finely chopped
Large handful of sage leaves, finely chopped
125g fresh breadcrumbs
Zest of 1 lemon, and juice of ½ lemon
1 egg, beaten
Salt and black pepper

Melt half of the butter in a small saucepan. Gently sweat the onion with the sage in the pan for 10 minutes over a low heat.

Put the breadcrumbs into a mixing bowl and add the onions and sage, lemon zest and juice. Melt the remaining butter and add this to the mixture, and bind the ingredients together with the beaten egg. Season well with salt and black pepper.

Use this to stuff either the neck or the body cavity. Don't forget to weigh the turkey after you have stuffed it. You need to include the stuffing weight in your overall cooking time.

If you have some extra stuffing left over, make it into stuffing balls and bake in a preheated oven at 180°C/gas mark 4 for 25 minutes on an oiled baking sheet until crisp and golden.

Pecan, apple and celery stuffing

I love the way that pecans remain really crisp in a stuffing mix. If you can't find pecans, use walnuts, but toast them for a few minutes first.

To make sure that the heat penetrates the turkey thoroughly during cooking, don't over-stuff it. Extra stuffing can be cooked separately as described on page 185. You can make this in advance. Pack into a plastic box and freeze.

For a medium-sized bird:
Olive oil, for frying
4 shallots, chopped
4 celery sticks
2 large Bramley apples
175g pecan nuts
150g breadcrumbs
2 large bunches of parsley, chopped
25g fresh thyme, chopped
½ teaspoon powdered cloves
½ teaspoon ground cinnamon
Zest and juice of 2 oranges
3 garlic cloves, finely chopped
110g melted butter
Sea salt and black pepper

Heat a little olive oil in a pan and add the chopped shallots. Sweat over a low heat until they are translucent and soft. Allow to cool.

Chop the celery and peel, core and chop the apples. Roast the pecans for 2–3 minutes in a moderate oven (180°C/gas mark 4) and chop roughly.

In a large mixing bowl, mix the breadcrumbs with the chopped herbs, spices, orange zest, chopped apples, celery, nuts and garlic. Add the shallots and orange juice. Stir in the melted butter and season well.

Use this to stuff the body cavity. Don't forget to weigh the turkey after you have stuffed it. You need to include the stuffing weight in your overall cooking time.

Pork and pancetta stuffing

This meaty stuffing is more filling and substantial than most. It has great flavour, with the saltiness of the pancetta and the smokiness of the sage.

To make sure that the heat penetrates the turkey thoroughly during cooking, don't over-stuff it. Extra stuffing can be cooked separately as described on page 185. You can make this in advance. Pack into a plastic box and freeze.

For a medium-sized bird:
50g butter
Olive oil
2 onions, chopped
150g pancetta
900g good free-range pork sausage meat
50g chopped sage
150g breadcrumbs
1 egg, beaten
Sea salt and black pepper

Melt the butter and a little oil together in a pan. Add the chopped onions and sweat over a low heat until translucent and soft. Allow to cool.

Finely chop the pancetta and mix into the sausage meat with the chopped sage and breadcrumbs. It is easiest to do this with your hands. Add the cooled onion and beaten egg and season well with sea salt and black pepper.

Then stuff either the neck or the body cavity. Don't forget to weigh the turkey after you have stuffed it. You need to include the stuffing weight in your overall cooking time.

Sausages with bacon

You'll never have enough sausages, so cook as many as you can fit into your oven.

For 8–10:
1kg dry cure streaky bacon
1.5kg free-range pork chipolatas

Take the rind off the bacon rashers with a pair of scissors, stretch each rasher with the back of a large knife and then halve each one lengthways.

Halve the chipolatas by twisting them firmly in the middle, which should divide them easily – skin and all. Then cut them at this divide and wrap a piece of streaky bacon around each one. If you want to prepare them in advance, pack into a plastic container and freeze at this stage.

To cook, fit rows of them into a baking tray, lightly oiled or lined with a silicone mat, and cook at 160°C/gas mark 2–3 for 25 minutes.

Warm Christmas salad

Some alternatives for vegetarians

For those who don't eat meat, this is a perfect dish for Christmas lunch. It has a great texture, with the crunchiness of the nuts and the sweet treacly taste of squash and roasted onions contrasting with the sharpness of the feta cheese.

For non-vegetarians, it is excellent as a main course or a side dish with cold turkey or ham after Christmas, and delicious with baked or fried speck or prosciutto crumbled over the top.

For 6:

1 good tablespoon groundnut or sunflower oil
2 butternut squash, deseeded and cut into large chunks
4 red onions, quartered
10 shallots, peeled and whole
Salt and black pepper
4 red peppers, deseeded and cut into long generous pieces
4cm piece of fresh root ginger, peeled and chopped
2 red chillies, deseeded and finely sliced
1 tablespoon soft brown sugar
6 cloves
½ white onion
1 garlic head
1 star anise
120g Puy lentils
200ml dry sherry or wine
400g cooked chickpeas
A little toasted sesame oil
75g toasted cashews
75g toasted pecans
240g cooked chestnuts (tinned, vacuum-packed or home cooked, see page 185)
4–6 sun-dried tomatoes, sliced
Handful of sultanas, soaked in sherry for 2 hours
250g feta cheese, crumbled
Large bunch of coriander, chopped

Preheat the oven to 190°C/gas mark 5.

Heat the groundnut or sunflower oil in a roasting pan. Add the butternut squash, red onions and shallots and season with salt and pepper. Cook these in the oven for 35 minutes before mixing in the peppers, ginger, chillies and brown sugar and returning to the oven.

Meanwhile stick the cloves into the half onion, cut the whole garlic head in half horizontally and put these and the star anise into a medium-sized saucepan with the lentils. Cover with 400ml cold water and 200ml dry sherry or wine, bring to the boil and cook over a medium heat for about 20–25 minutes. When they are nearly tender, add the cooked chickpeas and heat through thoroughly. Drain and season with salt and freshly ground pepper and remove the garlic, star anise and onion. Stir in a little sesame oil and put to one side.

When the peppers are starting to brown at the edges, add the toasted nuts, chestnuts, sun-dried tomatoes and sultanas to the roasted vegetables. When the vegetables are tender and beginning to caramelise at the edges, remove from the oven.

Put a bed of lentils and chickpeas on a large serving plate and scatter over the roasted vegetables, nuts and fruit. Fork it all through with a little sesame oil. Check the seasoning and add the feta cheese with plenty of chopped coriander.

Chicory gratin with winter garden salad

This wonderfully flavourful dish goes brilliantly with all the various Christmas Day veg.

For 8:
  ½ onion
  1 garlic clove
  6 tablespoons extra virgin
    olive oil, plus a little more
    for the dish
  600g chicory
  Salt and black pepper
  50g grated Parmesan cheese
  A few knobs of butter, to finish

For the cheese sauce:
  1 litre milk
  80g butter
  80g flour
  1 egg yolk
  250g mascarpone cheese
  100g grated Parmesan cheese
  Freshly grated nutmeg, to taste
  200g (or to taste) grated cheese,
    such as Cheddar, pecorino
    or Parmesan
  Salt and black pepper

For the winter garden salad:
  A mix of winter leaves, such as
    spinach, baby leaf mustard,
    rocket, and lettuce mixed with
    chervil and parsley

Preheat a medium (180°C/gas mark 4) oven.

Slice the onion and peel the garlic clove, crushing it with the side of a knife but leaving it whole. Heat the olive oil in a good-sized saucepan and cook the onion and garlic on a gentle heat until they are golden brown. Remove the garlic and add the chicory, cut in half or quarters lengthways (depending on size), to the pan. Once it's begun to wilt and brown – after about 5 minutes – take it off the heat. Season with salt and pepper.

To make the cheese sauce, bring the milk to the boil in a small saucepan. In another pan, melt the butter. Stir the flour into the butter, allow it to cook for a couple of minutes and then gradually add the hot milk. Then add the egg yolk mixed with the mascarpone, Parmesan and plenty of nutmeg, stirring continuously as you add the ingredients. Season with plenty of salt and pepper.

Layer the chicory and cheese sauce in a gratin dish. Finish with the remaining cheese sauce. Finally scatter the grated Parmesan over it and dot the top with the butter and a bit of extra nutmeg.

Cook in the preheated oven for 35–40 minutes.

Serve with the mixed winter garden salad leaves.

Fennel and Gorgonzola soufflé tart

This is one of the most delicious winter tarts you'll ever eat. Every mouthful has a different taste. The unusual treacly flavour of roasted bulb fennel is perfect with the rich cheese and the flaky pastry, and the crunch of walnuts adds all-important texture. Vegetarian or not, I'd be happy to eat this as a change for Christmas. A drizzle of truffle oil – diluted in a mild olive oil – makes a good last-minute addition.

This is wonderful served with many of the usual Christmas vegetables – Brussels sprouts, cumin carrots and saddleback potatoes.

For 6–8:
4–5 heads of fennel, depending on size
Extra virgin olive oil
About 110ml milk
20g unsalted butter
1 heaped tablespoon plain flour
3 large eggs, separated
125ml plain yoghurt
1 teaspoon Dijon mustard
Zest of 1 lemon
Salt and black pepper
20g Parmesan, grated
100g Gorgonzola
50g toasted walnuts, broken up

For the pastry:
110g unsalted butter
220g seasoned plain flour
1 egg yolk mixed with a little iced water

To make the pastry, rub the butter into the seasoned flour, or pulse in a food processor until the mixture resembles breadcrumbs. Add just enough of the egg mixture to bring the pastry together into a ball. Roll out and fill a 28cm flan tin (with a little extra pastry left hanging over the side to allow for shrinkage) and chill for 30 minutes.

Preheat the oven to 180°C/gas mark 4.

Prick the bottom of the tart with a fork, cover with a round of greaseproof paper or foil and weigh this down with some baking beans or rice. Bake the pastry case blind in the preheated oven for about 15 minutes. Keep the oven on afterwards, ready for roasting the fennel heads.

Blanch the fennel heads in boiling water for 2 minutes and then roast them on a baking tray in the preheated oven with a little olive oil, salt and pepper for about half an hour, until they are beginning to turn brown and caramelise at the edges, but they still have a bite. Keep the oven on for cooking the tart.

Heat the milk in a small saucepan until warm. Melt the butter in another small saucepan and stir in the flour to make a fairly stiff roux. Gradually whisk in the warm milk. Cover and put to one side to cool a little. Then, mix the egg yolks with the yoghurt and Dijon mustard in a separate bowl, and add the mixture to the roux, along with the lemon zest. Season with salt and freshly ground black pepper.

Sprinkle the pastry with the grated Parmesan (this acts like flour in the base and absorbs any moisture from the fennel bulbs) and lay the roasted fennel over the tart base. Break the Gorgonzola over the top and toss in the walnuts.

Whisk the egg whites until stiff and lightly fold into the roux. Spoon this over the fennel, cheese and walnuts and bake the tart in the oven for about 30 minutes or until risen, golden and set to the touch.

Christmas Day vegetables

Roast potatoes

Use 'Red Duke of York', 'Desiree' or 'King Edward' potatoes. All three make great roast potatoes, crunchy on the outside and fluffy in the middle.

If you're roasting your turkey or goose in the same oven, then put the potatoes on the top shelf, and while the bird is resting, turn the heat up (in the case of turkey) or down (in the case of goose) to the temperature specified below for the remainder of the cooking time.

For 6–8:
6 tablespoons goose fat or lard or sunflower oil
750g potatoes, peeled and chopped into generous chunks
Salt and black pepper
Some herbs (optional) – thyme, rosemary or sage

Preheat the oven to 200°C/gas mark 6. Cover the bottom of a baking tray with a thin layer of the fat or oil, and put in the oven for 5 minutes.

Meanwhile parboil the potatoes for 5 minutes in salted water. Drain them, dry them off over a low heat for a few minutes and shake them around a bit or use a fork to break up the outside flesh.

Season with salt and pepper and toss them in the hot fat or oil. You can scatter herbs over them – thyme, rosemary or sage – at this stage if you wish, making sure that the herbs as well as the potatoes are well coated with fat or oil, so that they don't burn.

Put the tray back in the oven and after 45 minutes the potatoes should be perfect.

Rosemary saddleback potatoes

These potatoes are half roasted, half baked, and excellent for those who feel like a change from roast potatoes.

If you're roasting your turkey or goose in the same oven, then put the potatoes on the top shelf, and while the bird is resting, turn the heat up (in the case of turkey) or down (in the case of goose) to the temperature specified below for the remainder of the cooking time.

For 6–8:
750g potatoes (waxy ones are good for this, as they hold together better as they cook)
6 tablespoons extra virgin olive oil
Leaves from 5 sprigs of rosemary
Salt and black pepper

Preheat the oven to 190°C/gas mark 5. Peel the potatoes, or keep the skins on if you prefer. Cut them into slices just under 5mm thick, stopping just before the bottom of the potato, so that each potato still remains in one piece but the slices fan out rather like the leaves of a book.

Put them on to an oiled baking tray and scatter the rosemary over them, pushing the leaves right down into the slices. Douse with olive oil – the flavours of the herbs and oil soak right into the potatoes, so it's really worth using extra virgin olive oil – and season with salt and pepper.

Put them in the preheated oven and roast for about 1–1½ hours until they're golden brown.

Parmesan salsify or parsnips

These are crunchy and sweet, and ideal with roast goose or turkey. You can use quartered parsnips, or even better – if you can find or grow them – whole, thin roots of salsify.

If you're cooking your turkey or goose in the same oven, then place the tray of parsnips near the top of the oven, and then while the bird is resting, turn the heat up (in the case of turkey) or down (in the case of goose) to the temperature specified below for the remainder of the cooking time.

For 6–8:
  Olive oil, for the tin
  600g salsify or parsnips
  100g fresh brown or white
    breadcrumbs
  100g Parmesan cheese, grated
  Seasoned flour
  2 eggs, beaten

Preheat the oven to 190°C/gas mark 5. Put an oiled baking tin into the oven and allow it to get really hot.

Peel the salsify or parsnips, and cut them into wedges. Then steam them for 10 minutes. Mix the breadcrumbs with the Parmesan.

Dip the hot roots in the seasoned flour and then into the beaten egg, and lastly roll them in the breadcrumb mixture.

Put them in the oiled baking tin and roast in the preheated oven for about 35 minutes, until tender and golden brown.

Sauté of leeks with Jerusalem artichokes

This is my favourite of all quick leek dishes, a result of my assistant Tam's winter rummage in the garden.

For 6–8:
  1 teaspoon cumin seeds
  Juice of ½ lemon
  700g Jerusalem artichokes,
    scrubbed
  30g butter
  1 tablespoon olive oil
  1kg leeks, washed and cut
    into slices
  Maldon salt and freshly ground
    black pepper
  Bunch of parsley, chopped

Toast the cumin seeds for a couple of minutes in a dry frying pan to bring out the flavour.

Fill a bowl with cold water and squeeze the lemon juice into it. Slice the artichokes thinly and put the slices into the acidulated water immediately.

Heat the butter and oil in a heavy-based pan. Drain the artichokes and pat them dry with kitchen paper. Add them to the pan and stir over a medium heat for a minute or two.

Add the sliced leeks, scatter in the toasted cumin seeds, season with salt and pepper and sauté gently without browning until the leeks are just cooked but still have bite.

Remove from the heat, adjust the seasoning and toss in some roughly chopped parsley.

Roast carrots with butter and toasted cumin

I make these carrots all the time through the winter. They have a fantastic flavour that is great with turkey but even better with the stronger taste of goose. You can roast them the day before and then sauté them with the cumin and butter just before you eat. The slow roasting brings out all the sweetness of the carrot roots.

For 6–8:
   900g carrots, peeled and whole
   Olive oil, for roasting
   2 tablespoons cumin seeds
   Large knob of butter
   Salt and black pepper

Roast the carrots whole – with a little olive oil drizzled over them – in a low oven at 160°C/gas mark 3 for a good hour.

Either leave the roasted carrots whole or slice them into chunky ovals. Then toast the cumin seeds for a couple of minutes in a dry frying pan to bring out the flavour. Add a large chunk of butter, add the carrots to the pan and toss with the cumin seeds.

Season and serve immediately.

Carrot and celeriac purée

An excellent, creamy, textured purée with a gentle flavour, an ideal contrast to the stronger tastes of Brussels sprouts or red cabbage. You can do this a day in advance, allow it to cool, cover it with foil and keep it in the fridge. Leave the foil on and reheat in a low oven (150°C/gas mark 2) for 10–15 minutes, dotted with a little butter.

For 6–8:
   1 large celeriac root
   900g carrots, scrubbed and halved
   50g butter
   Salt and black pepper
   Freshly grated nutmeg
   75ml single cream (optional)
   Cumin seeds, to serve

Peel the celeriac and cut it into 2–3cm chunks.

Bring a saucepan of water to the boil and either boil or steam the celeriac and carrots until just tender. Tip the vegetables into a food processor and pulse with the butter until you have a consistency you like. Season with salt and pepper, add grated nutmeg and stir in the single cream, if using.

Toast the cumin seeds for a couple of minutes in a dry frying pan to bring out the flavour.

When you are ready to serve it, warm it through and sprinkle over a few toasted cumin seeds.

Braised red cabbage with blackberries

The sweetness of the blackberries is fabulous in contrast to the sharpness of the cabbage. You can buy frozen blackberries at Christmas, or better still use wild blackberries you've gathered and frozen in the autumn.

For 6–8:

    50g butter
    Splash of olive oil
    500g shallots, chopped
    1 large red cabbage, finely shredded
    75ml red wine
    125ml balsamic vinegar
    75ml white wine vinegar
    500g cooking apples, peeled and cut into thickish slices
    6 cloves
    1 cinnamon stick
    4 heaped tablespoons soft brown sugar
    500g blackberries

Melt the butter in a large pan and add the olive oil and shallots, and sweat for a few minutes over a low heat.

Add the red cabbage, red wine, vinegars, apples, cloves and the cinnamon stick, and simmer, covered, for 45 minutes. Remove the lid and add the sugar, and cook for a further 20 minutes at least, until there is very little excess liquid and the cabbage is soft and glossy.

Stir in the blackberries and simmer gently for 2–3 minutes.

Brussels sprout purée with nutmeg

I remember having this as a teenager when we went to lunch with friends of my parents and, after having always hated Brussels sprouts, I was converted. The sprouts are best lightly cooked and then pulsed quickly in a food processor, so that you're left with some texture. For extra crunch and flavour, stir in a few chestnuts.

For 8:

    1kg Brussels sprouts
    150ml crème fraîche
    Freshly grated nutmeg, to taste
    10–15 cooked chestnuts (tinned, vacuum-packed or home cooked, see page 185), roughly chopped (optional)

Halve the sprouts and boil them for 3 minutes so that they're still quite firm and bright green. Drain them, add the crème fraîche and nutmeg, and coarsely mash in a food processor.

You can then add roughly chopped chestnuts to the sprout purée and heat in an open pan for a couple of minutes.

Brussels sprouts with pancetta and chestnuts

I love the look, texture and taste of this mixture. The saltiness of the pancetta and the sweetness of the chestnuts are a good contrast with the strong flavour of the Brussels sprouts – a brilliant green if not overcooked.

For 6–8:

    900g Brussels sprouts
    110g pancetta or streaky bacon, thinly sliced
    2 garlic cloves, finely chopped (optional)
    200ml balsamic vinegar
    200–300g cooked chestnuts (tinned, vacuum-packed or home cooked, see page 185)
    Salt and black pepper

Remove the outside leaves from the sprouts, trim the stems and rinse. Steam for 6–8 minutes, depending on size.

Cut the pancetta or bacon into little strips, put it into a dry sauté pan over a medium heat and cook until crisp, adding the garlic (if you want it) for a couple of minutes.

Add the balsamic vinegar and increase the heat; let the vinegar bubble up and reduce to a syrupy glaze. Add the Brussels sprouts and heat through. Lastly add the cooked chestnuts, turn them in the glaze and season with salt and black pepper.

Christmas Day puddings

Steamed Christmas pudding

Christmas pudding has one of the densest structures of anything you'll cook. That makes it rich and delicious, but it also means it takes a lot of boiling or steaming on Christmas Day.

Serve it with brandy butter (see right), brandy cream (see page 200) or cream, or indeed all three.

For at least 8–10:
1 Christmas pudding (see page 21)
Coins (optional)
Sprig of holly
A little brandy

If boiling, use a huge saucepan with a cushion of crumpled foil in the bottom. Sit the pudding on the foil and fill the saucepan to two thirds of the way up the pudding basin with boiling water. Cover tightly and simmer for 3 hours for a medium-sized pudding, or 4 hours for a large pudding, topping up with boiling water when necessary. Alternatively, steam the basin in a double saucepan or steamer for 3 hours for a medium-sized pudding, or 4 hours for a large pudding.

Take it out of the pan, loosen the pudding from the side of its bowl with a knife and invert it on to a warmed plate. Boil the coins you want to add and poke them in all the way through the pudding, pushing them right into the middle with a skewer. A sprig of holly is traditionally pushed in to the top and then the whole thing is set on fire as it's brought to the table. To do this, heat some brandy briefly in a pan or ladle. Just before serving, light the spirit with a match and pour it over the pudding.

To reheat the pudding after Christmas Day, wrap it up in foil and reheat in a hot oven (200°C/gas mark 6) for 15 minutes; or make Christmas pudding ice cream (see page 226).

Brandy butter

The Christmas classic. Use it with mince pies (see page 24) as well as Christmas pudding right the way through the festive season. It stores well in the fridge.

For 8:
175g unsalted butter, softened
175g caster sugar
Zest of 1 orange
Brandy, to taste

Beat the butter and sugar until light, pale and creamy and fold in the orange zest. Mix in as much brandy as you wish – for these quantities I'd use about 4 tablespoons.

Chill in the fridge. If you are making this well in advance, either wrap it well and freeze it or keep it in a covered container in the fridge.

Simple brandy cream

The fluffy, soft texture of this cream is excellent with Christmas pudding and a good change from brandy butter. This recipe will be plenty for twice as many people if you have brandy butter on offer too.

For 6–8:
570ml double cream
2 teaspoons caster sugar
½ teaspoon vanilla extract
1 tablespoon brandy
Zest of 1 orange (optional)

Combine the ingredients in a mixing bowl. Beat until the mixture reaches soft-peak stage and spoon into a bowl to serve.

Trifle

A traditional Christmas Day evening pudding. The secret of a good trifle is to have plenty of fruit and some bits of crunch, as well as sherry-soaked cake covered in lots of cream and custard. You can buy your cake and custard, but if you've got the time, your trifle will be all the better for making your own. You can make the cake well beforehand. Kept in an airtight container, it will last for weeks.

Top the trifle with pomegranate seeds and hazelnut praline (a crushed hazelnut cartwheel).

For 12 (to fill a 1.5 litre bowl):
200g Madeira sponge
(about half the cake below)
110ml sherry (optional)
80g Amaretto biscuits
300g fresh or frozen raspberries

For the Madeira cake:
50g self-raising flour
175g plain flour
175g unsalted butter
200g caster sugar
Zest of ½ lemon
Zest of ½ orange
4 eggs, beaten

For the custard:
500ml milk
180ml double cream
1 vanilla pod, split
9 egg yolks
90g caster sugar
1½ tablespoons cornflour

For the top:
275ml double cream
½ pomegranate
100g hazelnut cartwheel
(see page 32), crushed

First make the Madeira cake. Preheat the oven to 180°C/gas mark 4. Oil and line a 15cm cake tin with a removable base.

Sift the two flours together. Cream the butter, sugar and zests until pale and white. Add the beaten eggs, a little at a time, adding sifted flour each time to prevent the mixture from splitting. Finally tip in all the remaining flour and fold together. Pour the mixture into the tin and bake in the oven for 25 minutes. Lower the oven temperature to 160°C/gas mark 2½ and bake for another 50 minutes, covering the top lightly with foil if it is getting too brown.

Allow the cake to cool in the tin for a few minutes and then turn it out on to a wire rack.

Next make the custard. Put the milk, cream and vanilla pod in a saucepan and heat gently so that the vanilla infuses. Beat the egg yolks, sugar and cornflour with a whisk in a bowl. When the milk starts to bubble, pour it over the egg mix, whisking all the time. Then pour the mixture through a fine sieve to remove any lumps and the vanilla pod, and put back on a medium heat. Keep whisking until it has thickened and set aside to cool.

Next combine the trifle. Break up the Madeira sponge and put it in the bottom of the dish. Pour over the sherry, if using. Sprinkle the Amaretto biscuits over the sponge, and then the raspberries. If you're using frozen raspberries, don't defrost them first, as you want to keep the fruit whole. Pour over the cool custard. Cover with cling film and chill for a couple of hours, or even overnight.

Whip the cream until it makes soft peaks and spread carefully over the custard.

Remove the seeds from the half pomegranate by holding it over a container and bashing the skin with the back of a wooden spoon. Scatter the pomegranate jewels over the top of the trifle, along with the crushed hazelnut wheel, and serve.

Boxing Day

Boxing Day can be tricky. Christmas is over and – certainly for children – there's often a feeling of anti-climax. Many of us have had too much to eat and drink, the diversion of presents is over, and yet there we are, all still together, with tempers beginning to fray.

If the weather is decent, kick everyone outside – even the reluctant teenagers. Get everyone to go to the park, or if you live in the country, this is the moment for a long walk. While they do that, you can straighten the place up a bit. If you have had the central heating on full, it's worth spending half an hour topping up vases and watering indoor plants.

Leftovers are an inevitable by-product of Christmas, and they often make the most delicious food. Stock goes into creamy winter risottos and soups: light and sharp Thai noodle soup (see page 206) with plenty of coriander and lime juice is just what I feel like after a few days of over-indulgence, or something warm and comforting like spiced parsnip soup (see page 209).

Try making the nasi goreng, a spicy, fragrant, warm Malaysian rice salad, with leftover turkey (see page 213). Use the white meat for tacchino tonnato (see page 219) or old-fashioned croquettes (see page 220), and the brown meat for a rough puff-pastry turkey, leek and ham pie (see page 222).

When everyone's fed up with turkey, warm salads always go down well. Try duck breast salad, served in a plum sauce dressing (see page 211). It's also the perfect moment for a classic winter salad including strong, punchy cheese such as the spinach and Roquefort salad on page 215.

It's a good idea to have one or two extras up your sleeve to supplement leftovers. Sweet, clovey ham with Cumberland sauce (see page 220) is invaluable for when you've lots of people to feed, and can be eaten for lunch or dinner with celeriac remoulade (see page 218) and salted baked potatoes (run them under the tap, roll them in coarse salt, prick them all over and bake for about an hour until tender).

There isn't always a call for pudding between Christmas and New Year, but a winter fruit salad or a prune and Armagnac tart, which can both sit in the fridge for days, may come in handy (see pages 226 and 227). You can also fry up slices of Christmas pudding in butter and serve them with a dollop of vanilla ice cream, or use the pudding leftovers to make delicious, chewy Christmas pudding ice cream (see page 226).

Soups, risottos and other easy lunches

Turkey stock

If you've had turkey, you'll have turkey bones, which will make plenty of stock for soups. Turkey makes a strong stock, so you don't need to roast the bones to intensify the flavour before boiling. You'll only need to add salt when you come to use the stock in a recipe.

Turkey carcass
1 onion, unpeeled and quartered
2 carrots, scrubbed
2 celery sticks
Parsley stalks
2 bay leaves
10 peppercorns

Break up the carcass a little so that you can put it in a large saucepan with the vegetables. Cover with cold water and bring to the boil. Skim the surface and simmer for 2–3 hours. Strain and, if you want a stronger flavour, reduce by boiling in an open saucepan.

Keep the stock in the fridge or freeze to use later.

Thai noodle soup with spinach

This is my sister Jane's adaptation of a Thai classic. It's a delicious fresh-tasting soup which I could eat almost every day. It is midway between a spaghetti dish and a soup, perfect for a quiet evening in front of the telly. It's hard to eat elegantly, so perhaps avoid serving at a dinner party.

For 8 small bowls:
1 litre good turkey stock
    (see left) or chicken stock
1 x 400g tin of coconut milk
Juice of 1 lime
1 red chilli, deseeded and
    chopped finely
200g egg noodles
200g cooked and peeled king
    prawns
150g spinach
Splash of soy sauce
Splash of Thai fish sauce
2 large mushrooms, thinly sliced,
    to serve
4 spring onions, finely sliced,
    to serve
Lots of chopped coriander,
    to serve

Put the stock into a saucepan and add the coconut milk, lime juice and red chilli. Bring to the boil.

Cook the noodles separately (according to the instructions on the packet), and then add them and the prawns to the stock. Heat thoroughly, but do not boil. Add the spinach, sliced into fine strips, and allow it to just wilt momentarily in the liquid. Add a splash of soy sauce and fish sauce to taste.

Serve garnished with the mushrooms, sliced spring onions and chopped coriander.

Winter minestrone soup

If you fancy a quick soup for lunch and have stock and some slightly tired vegetables that need to be eaten, this is perfect. The quantities and ingredients can be adapted depending on what's to hand. If you want a thicker soup, add more solid ingredients and use less stock; or the other way around for a thinner soup.

For 4:
    3 tablespoons olive oil
    2 onions, chopped
    100g bacon or pancetta, chopped
    100g shredded green cabbage
    3 carrots or any root vegetable
    500ml turkey stock (see page 206) or bouillon
    Slurp of red wine
    5 large tomatoes, chopped, or 400g tin of chopped tomatoes
    Salt and black pepper
    400g tin of cannellini beans or any kind of beans or chickpeas
    160g leftover pasta, chopped (optional)
    Parmesan cheese and good olive oil, to serve

Heat the oil in a large saucepan and fry the onions and bacon until the onions have softened. Then add the cabbage, carrots (or other root veg), stock or bouillon, red wine, tomatoes, salt and pepper and cook for 10 minutes. Crush roughly with a potato masher and then add the beans and pasta (if using). Cook for another couple of minutes until the beans and pasta are warmed through.

Serve with a topping of Parmesan and a slurp of good olive oil.

Spiced parsnip soup

The flavour of this soup is really improved if you use a good strong stock – turkey is ideal – and you need to add lots of coarsely chopped coriander: its sharp, strong flavour is a good contrast to the creamy parsnip.

For 6:
    30g butter
    1 tablespoon sunflower oil
    1 onion, chopped
    1 teaspoon ground coriander seeds
    1 teaspoon ground cumin seeds
    ½ teaspoon ground turmeric
    ½ teaspoon chilli powder
    675g parsnips, chopped
    1.2 litres turkey stock (see page 206) or other good stock
    Salt and black pepper
    A little milk (optional)
    150ml single cream (optional)
    Large bunch of coriander, coarsely chopped
    Yoghurt, to serve

Melt the butter with the oil in a large heavy-based pan and add the chopped onion. Sweat the onion for 5 minutes, without allowing it to colour. Stir in the spices and cook gently for another 2 minutes.

Add the parsnips and the stock and bring to the boil. Reduce the heat, cover and simmer for about 30 minutes or until the parsnips are tender. Allow to cool slightly, season carefully with salt and pepper, and purée in a food processor or with a hand blender.

Return the soup to a clean pan, adding a little milk if necessary, depending how thick you would like the soup to be. Add the cream (if you want it) and warm through gently, without allowing the soup to boil.

Take off the heat and add a couple of good handfuls of chopped fresh coriander. Serve with a dollop of yoghurt.

Smoked haddock chowder

This is a terrific soup to make in advance and freeze, ideal for the times when you can't face cooking another meal.

For 4:
    1 bay leaf
    A few peppercorns
    1 blade of mace
    2 cloves
    750ml whole milk
    450g undyed lightly smoked haddock fillet
    50g butter
    3–4 spring onions or 1 leek, finely sliced
    1 dessertspoon plain flour
    6 small new potatoes, quartered
    Good bunch of parsley, chopped
    12 quails' eggs, lightly boiled
    150ml cream
    Salt and black pepper
    Juice of ½ lemon

Put the bay leaf, peppercorns, mace and cloves into a saucepan with the milk. Bring just to the boil, add the haddock (cut into 2 pieces, if it is too long) and simmer for 2 minutes. Take off the heat, cover and allow the haddock to cool in the liquid.

Strain, reserving the liquid, and lift out the fish. Gently flake the haddock, discarding the skin and any bones, and cover until you're ready.

Put the butter into a saucepan and sweat the onions or leek until soft but not brown. Stir in the flour and cook for a couple of minutes. Gradually whisk in the reserved liquid until the mixture is smooth. Add the potatoes and cook gently until the potatoes are just tender. (If the soup seems to be a little thick, add some water.)

Turn down the heat and add most of the parsley, quails' eggs (cut in halves), fish and cream, and warm through without boiling. Remove from the heat, season with salt and pepper, and add lemon juice and more parsley.

Oatmeal rolls

Oatmeal rolls are lovely stuffed with slices of turkey and cranberry and orange compote (see page 26). They're also perfect to eat with any soup. They are easy to make, but you need to soak the oatmeal, and the whole process takes a while. Try to do this before Christmas: make lots and put them in the freezer.

For 15 rolls:
225g medium-sized oatmeal
275ml milk
50g butter
450g strong white flour
1 teaspoon salt
1 teaspoon dried yeast
Beaten egg, to glaze (optional)

Soak the oatmeal in the milk for at least a couple of hours, or overnight. Then melt the butter and add to the oatmeal. Add all this to the flour, salt and yeast, and mix well. If the resulting mixture is too wet or too dry, add small amounts of flour (or water) until the dough holds together, rather than sticking to your hands. Knead until the dough becomes elastic and stretchy.

Leave to rise in an oiled plastic bag or a bowl covered with cling film in a warm place until the dough is twice its original size. (This could take 2–3 hours.) Then knock it back, cut it into 15 pieces and shape into rolls.

Put these on a floured baking tray. Cut a cross on each with a sharp knife and dust with flour or oatmeal. Leave to rise again for about half an hour. Preheat the oven to 220°C/gas mark 7.

Bake in the oven for about 20 minutes and then turn out on to a rack to cool. If you like a glazed finish, brush beaten egg over the rolls immediately after they come out of the oven.

Rosemary risotto

This is one of my favourite winter risottos. The strong flavour of the turkey stock is a good balance to the rosemary. I like this risotto really soupy (Italians call this all'onda, which means wavy), but you can reduce the amount of stock for a drier, firmer texture. I also like a buttery risotto, but reduce the quantity of butter to 100g if you prefer. Any leftovers make delicious risotto balls (see right) the next day.

For 4–5:
2 litres good turkey stock
(see page 206)
1 large red onion, chopped
1 garlic clove, chopped
Olive oil, for frying
150g unsalted butter
300g Arborio rice
1 glass of white wine
200g Parmesan cheese
4 tablespoons finely chopped
rosemary leaves
Salt and freshly ground black
pepper

Bring the stock to the boil and allow it to simmer gently.

Sweat the onion and garlic in a heavy-based saucepan with a little olive oil and a knob of the butter until it becomes translucent. Add the rice to the pan and stir it into the onion. Add a glass of white wine and allow it to bubble up until almost all the liquid has been absorbed. Add a ladleful of stock and keep stirring until it has been absorbed; then repeat this, adding a ladleful at a time until all the liquid has been absorbed. After about 18 minutes, check the bite of the rice: it should be al dente – tender but still firm.

A couple of minutes before you remove the pan from the heat, cut the rest of the butter into chunks and add it to the pan with the Parmesan and chopped rosemary. Season carefully with salt and pepper, and serve.

Risotto balls with mozzarella

We tend to have at least one risotto over any winter week – including Christmas – and I aim to make a bit too much so we can also have risotto balls the next day. I love the crunchy outside, then the creamy, comforting Parmesan-rich rice, with the melted mozzarella oozing out as you cut into the centre. Serve with a rich, reduced tomato and chilli sauce and buttery spinach, or a crunchy, lemon-dressed winter mixed leaf salad.

If you're in a hurry, you can make a quick version of this recipe, without the mozzarella, by rolling the risotto balls in polenta and then frying them in half olive oil, half butter.

For 4–6, depending on quantities:
Leftover risotto
1 or 2 eggs, depending on
quantity of risotto, beaten
1 or 2 balls of mozzarella cheese,
chopped into 2cm pieces
Olive oil and a knob of butter,
for frying

For the outer coating:
Seasoned plain flour
Plenty of white breadcrumbs
Sage or rosemary, finely chopped
1 egg, beaten

Stir one whole egg (or two if you're using a large amount) into your leftover risotto to help it combine.

Make golf-ball sized balls from the risotto. Push a nugget of mozzarella into the middle of each ball, and then re-form the shape. On a plate, roll the balls in the seasoned flour. Place the breadcrumbs on a plate and scatter with the sage or rosemary. Roll the risotto balls in the egg and then in the breadcrumbs and herbs.

Shallow fry the risotto balls, in batches, in olive oil with a knob of butter, until they are golden brown. Serve while still piping hot.

Duck breast salad with pomegranate

Some hearty winter salads

This is a lovely warm salad, with the rich duck in a sweet and sour sauce. You can serve the slivers of duck on top of any salad leaves, or even just baby raw spinach, but strong-tasting chicories, rocket and mustards work best: these act like horseradish or mustard, cutting through the richness of the meat.

For 6 as a starter:
  1 tablespoon fennel seeds
  Zest of 2 oranges
  2 tablespoons Hoisin or
    plum sauce
  Pinch of sea salt
  3 fat duck breasts
  6 small handfuls of mixed
    salad leaves
  2 small pomegranates or
    1 large pomegranate

For the dressing:
  2 dessertspoons sesame oil
  1 dessertspoon honey
  2 teaspoons Hoisin or plum sauce
  Juice of ½ lemon
  Splash of sherry

Mix the fennel seeds, orange zest, Hoisin or plum sauce and salt. Make a criss-cross pattern with a serrated knife on the duck skin and rub the mixture into the cuts and all over the duck breast. Leave to marinate for about half an hour.

Preheat the oven to 180°C/gas mark 4.

For perfectly cooked duck breasts, which are crisp on the outside and pink and juicy on the inside, fry the breasts, skin side down, in a dry pan on a medium heat until nearly all the fat is rendered – melted from beneath the skin – and the skin has turned golden brown. This will take about 10 minutes. Pour off the excess fat at least once and save it. It's delicious for cooking roast potatoes.

Transfer the breasts, in the same pan if you can, to the preheated oven for 8 minutes. Remove them from the oven, wrap them loosely on a plate in aluminium foil and leave to rest for at least 10 minutes. This is vital: it allows the flesh to relax and makes it deliciously tender.

While the duck is resting, arrange the salad leaves on plates and mix the ingredients for the dressing. Slice the breasts thinly and add them to the salad just before you eat. Drizzle the dressing over the top.

To remove the seeds from the pomegranates, slice the fruit in half and over a container bash the skin with the back of a wooden spoon. Scatter the seeds over the salad.

Nasi goreng

My absolute favourite leftovers dish. In fact, I sometimes buy lamb for it specially. It takes a little bit of time to make, but more than repays every minute of effort.

For 8–10:
  1 teaspoon cumin seeds
  1 teaspoon coriander seeds
  2 tablespoons groundnut oil
  2 onions, chopped
  2 garlic cloves, finely chopped
  5cm piece of fresh root ginger, peeled and chopped
  2 peppers, red or yellow, sliced
  2 fresh green or red chillies, finely chopped, or 1 teaspoon dried red pepper flakes
  450g cooked basmati rice
  450g cooked lamb, chicken or turkey
  200g frozen petit pois
  4 tablespoons soy sauce
  2 tablespoons Thai fish sauce
  Salt and pepper
  250g large cooked prawns
  8–10 spring onions, finely sliced
  1 tablespoon toasted sesame oil
  1 tablespoon garam masala
  Toasted peanuts or cashews, roughly chopped, to serve
  Bunch of fresh coriander, chopped, to serve

For the omelette:
  50g butter
  4 eggs
  A few drops of soy sauce
  Salt and black pepper

In a small frying pan, toast the cumin and coriander seeds for a couple of minutes. Then crush them, using a pestle and mortar, and put them to one side.

To make the omelette, heat the butter in a small omelette pan. Beat the eggs with a few drops of soy sauce and season with salt and pepper. Add the eggs to the pan and cook the omelette until just firm. Remove it from the pan and roll it up.

Heat the groundnut oil in a large, shallow, heavy-bottomed pan and gently – on a low heat – sweat the onions until they are translucent. Add the garlic, ginger, peppers and chillies or red pepper flakes and cook for another 5 minutes. Add the cumin and coriander seeds and then the cooked rice, meat and peas. Turn up the heat and stir-fry for a couple of minutes. Add the soy and fish sauces and season carefully with salt and pepper. Add the prawns to the pan and stir again for a few minutes to heat them through.

Take off the heat, add the spring onions and sesame oil, and stir in the garam masala. Slice the omelette roll into strips. Pile the mixture on to a dish and decorate with plenty of toasted nuts, omelette strips and chopped coriander.

Grilled goats' cheese salad

Winter is the season when chicory and endive are at their best, and they make wonderful Christmas salads.

For 6:
  100g pancetta, chopped
  1 garlic clove, crushed
  1 small French baguette
  2 tablespoons runny honey
  200g small mature goats' cheese, with rind (rather than fresh)
  Salt and black pepper
  6 sprigs of thyme
  3 small handfuls of mixed mild salad leaves
  3 small handfuls of bitter leaves, such as dandelion, any chicory and frisée
  2 tablespoons pine nuts, toasted

For the dressing:
  1 garlic clove, finely chopped
  1 tablespoon red wine vinegar or balsamic vinegar
  4 tablespoons olive oil
  1 teaspoon Dijon mustard
  Salt and black pepper

Fry the pancetta in its own fat, with the garlic. Remove the pancetta once it begins to brown and let it cool. Discard the garlic.

Slice the French baguette into 1cm-thick ovals and toast these on one side. Heat the honey.

Cut the goats' cheese into thick slices and put one per piece of bread on the untoasted side. Season with salt and pepper and drizzle the honey over the cheese. Put a sprig of thyme on the top and put the bread under the grill until the cheese begins to melt.

Tear up the salad leaves and make the dressing, combining all the ingredients together and whisking with a fork. Dress the leaves and put on individual plates. Scatter over the pancetta and the pine nuts, and add the toasted goats' cheese.

Spinach and Roquefort salad

Raw baby spinach is excellent during the winter. Make a classic French salad with strong-flavoured Roquefort, topping it with a few crunchy strips of prosciutto, croutons and almonds.

For 4:

75g prosciutto (or any dry-cured ham), sliced
75g almonds
220g baby spinach
Good handful of small sorrel leaves, stems removed (if you can find them)
100–150g Roquefort cheese

For the croutons:

2–3 thick slices from a wholemeal or granary loaf
Olive oil, for frying
Splash of balsamic vinegar
Salt and black pepper

For the dressing:

2 teaspoons Dijon mustard
1 teaspoon caster sugar
1 dessertspoon red wine vinegar
100ml sunflower oil
3 tablespoons extra virgin olive oil
Salt and black pepper

Preheat the oven to 180°C/gas mark 4.

First make the croutons. Cut the slices of bread into large cubes. Heat some olive oil in a small frying pan and, when the oil is hot, cook the bread cubes until golden and crisp. Dry on kitchen paper. Add a splash of balsamic vinegar and season with salt and pepper while hot.

Put the prosciutto slices on an oiled baking sheet and bake in the preheated oven for about 10–15 minutes, until crisp.

Halve the almonds and toast them in a dry frying pan for a few minutes, tossing them once or twice as they cook.

To make the dressing, whisk the mustard, sugar and vinegar together in a jug, using a hand mixer. Gradually add the two oils in a stream while whisking and season carefully with salt and black pepper.

Put the spinach and sorrel leaves in a large shallow bowl and toss in just enough of the dressing to coat the leaves. Cut – or break up – the Roquefort into small cubes.

This salad is best served on individual plates. Make a good mound of the leaves on each plate and scatter the Roquefort cubes over them. Add the croutons and almonds. Lay the prosciutto slices over these and drizzle a little more dressing over the top.

Winter salad with pecorino, Gorgonzola and walnut oil

A big plate of this is the perfect thing for a lunch over Christmas, or as a light dinner. Use any good winter leaves – corn salad, chicory, endive and winter lettuce – as the base. Add slivers of pecorino and chunks of blue cheese, with a scattering of walnuts, pear and apple.

For 4 as main course:

4 handfuls of mixed winter salad leaves
1 pear
1 apple
Squeeze of 1 lemon
1 handful of walnut halves (4–5 walnuts per plate)
150g Gorgonzola, cut into small chunks
75g pecorino, cut into fine slivers

For the dressing:

5 tablespoons walnut oil
Lemon juice, to taste
Salt and black pepper

To ensure that everyone gets a good scattering of ingredients, this is best made on individual plates.

Wash and dry the winter salad leaves and divide them between the plates. Slice the pear and apple and squeeze over the lemon juice to stop the flesh discolouring. Scatter these and the walnuts, Gorgonzola and pecorino over the top of the salad leaves. Mix the walnut oil with lemon juice to taste and season with salt and pepper. Dress the salads just as you're going to eat.

Pork and chestnut terrine

This is excellent for a buffet lunch or supper. As you cut a slice, the chestnuts' sweet taste and distinctive texture make a good contrast to the rich, sagey meat.

It is lovely eaten with bread, but I think it's even better with small salted baked potatoes (see page 204).

Making it a couple of days in advance improves the taste. It stores very well – for up to a week in the fridge. If you leave out the bacon and garlic, it is also perfect for freezing.

For 2 terrine dishes:
- **500g very fresh pig's liver**
- **250g pork belly**
- **1 small onion**
- **2 garlic cloves, crushed**
- **10–15 vacuum-packed cooked chestnuts, left whole**
- **50g fresh breadcrumbs**
- **1 tablespoon chopped sage**
- **½ wine glass of port or brandy**
- **Good pinch of freshly grated nutmeg**
- **Salt and freshly ground black pepper**
- **Warm water**
- **5 rashers rindless streaky bacon to line the dishes, 'stretched' with the back of a knife (optional), or butter or lard, for greasing**

Peel any membrane from the liver and trim out any tough ventricles.

Put the pork belly, onion and liver through a mincer, using the coarse plate, or pulse together in a food processor. Don't chop it too finely as you want your pâté to have some texture. Transfer to a bowl. Add the garlic, chestnuts, breadcrumbs, sage, port or brandy and nutmeg, and mix well. Season with salt and black pepper.

Fill a deep baking tray with warm water to a third of the way up the side. Preheat the oven to 170°C/ gas mark 3, and place the tray in the oven while it heats up (about 10 minutes).

Line two 1-litre ovenproof dishes or terrine dishes with the bacon, if you are using it, or simply grease them with a bit of butter or lard. Divide the mixture between them and cover with greased aluminium foil. Place the dishes in the water-filled baking tray and cook in the centre of the oven for about 2 hours. The pâté will be cooked when it comes away from the side of the dish and is firm to the touch.

Allow to cool in the dish, then refrigerate and turn out when thoroughly chilled.

Chicken liver pâté with pickled plums

The richness of good chicken livers is a perfect contrast to the spicy tartness of these plums. Serve this pâté with toasted fennel seed bread (see page 154) or grissini smeared in unsalted butter. Only eat livers from decently raised chickens. You can tell by the texture: a slow-raised chicken will have a firm liver, while an immature, force-fed bird will have a liver of mush. Turkey liver (which should come with the giblets) has a stronger flavour, but you could use this too, supplementing it with chicken livers.

For 8–10:
**450g organic chicken livers
(or the liver from your turkey
plus chicken livers)
Milk
Olive oil, for frying
1 onion or 2–3 shallots, chopped
150g streaky bacon, chopped
2 garlic cloves, finely chopped
10 fresh sage leaves, ripped into
pieces
1 dessertspoon thyme, chopped
Pinch of mixed spice
Salt and black pepper
175g butter, and a little more
to seal the pâté in its bowl
Good bunch of parsley
Splash of dry sherry**

For the pickled plums:
**600g plums
200ml malt vinegar
1 cinnamon stick
6 cloves
2 star anise
350g granulated sugar**

First make the pickled plums. Halve and stone the plums. Put the vinegar, spices and sugar into a saucepan and stir gently over a low heat to dissolve. Add the plums and simmer until the fruit is just softened but still holding its shape. Carefully lift out the fruit

and put it into a bowl. Boil the poaching liquid for 10 minutes and pour it over the fruit. Leave for a few hours or overnight.

Clean the chicken (and turkey) livers, cut out any white spots and damaged areas, and carefully remove the gall bladder. This is the little greenish sac situated in the liver which, if burst, will taint the meat. Leave in a bowl of milk for 2 hours minimum, lift out and dry.

Heat a little olive oil in a pan over a low heat and fry the onion or shallots and bacon for 5 minutes. Add the garlic, ripped sage leaves, thyme, mixed spice and salt and pepper. Add the livers and sauté until they are cooked but still a little pink in the middle. Take them off the heat.

On a large board, chop the livers to the texture you like and mix with the butter, some parsley, a splash of dry sherry and some olive oil. You can do all this in a food processor if you want a smooth texture, but I prefer it coarse. Check the seasoning. Press the pâté into a pâté dish and cover with a thin layer of melted butter. Serve with the pickled plums and plenty of toasted fennel seed bread or grissini.

Celeriac remoulade with horseradish

Remoulade is a wonderful starter on its own and it's fantastic with pork and chestnut terrine (see page 216) or slices of crunchy fried prosciutto.

For 6:
**1 medium-sized celeriac
Lemon juice, for acidulation
Large bunch of parsley, coarsely
chopped, to serve**

For the mayonnaise:
**1 whole egg and 1 extra yolk
½ teaspoon mustard powder
1 garlic clove, crushed (optional)
Pinch of salt and black pepper
200ml good sunflower oil
100ml olive oil
1 teaspoon fresh grated
horseradish
Lemon juice or white wine
vinegar, to taste**

To make the mayonnaise, put the egg, extra yolk, mustard powder, garlic (if using), salt and pepper into a bowl. Froth up with an electric hand whisk. Add the oils in a stream while whisking, until the mixture becomes thick. Add the horseradish and lemon juice or vinegar and then season again. This can be stored in the fridge for a few days.

(If the mayonnaise curdles at any point, start the whole process again with a third egg yolk, whisking it in a clean bowl and adding the curdled mixture in a slow stream while processing or whisking.)

Peel the celeriac root and slice it as thinly as you can into big round discs. Then slice these into juliennes (matchsticks). As you cut them, put them into a bowl of water acidulated with a good squeeze of lemon juice to stop them turning brown.

Drain them, pat them dry and place in a bowl. Stir in just enough mayonnaise to coat and season. Serve with parsley scattered over.

Tacchino tonnato

This is an adaptation of *vitello tonnato*, that wonderful cold veal (or pork) dish, which also works brilliantly with the white meat of turkey. Don't be tempted by coronation chicken (or turkey): make this instead. The flavour improves with keeping, so if possible make this the day before you are going to eat it.

For 6:
- 200g tin of good tuna in olive or sunflower oil
- 5 anchovy fillets
- 275ml oil (half-and-half olive and sunflower, or just sunflower if you prefer)
- 3 tablespoons lemon juice or vinegar
- 3 tablespoons capers
- 1kg cooked white turkey meat
- Olives, to serve
- Whole capers, chopped, to serve
- Parsley, to serve
- Lemon slices, to serve

For the mayonnaise:
- 1 whole egg and 1 extra yolk
- 1 teaspoon mustard powder
- 200ml good sunflower oil
- 100ml olive oil
- Lemon juice or white wine vinegar, to taste
- Good pinch of salt and black pepper

To make the mayonnaise, put the egg, extra yolk and mustard powder in a bowl. Froth up with an electric hand whisk. Add the oils in a gentle stream while whisking, until the mixture becomes thick. Flavour with fresh lemon juice or vinegar and salt and pepper to taste.

Put the tuna, anchovy fillets, oil, lemon juice or vinegar and capers in a food processor and pulse until creamy. Mix with the mayonnaise. Thin the mixture to the consistency of single cream by adding a little boiling water if necessary.

Slice the meat very thinly and carefully. Place a little of the mayonnaise sauce in the bottom of a dish and arrange the slices of meat over it in layers, covering each layer with a layer of sauce as you go. Keep some extra sauce in reserve for when you serve the meat in case you need to put a bit more on the top. Cover well with aluminium foil and put in the fridge for several hours or for up to 3 days.

Serve at room temperature on a large flat serving plate. Decorate with olives, whole capers, parsley and lemon.

Turkey croquettes

This dish may sound rather Edwardian, but with the crunchy outside and creamy middle, everyone loves it. You can add some ham to the mixture for extra flavour, if you wish. Serve the croquettes with a reduced tomato sauce.

For 6:
**250g cooked turkey, white
  or brown
1 onion, chopped
Butter and oil, for frying
25g flour
275ml turkey, chicken or
  vegetable stock
30ml double cream
1 egg, beaten
Lemon juice, to taste
Bunch of parsley, chopped
Bunch of tarragon, chopped
Salt and black pepper**

For the crust:
**Seasoned flour
1 egg, beaten
125g toasted breadcrumbs**

Chop up the leftover turkey in a food processor, pulsing just a couple of times so that it's not too mushy. Alternatively, finely chop it by hand. Fry the onion gently in a little butter. Add the flour and then the stock, cream, chopped turkey, egg and a little lemon juice. Add the chopped herbs and season with salt and pepper.

Spread the mixture on to a large plate, cover with cling film and leave to cool and thicken in the fridge for an hour or two.

Roll the mixture into cylinders about 8cm long. Roll these in first the seasoned flour, then the egg and lastly the toasted breadcrumbs. Fry until golden in a little oil and butter for about 5 minutes, turning regularly, and keep warm in a low oven (150°C/gas mark 2). You can freeze any mixture you don't use.

Ham glazed with honey and cloves

An excellent stalwart dish to have on hand over Christmas. You can have it warm when it's first cooked and then cold for lunch for several days afterwards. Serve with cranberry and orange compote (see page 26), Cumberland sauce (see right), salted baked potatoes (see page 204) and celeriac remoulade (see page 218).

For 10–12:
**4.5kg boned gammon
Bay leaves
4 tablespoons Dijon mustard
4 tablespoons demerara or soft
  brown sugar
Cloves
200ml cider, or orange or apple
  juice**

Soak the boned gammon overnight in cold water.

Preheat the oven to 170°C/gas mark 3½.

Drain and wrap the joint with a couple of bay leaves in a loose, sealed parcel of aluminium foil and place in a large roasting tin with a little water in the bottom. Roast for 30 minutes per 450g in the oven, removing it from the oven 20 minutes before the end of the cooking time.

Increase the oven temperature to 200°C/gas mark 6. Take the foil off the gammon and with a very sharp knife strip off the rind, leaving an even layer of fat on the joint. Score the fat in a criss-cross pattern.

Mix together the mustard with the sugar and spread it over the fat with a palette knife. Push a clove into the middle of each diamond shape. Return the gammon to the tin, fat side uppermost. Pour over the cider or juice and put the gammon back into the oven for about 20 minutes, basting at least a couple of times, until the glaze has caramelised.

Cumberland sauce

The classic accompaniment to ham.

For 8:
**4 oranges
550g redcurrant jelly
2 lemons
300ml port
1 dessertspoon French
  mustard
1 dessertspoon arrowroot
  dissolved in 2 tablespoons
  cold water
Salt and black pepper**

Using a zester, grate long strips of orange rind from two of the oranges. Put these in a small saucepan, cover with water and simmer for 10 minutes until tender. Drain and set aside.

Put the redcurrant jelly into a medium-sized pan and add the squeezed juices of all the oranges and the two lemons. Whisk this over a gentle heat until the jelly has melted and add the port and mustard. Bring to the boil and simmer for 2–3 minutes. Take off the heat and add the dissolved arrowroot. Bring back to the boil, while whisking, and wait for the sauce to thicken slightly. Remove from the heat, add the orange zest and allow the sauce to cool, stirring occasionally to prevent a skin forming. Season with salt and pepper.

Cumberland sauce keeps very well for several days and it freezes beautifully.

Pies and tarts

Turkey, leek and ham pie with rough puff pastry

Properly made, there is nothing better than a good pie with crumbly, buttery pastry and lots of delicious juice. This is an excellent use of leftover ham and the brown meat of your Christmas turkey. Serve this with mashed potato and roast carrots with butter and toasted cumin (see page 195).

For 6–8:
1 onion, studded with cloves
1 bay leaf
500ml milk
50g butter, plus a knob for frying
500g leeks, sliced
Salt and black pepper
A little white wine or sherry
50g flour
Freshly grated nutmeg
250g cooked ham, chopped
250g cooked turkey, chopped
Large bunch of parsley,
**   chopped**
Beaten egg yolk, to glaze

For the pastry:
150g unsalted butter
150g lard
350g plain flour, sifted
A little very cold water

First make the pastry. Rub half the butter and half the lard into the sifted flour until the mixture resembles breadcrumbs. Add enough of the water to form the pastry into a ball. Roll out the pastry and dot it with a third of the remaining butter and lard. Fold one side over into the middle and then the other. Turn it and roll it out again, and repeat the process twice, until all the remaining butter and lard have been incorporated. Cover with cling film and chill for 30 minutes.

Put the studded onion and bay leaf with the milk into a small saucepan and bring to the boil. Cover and put to one side for half an hour to infuse.

Preheat the oven to 180°C/gas mark 4.

Put the knob of butter into a pan over a low heat and when it has melted add the chopped leeks, salt and pepper and a little wine or sherry, and sweat until softened.

Melt the 50g butter in a saucepan and make a roux by stirring the flour into the butter and allowing it to cook gently for a couple of minutes, while you continue to stir, until the mixture forms a smooth paste. Gradually add the strained infused milk, stirring constantly, until you have a smooth béchamel. Remove from the heat and add the nutmeg, leeks, ham and turkey. Season again with salt and pepper and add the chopped parsley.

Roll out the pastry on a floured surface and use two-thirds of it to line a pie dish. Fill with the turkey and ham mixture and cover with the remaining pastry. Dampen the edges and seal by pinching together.

Brush the top with a little beaten egg yolk and bake in the preheated oven for 40 minutes until golden brown.

Mary's smoked haddock Florentine

The ultimate fish pie – a Mary Berry recipe – incorporating spinach and mushrooms. Serve it with the traditional accompaniment of lots of sweet, buttery peas.

This is a great dish to make in advance, as it can be frozen (without the eggs) for up to a month. Mary uses ordinary eggs, but you could also try it with quails' eggs.

For 10:

A knob of butter
450g button mushrooms, thickly sliced
700g fresh young spinach
Salt and black pepper
Freshly grated nutmeg
6 eggs, hard-boiled, or 12–18 quails' eggs, lightly boiled
1.1kg undyed smoked haddock fillet
40g fresh breadcrumbs
75g Parmesan cheese
A little cornflour

For the béchamel:

1.2 litres milk
1 onion, peeled and halved
1 bay leaf
Parsley stalks
Salt and black pepper
100g butter
100g plain flour
100g mature Cheddar, grated
2 teaspoons Dijon mustard

Put the milk for the béchamel into a saucepan, and add the onion halves, bay leaf and parsley stalks. Bring to just under boiling point and then take off the heat. Cover and allow to infuse for half an hour or so. Season with salt and pepper.

In a separate saucepan, melt the butter, pull the pan off the heat, stir in the flour and add the strained, infused hot milk. Return the pan to the heat and slowly bring to the boil, stirring continually until the sauce has thickened. Cover the pan with a lid to prevent a skin from forming.

Preheat the oven to 220°C/gas mark 7.

Melt the knob of butter in a large, deep frying pan and fry the mushrooms briskly for a minute or two. Add the spinach to the mushrooms and cook gently until it has just wilted. Drain the spinach and mushrooms and season well with salt, pepper and nutmeg.

Mix 6 tablespoons of the béchamel sauce with the spinach and mushrooms and spread the mixture on the base of a shallow, buttered ovenproof dish, about 38cm x 30cm. Cover with the hard-boiled eggs, quartered, or the lightly cooked quails' eggs, halved.

Cut the haddock into manageable-sized pieces and sit these on top of the eggs. Add the grated Cheddar and Dijon mustard to the remaining sauce and pour over the raw fish. Sprinkle the breadcrumbs mixed with the Parmesan over the top. Bake in the preheated oven for about 35 minutes, until golden.

Shallot tatin with leftover cheese

You can make this fantastic tart with onions, but the sweetness of the shallots is what makes this recipe particularly delicious. It's ideal over Christmas – a brilliant use of all those hard bits of leftover cheese. Serve it with a winter green salad.

For 6:
  450g shallots
  175g leftover soft cheese, such as Brie or Camembert
  40g butter
  2 tablespoons olive oil
  1 tablespoon soft brown sugar
  Salt and black pepper
  500g puff pastry

Preheat the oven to 200°C/gas mark 6.

Peel the shallots, leaving them whole, and cut the cheese into thickish slices. Bring a pan of water to the boil, add the shallots and cook them for 5–7 minutes if they are small and 10 if they are larger. Drain and put to one side.

Heat the butter and oil in an ovenproof pan or a frying pan with a detachable handle. When the butter has melted, sprinkle in the sugar and allow it to dissolve gently before adding the shallots. Season well with salt and pepper and allow the shallots to cook until a rich golden caramel. Remove from the heat.

Roll out the pastry on a floured board to a circle a bit bigger than the pan. Spread the slices of cheese over the shallots and lay the pastry over the top, pressing it down slightly all around the edge.

Bake the tart in the preheated oven for about 25 minutes, or until risen and golden.

Allow to cool a little and then put a large serving plate over the pan and invert it quickly so that the shallots are on the top, with the pastry underneath. Serve the tart warm.

Sweet red pepper and feta tart

A punchy-flavoured tart similar to the classic French onion and anchovy tart called a *pissaladière*, but with greater sweetness from the peppers. This makes an easy winter lunch with a good pile of rocket salad.

For 6–8:
  1 large onion, chopped
  Olive oil
  6 red peppers (or a mixture of red and yellow)
  2 garlic cloves, crushed
  1 tablespoon white balsamic vinegar
  1 dessertspoon caster sugar
  8–10 black olives, stoned and halved
  50g anchovies, chopped
  Small bunch of thyme, leaves stripped and chopped
  200ml single cream
  3 eggs, beaten
  Salt and black pepper
  200g feta cheese

For the pastry:
  110g unsalted butter
  220g seasoned plain flour
  1 egg yolk mixed with a little iced water

First make the pastry. Rub the butter into the seasoned flour or pulse in a food processor until it resembles breadcrumbs. Add just enough of the egg and water to bring the pastry together into a ball. Line a 28cm tart tin with the pastry and chill for 30 minutes.

Preheat the oven to 180°C/gas mark 4.

Prick the bottom of the tart with a fork, cover with a round of greaseproof paper or foil and weigh this down with some baking beans or rice. Bake the pastry case blind in the preheated oven for about 15 minutes. Keep the oven on, ready for baking the filled pastry case.

In a heavy-based saucepan, sweat the chopped onion in olive oil for 5–10 minutes over a gentle heat and put to one side. Halve and deseed the peppers and grill or roast them until they have blackened. Put them into a plastic bag when you remove them from the heat and after a few minutes the skins will be easy to remove.

Slice the peppers and put them into the saucepan with the softened onions and the crushed garlic. Add a drizzle of oil and the balsamic vinegar and sugar and cook over a gentle heat for 5 minutes or so, until the peppers are soft but still have a bite. Remove from the heat and add the black olives, anchovies and thyme.

In a separate bowl, combine the cream and eggs, and season well. Spread the pepper mixture over the pastry, crumble over the feta cheese and pour on the cream and egg mixture. Bake in the preheated oven for about 30 minutes, or until set and golden.

Post-Christmas puddings

Winter fruit salad

This salad is made from dried fruit, which can sit for days in its marinade. It sounds unpromising, but is wonderful for a big party. Eat it with plain yoghurt, ice cream or sorbet.

For 8–10:
    450g granulated sugar
    1 litre tea (Earl Grey is ideal),
        freshly brewed
    1 cinnamon stick
    6 cloves
    1 lemon, sliced
    1 orange, sliced
    600g dried fruit, a selection –
        I suggest about 100g each
        of apricots, peaches, pears,
        large raisins, prunes and apple
        rings, stoned and soaked
        if necessary
    3–4 tablespoons brandy

Add the sugar to the freshly brewed tea. Add the spices, lemon and orange. Put the dried fruit in a large saucepan and pour the tea over it. Bring slowly to the boil, simmer for a couple of minutes and take off the heat.

Transfer everything to a large bowl. Add the brandy and allow the fruit to steep in the liquid for 2–3 days before serving.

Christmas pudding ice cream

A great way of using leftover Christmas pudding. I love the slightly chewy texture of this ice cream, with the sweetness cut through with a shot of rum.

For 8–10:
    568ml milk
    100g caster sugar
    A few drops of good vanilla
        extract
    220g sweetened condensed milk
    Pinch of salt
    475ml whipping or double cream
    150g Christmas pudding,
        broken up
    Slosh of rum, to taste

Heat the milk with the sugar and vanilla, and bring to boiling point. Remove from the heat and cool. Add the condensed milk, salt and cream.

Put in an ice-cream maker and freeze/churn the mixture for 20 minutes. Fold in the Christmas pudding and add the rum to taste. Put in a container and freeze. Or, if you haven't got a machine, pour into a plastic container and freeze for 2 hours. Remove from the freezer and stir well. Return to the freezer and repeat this process twice, stirring at 2-hourly intervals, before serving.

Campari and mango sorbet

The sweetness of the mango sorbet is a delicious contrast to the tartness of the Campari. Put a dollop of each type together on a plate, and serve with a few fresh lychees.

For 6:
For the Campari sorbet:
150ml Campari
600ml fresh orange juice
500ml stock syrup (see below)

For the mango sorbet:
4 mangoes
300ml stock syrup (see below)
Juice of 1 lemon

Make the stock syrup for both your sorbets by mixing 800ml water with 800g caster sugar. Dissolve the sugar slowly, over a gentle heat, stirring as you heat. Boil for 3–4 minutes. Allow to cool and store in the fridge until needed.

First, the Campari sorbet. Combine the Campari, orange juice and sugar syrup thoroughly. Pour into an ice-cream maker and freeze/churn for about 20 minutes. Transfer to a plastic container and freeze. If you don't have an ice-cream maker, transfer the mixture to a stainless steel bowl and freeze, covered, for about an hour. Then stir it with a fork to break up the ice particles and return to the freezer. Repeat this process twice more at hourly intervals, then transfer the sorbet to a plastic container, seal and freeze.

To make the mango sorbet, liquidise the mango flesh with the syrup, stir in the lemon juice and freeze/churn for 20 minutes. Transfer to a plastic container and freeze. If you don't have an ice-cream maker, follow the steps described above for the Campari sorbet.

The sorbets are best when they're as fresh as possible and should be eaten within one month.

Prune and Armagnac tart

This winter almond tart is based on a recipe from the River Cafe, which Rose Gray demonstrated at our cookery school one summer with fresh apricots. You can make it with almost any fruit, but one of the very best versions is with Armagnac prunes. The tart is most delicious if you use prunes that have been soaked in Armagnac for a while. You could, however, prepare the prunes the night before. To do this, soak 25 dried, stoned prunes (approximately 175g) in Earl Grey tea overnight, drain, and then soak in Armagnac (enough to cover them) for 3–4 hours before you start cooking.

Serve this with a good vanilla ice cream.

For 8–10:
300g unsalted butter, softened
300g caster sugar
300g blanched whole almonds, coarsely ground
3 eggs
25 prunes in Armagnac (see page 29), and a few tablespoons of the brandy prune juices
1 teaspoon vanilla extract

For the pastry:
110g unsalted butter, cut into cubes
175g plain flour
2 egg yolks
50g caster sugar
Pinch of salt

To make the pastry, rub the butter into the flour or pulse in a food processor until it resembles coarse breadcrumbs. Add the egg yolks, sugar and salt and pulse/mix again until the pastry comes together into a ball. Wrap it in cling film and chill for an hour.

Next place the pastry in a 30cm tart tin. A signature technique of the River Cafe is to grate the cold pastry, with a coarse cheese grater, into the tin and then spread it out with your fingers. This gives a rough texture to the pastry, making it very biscuity. Return to the fridge for half an hour.

Preheat the oven to 180°C/gas mark 4.

Prick the bottom of the tart with a fork, cover with a round of greaseproof paper or foil and weigh this down with some baking beans or rice. Bake the pastry case blind in the preheated oven for about 15 minutes. Allow to cool. Keep the oven on.

Now make the filling. Using an electric hand whisk, beat the butter and sugar together until pale and light. Add the ground almonds, beat to combine and then add the eggs, one by one, mixing well. Finally add a few tablespoons of the brandy prune juices and vanilla extract.

Pour this mixture into the tart tin. Push the prunes into it and place in the preheated oven. Turn the heat down to 150°C/gas mark 2 and cook for 40–50 minutes until golden brown.

Post-Christmas drinks

Bloody Mary with horseradish

There's nothing better than a Bloody Mary when you're feeling a bit the worse for wear. In fact, I'm almost always on for a Bloody Mary however I'm feeling, and they can practically replace a meal. The best are spiced up with fresh horseradish and sharpened with plenty of lemon juice.

For 4 medium glasses:
 175ml vodka
 Dash of dry sherry
 500ml tomato juice
 Juice of 1 lemon
 1 teaspoon fresh grated horseradish
 Tabasco and Worcestershire sauce, to taste
 Celery salt, to taste
 Freshly ground black pepper
 Ice, to serve

Combine the ingredients in a shaker and pour into individual glasses. Serve with ice.

A good Bullshot

We served Bullshots rather than champagne at our New Year's Eve wedding in Scotland as people arrived from the chilly church. They're perfect when you have lots of people who need warming up.

For 4:
 330ml tinned beef consommé
 1 tablespoon lime or lemon juice
 Celery salt, to taste
 Freshly ground black pepper
 1 tablespoon Worcestershire sauce
 Tabasco, to taste
 175ml vodka

Heat the consommé until piping hot and remove from the heat. Add the flavourings to taste and the vodka last of all.

Put into a jug and serve immediately or keep in a Thermos for later.

New Year's Eve

New Year's Eve means another feast. If you've used amaryllis or hyacinths, your table flowers should still be looking good, so with no worries about decorating, you can concentrate your time and thoughts on the food. Many of us have a holiday between Christmas and New Year, so planning and cooking can be quite leisurely and, unlike Christmas Day, there are fewer conventions to stick to.

For a New Year's Eve dinner, what about a plate of oysters on top of a pile of ice sitting in the middle of the table, followed by a rib of beef with fresh horseradish? There's an 'r' in both December and January, so native oysters are free from creamy spawn, and at their most delicious. Oysters are a palaver to open, but once you are in the swing you should be able to tackle a couple of dozen in half an hour with a short, stout oyster knife. Insert the knife to one side of the hinge muscle and you'll feel it give immediately.

If you're wary of oysters, try cockles and mussels in ginger and chilli (see page 235). I enjoy the rigmarole of these. They bring a lovely sociable slowness to the meal, with everyone picking through in search of juicy shellfish.

Making pasta is like shucking beans and peas: the ideal group activity when you have lots of people sitting around in a kitchen chatting as they prepare food. Agnolotti – large ravioli – with spinach and ricotta in a speck and cream sauce (see page 236) make ideal party food.

For something more substantial, try juniper fillet of venison with fresh pear chutney (see page 240) or a wonderful rich carbonnade of beef (see page 241). A traditional British winter favourite, steak and kidney pudding (see page 243), is also fantastic; or go for Moroccan, fragrant-spiced shoulder of lamb with couscous (see page 244). For those who prefer fish for their main course, I've included braised squid and chorizo stew, and salmon coulibiac (see page 238), both excellent for feeding lots of people.

I think a pudding is a must on New Year's Eve, and best of all are Mrs Titley's chocolate and coffee éclairs (see page 246). There's also Sussex pond pudding (see page 249) and summer pudding with a winter twist (see page 251). Or, if cheese is your thing, make the Italian winter buffet finale: panettone or pandoro inter-layered with Gorgonzola (see page 252). Surround this with candles, nuts and fruit. It both looks and tastes magnificent.

First courses

Salmon terrine

This is a very old-fashioned dish that reminds me of childhood. It comes from *English Country House Cooking* by my aunt, Fortune Stanley. We always used to spend Christmas with her when I was a child. It is ideal for lunch, or as the first course of a big dinner, served with a few winter leaves in an oil and lemon dressing.

For 10–12:
  1 large brown loaf (slightly stale is best)
  A little soft butter
  450g smoked salmon, sliced
  Freshly ground black pepper
  Juice of 1–2 lemons, to taste
  110g cream cheese
  Lots of chives and parsley, chopped, to taste

Using the longest serrated bread knife you have, slice the wholemeal loaf lengthways, not across the width, as thinly as you can. Remove the crusts. Not forgetting the corners, butter the bread and cover with the smoked salmon.

Season with freshly ground black pepper and lemon juice, to taste. Reassemble the layers as a loaf, pressing down gently as you go, so that the loaf sticks together.

Mix the soft cream cheese with chopped chives and parsley. Gently spread the cheese all over the loaf, starting at the sides and finishing with the top. Using a palette knife dipped in cold water, smooth the sides and top. Put in the fridge to harden.

After an hour or so, wrap the loaf in cling film, put it into a loaf tin and weight it down to compress the layers for a few hours or overnight. This is best made the day before it is eaten.

To serve, slice it as you would a normal loaf.

Sweet and sour cockles and mussels

I love mussels and cockles cooked almost any way, but this quick and simple dish tastes fresh and light – and is ideal after a period of lots of rich food. Mitch Tonks, the fish guru, cooked this for me and I have made it countless times since.

For 6–8:
  1kg mussels
  1kg cockles
  2 glasses of dry white wine
  1 onion, finely chopped
  2 garlic cloves, finely chopped
  2cm piece of fresh root ginger, peeled and finely sliced
  25g butter
  2 tablespoons olive oil
  1 teaspoon dried chilli, or 1 fresh red chilli, deseeded and finely chopped
  6 tablespoons red wine vinegar
  3 tablespoons caster sugar
  Lime juice, to taste
  Fresh coriander, chopped

Scrub the mussels and cockles, remove the fibrous beard that attaches each mussel to its rock, and tip into a large pan with the white wine.

In another pan sweat the onion, garlic and ginger in the butter and oil. Add the chilli, red wine vinegar and caster sugar, and cook until the onion is translucent.

Cover the pan containing the shellfish and bring to the boil. After 5 minutes, take the pan off the heat and discard any shells that have not opened.

Add the onion mixture to the shellfish and mix thoroughly. Add lime juice to taste and serve with plenty of chopped coriander.

Spinach and ricotta agnolotti

My mother learned to make pasta some 30 years ago at the Due More restaurant in Asolo in the Veneto, and I have been back there recently to do the same. Making pasta is easy, but it isn't quick. It's a multi-stage process that is best done when there are lots of people who can be called on to help; between Christmas and New Year is just the time. I like to have three people around: one person feeding the pasta dough into the machine, someone else turning the handle and a third person catching the sheets as they emerge.

If you don't want to eat meat, this recipe is the perfect celebratory food: leave the speck out and use freshly grated nutmeg. You can serve three or four agnolotti (large ravioli) per person as a first course or more for a main.

When buying the flour for the pasta, try to find De Cecco semola di grano duro rimacinata 176: this flour is a nice pale golden yellow, quite grainy and almost like a fine polenta, but not made with cornmeal.

For 40–50 agnolotti:
200g spinach
250g ricotta
Salt and black pepper
Freshly grated nutmeg, to taste
1 egg, beaten
1–2 tablespoons olive oil
**Plenty of grated Parmesan
  cheese, to serve**

For the pasta:
500g hard-wheat pasta flour
2 pinches of fine salt
5 eggs

For the sauce:
**12 fine slices of speck or
  prosciutto (optional)**
Drizzle of olive oil
**500ml double cream or Italian
  panna**

First make the pasta. Tip the flour and salt into a round pile in the middle of a big table, making a dip in the centre. Break the eggs into the dip and start bringing the flour into them with a fork. Once they are combined, knead the dough with your hands for about 10 minutes until it becomes elastic and soft and has the texture of play dough. Every now and then, throw the ball of dough from a height, letting it thud down on to the table: the force will knock the air out of the dough and help it soften. You will end up with a lump of smooth, golden dough about 15–20cm long and 8cm high (about the size of a large Cornish pasty). Allow the dough to rest – but not in the fridge – for half an hour or so.

Cut the dough into five chunks. Flatten each chunk with the palm of your hand and start to feed it into a pasta machine. In the beginning the roller must be on the widest setting. Do this six or seven times on the first setting and then once only as you progress through settings 2, 3, 4, 5 and 6. With every rolling, the dough will become silkier. If it begins to get a little sticky, dust it generously with flour. If you don't have a pasta machine, you can do this by hand, but it takes a lot of rolling to achieve the right texture and thinness.

When you have reached 6 on the gauge with each sheet, lay the long, thin sheets on to clean tea towels dusted with flour. It's important at this stage to have a big table, plenty of clean tea towels and enthusiastic helpers. Make sure the sheets are well spaced and not overlapping, so that they can dry out a bit. You'll know if they are thin enough if, when they are laid flat, you can clearly see the pattern of the tea towel through them. The texture should be satiny smooth. If one of the sheets gets too long in the rolling and is unmanageable, cut it in half

crossways and thread the half section back through the machine.

It is possible to freeze the pasta at this stage, rolled carefully in a tea towel or greaseproof paper to keep the sheets apart.

Rest the pasta for half an hour and then start to make the agnolotti squares. Wilt the spinach in salted, boiling water. Drain, and press all the liquid from the leaves using a spoon in a colander or sieve. Chop the spinach finely and mix with the ricotta, salt, pepper and nutmeg to taste.

Put a teaspoon-sized dollop of the mixture at 4–6cm intervals across one sheet (depending on the size of pocket that you want). With a pastry brush, paint the beaten egg all around the dollops and place another sheet on top. Gently press around each mound, working outwards to exclude any large air pockets. Then to make your agnolotti squares, cut between the mounds, using a serrated pastry wheel (a zigzag edge makes them look good).

Preheat the oven to 160°C/gas mark 2½. To cook the agnolotti, fill a very large pan (about 3 litres, wide and shallow is best) with salted water and a tablespoon or two of olive oil. Bring this to the boil and drop in the pasta, just 8 shapes at a time. The agnolotti will be cooked after 3–4 minutes. Lift them out carefully with a slotted spoon and keep them warm in the preheated oven in a little butter or oil until the others are ready.

To make the sauce, roughly chop the speck or prosciutto and gently fry in a little olive oil until just beginning to crisp. Pour over the cream or panna. If you're not using speck or prosciutto, just warm the cream through, adding extra nutmeg.

Divide the pasta between warm bowls and pour over the sauce. Serve with a bowl of grated Parmesan.

Main courses

Coulibiac of salmon

This salmon and puff pastry recipe is ideal for feeding lots of people.

For 6–8:
  900g fresh salmon
  50g long grain rice
  Vegetable or chicken stock
  50g butter
  1 large onion, finely chopped
  225g button mushrooms, chopped
  **2 hard-boiled eggs, shelled
    and chopped**
  **2 tablespoons parsley, finely
    chopped**
  **Salt and freshly ground black
    pepper**
  700g puff pastry
  1 egg, beaten

Preheat the oven to 200°C/gas mark 6.
Cut the salmon into small chunks, about 1cm in size.

Cook the rice in the stock and drain. Melt the butter in a saucepan and sweat the onion in it for about 5 minutes until it is soft and translucent. Then add the mushrooms, and cook for another minute or two. Set aside.

In a small bowl, mix the hard-boiled eggs and parsley, and season.

Put a piece of baking paper on a baking tray. Divide the pastry in half, and roll out one piece into a rectangle about 35cm x 25cm. Lay this on the baking tray. Cover it with the rice, leaving a margin of about 4cm round the edges. Arrange the salmon chunks on top. Follow this with the eggs and parsley mixture, and lastly the mushroom and onion mixture.

Roll out the other piece of pastry to the same size. Brush the margin of the first piece with beaten egg, and put the second piece on top. Press the edges together firmly and trim off any bits that overhang. Slash 5–6 times diagonally across the top and brush all over with beaten egg.

Bake in the oven for 35–40 minutes. Serve either hot or cold.

Braised squid and chorizo stew

I love the mix of textures and flavours in this robust dish. Serve it with saffron rice or crusty bread and a winter leaf salad with oil and lemon dressing. This is an excellent dish for a party: very easy and ideal for feeding lots of people.

The flavour of this recipe improves if it is prepared the day before. Refrigerate the stew, and when you want to eat, reheat gently for 10 minutes, adding the peas 5 minutes before it is ready.

For 6:
  1 onion, finely chopped
  2 garlic cloves, finely chopped
  1 celery stick, finely chopped
  200g chorizo, sliced
  Olive oil, for frying
  1 teaspoon tomato purée
  Pinch of saffron
  2 small dried bird's eye chillies
  **1 tablespoon ground cumin
    or harissa powder**
  2 x 400g tins of tomatoes
  1kg squid, cleaned and sliced
  800g tinned chickpeas
  2 tablespoons caster sugar
  200ml red wine
  200g frozen peas
  Juice of 1 lemon
  Handful of chopped parsley

In a heavy-bottomed pan gently sweat the onion, garlic, celery and sliced chorizo in the olive oil. Add the tomato purée and cook for a further minute before adding the saffron, dried chillies, cumin or harissa, tomatoes, squid, chickpeas, sugar, wine and 200ml water. Simmer gently for 45 minutes.

Five minutes before the end of the cooking time – or, if you have made the stew in advance and are reheating it, before you want to eat – add the peas.

Finish by adding the lemon juice and plenty of chopped parsley.

Loin of pork with fennel and cider

An ideal dish to leave in the oven and ignore for two or three hours while you get on with something else. Serve on its own or with creamy potato and celeriac mash.

For 4–6:

1.5kg loin of pork, boned and rolled
2 tablespoons fennel seeds
Salt and black pepper
3–4 heads of Florence fennel, depending on size
2 onions
1 head of garlic, sliced in half
3 dessert apples, peeled and quartered
1 tablespoon soft brown sugar
450ml cider
Olive oil

Preheat the oven to 200°C/gas mark 6.

If you like crackling, remove the skin from the pork. Wash it, then dry and score well. Rub in plenty of salt and a tablespoon of fennel seeds. Place on to a baking tray.

Tie the joint securely and place it in a roasting dish. Rub the remaining fennel seeds into the joint and season with salt and pepper. Roughly chop the fennel and onions, and place around the pork with the garlic, apples and sugar. Season well. Pour in the cider and splash over some olive oil.

Cook in the hot oven for the first few minutes, and then reduce the temperature to 160°C/gas mark 2½. Allow 35 minutes per 450g plus another 35 minutes, until the pork is tender. Roast the crackling at the same time, until crisp. (If it is ready before the joint, keep it warm until you're ready to serve.) Snip into long strips.

Lift out the pork, fennel and onions and sieve the juices with the apples. Cut the meat into thick slices and serve with a piece of the fennel, the onions and some juice, with the strips of crackling over the top.

Flash roast fillet of venison with fresh pear chutney

Venison is readily available in the winter, and very good value compared with beef. The fillet is tender and juicy, ideal with the strong flavour of juniper. It's good served with this fresh pear chutney, a dish the great game cook Clarissa Dickson Wright taught me; and also with roast or saddleback potatoes (see page 192) and roast carrots with butter and toasted cumin (see page 195).

For 4–6:

1 fillet fallow deer or
2 fillets roe deer
230ml white wine, for marinating
1 wine glass of sherry
1 bunch of thyme
Salt and roughly ground black pepper
10 juniper berries, crushed
3 garlic cloves, peeled and sliced
Olive oil
Knob of butter

For the chutney:

4 pears
2 small chillies, deseeded and chopped
2 garlic cloves, finely chopped
Thumb-sized piece of fresh root ginger, peeled and chopped
2 cinnamon sticks
Pinch of ground cloves
100g sugar
4 tablespoons apple cider vinegar

First make the chutney. Peel, core and roughly chop the pears. Put all the ingredients together in a small pan and cook gently, stirring until the sugar has dissolved, and then simmer until the pears are soft. This will take 15–20 minutes, depending on the ripeness of the pears. Keep in a jar in the fridge. (It will last a couple of weeks.)

Marinate the fillet overnight whole in the white wine, sherry, some of the thyme, salt, pepper and the crushed juniper berries.

Wash and dry the fillet, reserving some of the marinade. Make six little slits in it and push in the garlic clove slices, and some finely chopped thyme. Sprinkle salt and roughly ground black pepper over the fillet.

You can cook the meat in either an iron frying pan or a griddle. If using a frying pan, heat a mixture of olive oil and a little butter in the pan. If using a griddle, rub the meat with olive oil. Put in the fillet and brown each side for 5 minutes; then turn down the heat and cook for a further 10 minutes, turning the fillet every so often, and adding a little of the marinade to stop it burning.

Take the meat off the heat and wrap it in aluminium foil. Leave it to cool for 20 minutes before carving, and serve with the pear chutney.

Carbonnade of beef

A delicious, rich, slow-cooked stew, ideal for feeding lots of people on New Year's Eve. This recipe of Tam's is twice as good made a day or two in advance, and then reheated gently. It also freezes brilliantly (but allow plenty of time for thawing).

For 8–10:
2kg best lean chuck steak, uncut
75g plain flour
Salt and freshly ground pepper
4–5 tablespoons groundnut oil
2 bay leaves
3 garlic cloves, finely chopped
About 3 tablespoons tomato
  purée
1 heaped tablespoon sugar
Small bunch of thyme, stripped
  and chopped
550ml brown ale
4 large onions, quartered
450g or more carrots (optional
  – they make it go further)
400g chestnut mushrooms,
  wiped clean
Butter and flour, for thickening
  (optional)
Bunch of parsley, chopped,
  to serve
Baguette, sliced, to serve
Dijon mustard, to serve

Preheat the oven to 160°C/gas mark 2½.

Trim the meat and cut into large chunks. Put the flour, salt and pepper into a large plastic bag or bowl, add the meat and toss to coat.

Put about 4–5 tablespoons of groundnut oil into a large heavy-based, ovenproof pan and heat. Add the meat and brown it quickly on all sides. Add the bay leaves, garlic, tomato purée, sugar, thyme and ale, and bring to the boil. Cover and cook in the preheated oven for about 1½ hours.

Add the onions and carrots (if using) and cook for another 45 minutes. Add the whole mushrooms and continue cooking for another 15–20 minutes. Taste and season with salt and pepper as required.

If you want to thicken the sauce, mix a little melted butter and flour into a smooth paste and add to the hot liquid, stirring until it has dissolved.

To serve, scatter chopped parsley over the carbonnade. Bake a few slices of a baguette, enough for one slice per serving, and spread them with Dijon mustard. Sit a slice of baguette over the top of each serving of carbonnade.

Steak and kidney suet pudding

You don't want to eat this too often, but once in a while, there's nothing better. Serve with mashed potato, braised red cabbage (see page 196) and roast carrots with butter and toasted cumin (see page 195).

For 6–8:

2 onions, finely chopped
Sunflower oil, for frying
1.35kg chuck steak, cut into chunks
250g ox or lamb kidney, sliced lengthways and with the core and membrane removed
4 tablespoons well-seasoned flour
Handful of chopped mixed herbs, such as thyme, winter savory, parsley, rosemary or lavender

For the suet crust:

225g self-raising flour
225g plain flour
½ teaspoon salt
1 heaped teaspoon baking powder
275g suet (vegetarian or meat)
275ml cold water

To make the suet crust, sift the flours with the salt and baking powder and rub in the suet. Mix with enough of the cold water to make a soft dough. Roll out two-thirds of the dough to line a greased 2-litre pudding basin. Reserve the rest to cover the pudding, rolled out to cover the top and the rim.

Gently fry the onions in a little oil until translucent. Toss the beef and kidney in the flour and arrange in the pudding basin with a handful of herbs and onions. Add enough cold water to reach three-quarters of the way up the basin (about 150ml) and cover the top and the rim with the reserved dough, dampening the edges and pinching them to seal. Trim away any extra dough and cover with a double layer of greaseproof paper tied securely with string.

Put the basin in a saucepan and pour in boiling water until it reaches one-third of the way up. Cover and steam the pudding for 4 hours, topping up the saucepan with boiling water when needed.

When serving, have a small jug of boiling water ready. Cut the pudding like you would a cake, slicing from the top downwards; you'll need a serving spoon to collect the mixture that tumbles out. When you have removed the first portion pour in a small amount of the water. This, added to the concentrated juices, will give a good gravy.

Moroccan lamb with couscous

I learnt this recipe in Marrakech, and it's wonderfully imprecise. You can add all these spices or only some, but don't leave out the cumin: that's the one that really gives the characteristic flavour. You can leave it cooking slowly in the oven while you're out for a walk, or it is even better made the day before. It's good served with a selection of slow-roasted winter roots or a peppery leaf salad.

For 4:
  750g boned lamb shoulder, trimmed of excess fat and skin (a large half shoulder), or you could use 4 small lamb shanks
  3 teaspoons cumin seeds
  1 teaspoon coriander seeds
  1 tablespoon olive oil
  2 onions, chopped
  1 teaspoon ground cinnamon
  2 teaspoons freshly grated ginger
  1 teaspoon turmeric
  2 garlic cloves, chopped
  1 teaspoon smoked paprika
  Zest and juice of 1 lime
  120g prunes, stoned and soaked
  50g pine nuts, toasted
  400g tin of tomatoes
  Salt and black pepper
  Handful of fresh coriander, chopped
  Handful of mint, chopped

For the couscous:
  500ml good stock
  275g couscous
  Salt and black pepper
  Handful of mint or coriander
  Handful of parsley
  Zest and juice of ½ lemon or lime

Preheat the oven to 180°C/gas mark 4.

Trim and prepare the lamb and cut into large chunks (or get your butcher to do this for you). If you're using shanks, leave them whole.

Fry the cumin and coriander seeds in a non-stick pan until they begin to pop, and grind to a powder. I use an electric coffee grinder for this, but you could also use a pestle and mortar.

In a heavy-bottomed ovenproof pan or casserole dish heat the oil and cook the onions for a few minutes over a low heat. Lift them out on to a plate and brown the pieces of lamb (or shanks) quickly over a high heat.

Reduce the heat and add the ground cumin and coriander seeds and the cinnamon, ginger and turmeric, stirring to combine the flavours. Return the onions to the pan and cook gently for 2–3 minutes.

Add the garlic, paprika, lime zest and juice, prunes, pine nuts and tomatoes, cover and cook in the preheated oven for 2 hours. Season carefully with salt and pepper.

Eat there and then, or allow to cool completely and gently reheat when required. When you are about to eat, stir in the chopped coriander and mint.

To make the couscous, bring the stock to the boil, put the couscous into a deep bowl, pour over the stock, stir, cover and leave for 5–10 minutes to allow the grains to soften. Season well with salt and pepper and add the chopped herbs and lemon or lime zest and juice.

Slow-cooked lamb with potatoes

This is one of my favourite Elizabeth David recipes. It needs to be slowly cooked for at least four hours so the meat has melted right down and the potatoes are crunchy on top. An hour before the end of cooking, you can also add chopped carrots, aubergines or fennel with the potatoes.

If you have cooked this in advance, or you have leftovers, add 150ml white wine before reheating for 30–40 minutes at 150°C/gas mark 2.

Serve with redcurrant or rowan jelly (see page 25).

For 4–6:
  16 thin slices of pancetta
  6 lamb chump chops
  Olive oil
  Salt and black pepper
  Rosemary or thyme, finely chopped
  1 head of garlic, broken into cloves (leave the skins on)
  6 potatoes, peeled and cut into cubes
  8 shallots, chopped

Preheat the oven to 200°C/gas mark 6.

Cut four of the pancetta slices into strips. Trim any excess fat from the chops. Heat some olive oil in a large heavy-based ovenproof pan and line the bottom of the pan with the rest of the pancetta slices. Sit the chops on top, season well and sprinkle over the chopped herbs, the strips of pancetta and the garlic cloves. Cover the lamb with the potatoes and shallots and pour over a generous glug of olive oil.

Put the pan, uncovered, into the hot oven for 20 minutes and then lower the heat to about 150°C/gas mark 2, cover the pan and cook for a further 3½ hours, by which time the potatoes should be golden and will have absorbed most of the oil.

Beef olives

I was brought up on beef olives: thin slices of beef pounded out to large rectangles and wrapped around almost any stuffing. This is one of my favourite winter meat dishes, filled with chilli, pine nuts, olives and capers. It is best served with mashed potato or rice and plenty of braised red cabbage (see page 196).

I like eating the beef olives just with their own gravy, but in France they usually serve them with a rich tomato sauce.

For 4:
- **1 onion, chopped**
- **1 garlic clove, finely chopped**
- **1 tablespoon olive oil, plus some for frying**
- **100g chopped celery**
- **50g sweet red peppers, deseeded and chopped**
- **1 red chilli, deseeded and finely chopped, or 1 level teaspoon chilli flakes**
- **100g mushrooms, chopped, plus 2–3 sliced mushrooms for braising**
- **50g pine nuts, toasted**
- **50g olives, chopped**
- **50g capers, rinsed**
- **50g breadcrumbs**
- **1 tin of anchovies, drained and chopped**
- **A few prunes, chopped**
- **Salt and black pepper**
- **450g topside, in 8 slices, pounded to about 5mm thick**
- **A little seasoned plain flour**
- **30g butter**
- **570ml red wine or half-and-half good stock and wine**
- **2 bay leaves**

Preheat the oven to 180°C/gas mark 4.

Sweat the onion and garlic for 2–3 minutes in a little oil in a large frying pan and add the celery, red peppers, chilli or chilli flakes and chopped mushrooms, and sauté for another 3–4 minutes. Turn the mixture into a bowl and add the toasted pine nuts, olives, capers, breadcrumbs, anchovies and prunes. Mix thoroughly. Season well with salt and pepper.

Cut each slice of beef in half and divide the stuffing between the pieces. Roll them up into tube shapes and tie at both ends with trussing string, or secure with cocktail sticks. Dust with seasoned flour.

Heat the olive oil and butter in a heavy-based ovenproof pan and brown the beef rolls. Take off the heat and add the wine (or stock and wine), bay leaves and sliced mushrooms. Cover and bake in the preheated oven for 1 hour.

Remove from the oven, and take out the beef olives with a slotted spoon. Keep them warm. Put the liquid over a high heat and allow it to bubble up and cook, to reduce a little, before serving with the beef olives.

Puddings for a new year

Mrs Titley's chocolate and coffee éclairs

These éclairs are the best you'll ever eat. They are ideal for a big family party – make two-thirds chocolate and one-third coffee – over Christmas or New Year. You can make the cases several days beforehand and store them in an airtight container.

A piping bag with a 1cm plain nozzle is very useful for this recipe.

For 8:
  40g butter
  Pinch of salt
  75g plain flour
  2 eggs
  1 teaspoon vanilla extract
  275ml double cream

For the icings:
  50g dark chocolate
    (at least 70% cocoa solids)
  1 tablespoon golden syrup
  Splash of double cream
  1 tablespoon instant coffee
  2 tablespoons boiling water
  4 tablespoons icing sugar, sifted

Preheat the oven to 180°C/gas mark 4.

To make the choux pastry, put the butter and salt in a saucepan with 150ml water and heat slowly to melt the butter. Add the flour all at once, keeping the pan on the heat, but as the mixture thickens remove from the heat and beat really well until it comes away from the side of the pan leaving the surface clean. Allow to cool slightly.

Add the eggs and beat them slowly but thoroughly into the mixture. (You can do this in a food processor, using the beater attachment, or by hand.) Add the vanilla extract and beat well until the mixture is smooth and glossy.

On a baking tray covered with non-stick or silicone liner paper either shape the choux pastry with two spoons or put the mixture into a piping bag with a 1cm plain nozzle and pipe it. Make the éclairs roughly 8–10cm in length, with space in between for expansion.

Place in the preheated oven and cook for 20–25 minutes until they are pale brown and well risen. Allow to cool on a wire rack and make a hole in the sides to release the steam.

To make the chocolate icing, melt the chocolate in a bain-marie with the tablespoon of syrup, add a splash of double cream and stir to mix. To make coffee icing, mix the tablespoon of instant coffee with 2 tablespoons of boiling water; then add the icing sugar and stir thoroughly.

If you want to make the chocolate icing shinier, add a little more syrup; and you can add a dessertspoon of syrup to the coffee icing to take away any bitterness.

Whip the double cream until it holds soft peaks. Slit the sides of the éclairs and pipe in the cream. Spread the icing over the tops. Ice some with the chocolate icing and some with the coffee.

Sussex pond pudding

I had this pudding several times with the late Christopher Lloyd at Great Dixter and I love it for that. It is exactly the sort of food he used to cook – very British and traditional, and absolutely delicious. The pudding tends to collapse as you turn it out, but it tastes fantastic.

For 8–10:
  225g self-raising flour
  115g suet (vegetarian or meat)
  Zest of 1 lemon
  125ml milk and water mixed,
    half and half
  150g butter, cold
  150g soft brown sugar
  2 large unwaxed lemons, pricked
    in several places with a fork
  Double cream, to serve

Combine the flour, suet and zest in a large mixing bowl and add the liquid to make a soft dough. Roll it out into a large circle, keeping back one-third of the dough for the lid. Place in a buttered 1.4-litre pudding basin, letting any extra hang over the edge.

Cube the butter, put half into the pudding basin and cover with half the sugar. Sit the two whole lemons on the sugar and layer the remaining butter and sugar on top of the lemons.

Place the circle of dough you have reserved for the lid on top of the pudding and seal it well by pinching the edge of the lid with the dough lining the basin. Trim away any excess.

Make a pleat down the centre of a double layer of greaseproof paper, to allow for expansion during cooking, and cover the basin with the paper, securing it with string.

Sit the pudding basin in a large saucepan with enough boiling water to reach one-third of the way up the sides, and cover. Steam for 3½ hours, topping up the saucepan with boiling water when needed. Serve really hot with cream.

Date and toffee pudding

This recipe, given to me by Adrian Gill, is a gooey, date-rich version of sticky toffee pudding. Children love it, and it goes down well with adults too.

Both the pudding and the sauce freeze well.

For 8–10:
  500g dates
  220ml boiling water
  2 teaspoons bicarbonate of soda
  150g butter
  450g sugar
  3 eggs, beaten
  3 teaspoons vanilla extract
  375g plain flour
  4 teaspoons baking powder

For the sauce:
  150g butter
  150g brown sugar
  8 tablespoons double cream

Preheat the oven to 170°C/gas mark 3.

Cover the dates in the boiling water with the bicarbonate of soda. In a large mixing bowl, cream the butter and sugar together until light, then add the beaten eggs slowly, along with the vanilla extract. Sieve the flour and the baking powder into the bowl and mix well. Fold in the dates and liquid.

Grease and line a shallow tin. Pour in the mixture and cook in the preheated oven for 35 minutes, until firm to the touch.

To make the sauce, melt the butter and sugar over a low heat until dissolved and then add the cream. Bring to the boil and remove from the heat. Serve with the date pudding.

Iced berries with hot white chocolate sauce

This is a very simple recipe from the Ivy restaurant. I have upped the proportion of fruit to chocolate so that it doesn't feel so wicked. It's still rich, so I'd do a plate like this to serve 10–12 at the end of a large meal.

For 10–12:
    1.2 kg frozen berries

For the sauce:
    600g good white chocolate
    600ml double cream

To make the sauce, place the chocolate and the cream in a bowl over a pan of simmering water for 10–15 minutes, stirring every so often. It will melt and then thicken as the cream cooks.

Five minutes before serving, put the frozen berries on to individual plates, or one large plate, and leave at room temperature to lose a little of their chill. Transfer the hot chocolate sauce to a serving jug and pour over the fruit on the big plate, or get your guests to pour however much they want on to their own individual plates.

Winter pudding

A winter version of summer pudding, with fruit filling a bread case, but using frozen blackberries, and with cranberries and apples instead of soft summer fruit. Serve it with extra juice and plenty of runny cream.

For 4–6:
    A loaf of good white bread,
        panettone or brioche
    150g sugar
    1 cinnamon stick
    5 cloves
    600g frozen blackberries
    100g cranberries, fresh or dried
    300g Bramley apples
    Cream, to serve

Rinse (but don't dry) an 800ml pudding basin or soufflé dish with cold water. (This will make the pudding easier to turn out and help spread the juice evenly.) Slice the bread, panettone or brioche and cut off the crusts. Use the slices to line the pudding basin, making a circle to cover the top.

In a saucepan, dissolve the sugar in 570ml water, add the spices and bring to the boil. Cook for a couple of minutes. Add the fruit, gently bring to the boil and simmer for about 5 minutes. Taste for sweetness and with a slotted spoon ladle the fruit into the lined pudding basin, leaving the spices in. Add enough of the liquid to come to the top of the basin and reserve the extra juice. Cover with the circle of bread, panettone or brioche.

Put a small plate (that fits inside the top of the pudding basin or soufflé dish) over the pudding and cover with a weight. Put into the fridge overnight.

Before serving, turn out the pudding on to a large round dish and pour over some of the reserved juice and any fruit that wouldn't fit into the basin. Serve with a jug of cream.

Mrs Root's lemon soufflé

Another nostalgic dish for me, and one of my absolute favourite party puddings. It's an extremely lemony mousse, which was often made for us by a wonderful woman, Mrs Root, or 'Rootie', my mother's housekeeper, when we were children. She used to make it in a bain-marie, but this is a quicker and simpler version. Note that it contains uncooked egg.

You can make this the day before, and leave it somewhere cool, covered in cling film. The fridge is too cold a place to store it, and will cause the gelatine to harden.

For 8:
Zest and juice of 3 lemons
15g gelatine (equals 4 large leaves of gelatine)
3 large or 4 medium eggs, separated
115g caster sugar
300ml double cream

In a small pan, mix the lemon zest and juice and soak the gelatine in this mixture, warming it a little to dissolve completely.

Beat the egg yolks and caster sugar until foamy; then add to the gelatine and lemon mixture.

Whip the cream, and then wash and dry the beaters and beat the egg whites to stiff peaks. Fold the egg yolk mixture and the whipped cream together. Then gently fold in the egg whites.

Pour the soufflé into a shallow bowl and leave to set for 4 hours, or overnight, before serving.

Panettone or pandoro with Gorgonzola

This looks and tastes magnificent. Think of it as a communal birthday cake and surround it with candles. This is a traditional end to a Milanese party meal, and is often part of a large buffet dinner.

For 10–12:
1 large panettone (with fruit) or pandoro (star shaped without fruit)
300g mascarpone cheese
300g Gorgonzola cheese
Icing sugar, to serve

Beat the mascarpone with the Gorgonzola to make a smooth, thick cream.

Slice the panettone or pandoro horizontally into approximately 1.5cm slices. Ideally cut an even number of slices, and keep them in shape order. Spread the cheese mixture on every other layer: i.e. spread the top side of the large slice at the bottom and cover with the next one, then spread the next slice after that and do the same all the way up. (In other words, don't spread every slice with the mixture.) This makes the cake into 'sandwiches', which can be served whole, or halved if you are less hungry.

If you are using a star-shaped pandoro, it looks lovely if you twist each layer slightly, making a spiral.

When you have reached the top, put the cake on to a large platter and sprinkle the whole thing with sifted icing sugar.

Flower suppliers

For evergreen trees and foliage:
Tregothnan
The Woodyard
Tregothnan
Truro
Cornwall TR2 4AJ
www.tregothnan.co.uk
Tel: 01872 520 000

For ordering boxes of scented narcissi to be delivered:
Isles of Scilly Scented Narcissi
www.scentednarcissi.co.uk
Tel: 01720 423 767

For flowers, decorations, candles, vases, floristry kit, flower floats,
Florafix, magic balls and gingerbread house kits:
Sarah Raven's Cutting Garden
Perch Hill Farm
Willingford Lane
Brightling
Robertsbridge
East Sussex TN32 5HP
www.sarahraven.com
Tel: 01424 838 000

For orchids and orchid compost:
McBean's Orchids
Cooksbridge
East Sussex BN8 4PR
www.mcbeansorchids.co.uk
Tel: 01273 400 228

For cacti:
Abbey Brook Cactus Nursery
Bakewell Road
Matlock
Derbyshire DE4 2QJ
www.abbeybrookcacti.com
Tel: 01629 580 306

Food suppliers

For the turkey:
www.kelly-turkeys.com
Tel: 01245 223 581

For the goose:
www.goodmansgeese.co.uk
Tel: 01299 896 272

For fresh salmon (ask for sustainably raised):
www.fishinabox.co.uk
Tel: 01952 820 966
Or:
www.hebrideansmokehouse.com
Tel: 01876 580 209

For smoked salmon:
www.dunkeldsmokedsalmon.co.uk
Tel: 01350 727 639

For seafood:
www.channelfisheries.com
Tel: 01803 858 126

For sausages:
www.thenetherfieldcentre.co.uk
Tel: 01424 838 252

For black pudding:
www.charlesmacleod.co.uk
Tel: 01851 702 445

For drinks, including pisco:
www.thedrinkshop.com
Tel: 0800 169 6760

C

Acknowledgements

The idea for this book came from my discussions with my agent Caroline Michel, and Richard Atkinson at Bloomsbury, and I'm so glad it did. Warm thanks to both of them for their encouragement.

The photo sessions for the book were complicated and involved the whole team at Perch Hill. Bea Burke, Colin Pilbeam and Tessa Bishop did the growing and picking, and Bea, Colin, Tessa, Liz Craig, Denise Betteridge, Caroline Owen Lloyd and Tam Lawson worked on the flowers and decorations. Tam also led the way on recipe testing with Debbie Staples and Liz Wood. Huge thanks to everyone there. Overall, I have relied enormously on the talents and knowledge of Tam, who has contributed a huge amount to the ideas, recipe research and writing throughout the book. Warm love and thanks to her.

Once I'd drawn together the collection of Christmas recipes, I ran them past several friends and family to see if the ideas would inspire them to try new things for decorating and eating over Christmas. Tam and I talked through every detail. The ears of Lou Farman, Juliet Nicolson and Charles Anson were also endlessly bent and my twin sister Jane read and commented on every recipe. She was invaluable in stopping me from getting too highfalutin (if you can't get an ingredient in an Edinburgh supermarket, then maybe don't include it). She then produced one of the most delicious but highfalutin recipes of the lot, made with frozen strawberries from her allotment (see Strawberry white chocolate truffles, page 32). Loving thanks to all these people for their help, encouragement and support.

As far as the words go, Kate Hubbard worked skilfully on the early manuscript. Claire Smith made sure everything was clearly and correctly explained. Huge thanks to them both. Natalie Hunt at Bloomsbury then did a fantastic job checking every last detail, helped by Anne Askwith, Christine King and Margaret Gilbey.

For how the book looks I am grateful to Stuart Smith and Victoria Forrest from Smith Design, and again Richard Atkinson at Bloomsbury, who cares as much as I do about the overall style and beauty of the finished book. Thanks also to Sarah Morris for her terrific work on the cover, and to Lisa Fiske for all the care taken over the production.

This is the fifth book I've done with Jonathan Buckley. Since we started working on *The Bold and Brilliant Garden* twelve years ago, we have become great friends, and I think the combination of the two of us works well. We're both semi-workaholics, but still manage to have a nice time. Thanks so much Walt.

For specific recipes, huge thanks to Tam for her contributions and to her husband Michael, a great baker, for his cornmeal rolls (page 146) and oatmeal rolls (page 210). The idea for panettone or pandoro with Gorgonzola (page 252) came from Tam's daughter, Kate Dawson.

Thank you to Debbie Staples for her easy chocolate truffles (page 34) and rose Turkish delight (page 34), and for her Granny's recipe for rough puff pastry (page 222). Thanks also to Jan Pearson for her gingerbread house (page 39). This recipe has been passed down to her by a friend, Jeanne Richardson, who lives in Norway.

The idea for the Paper White table centre comes from a distant cousin, and has become a family tradition, passed down from one generation to the next. The florist Paula Pryke, who I worked with years ago at Sainsbury's magazine, was the inspiration behind the hyacinth napkin ring (page 86) and the rosemary covered vase (page 89).

The party logistics and catering advice was checked over by two fantastic party organisers: Georgina Holt and Dede McGillveray. Thank you to Teresa Wallace for the very cheesy biscuits (page 125), roasted almonds (page 126) and turkey croquettes (page 220), and to Andrew Wallace for the idea for pisco sours (page 137) at Christmas. Thanks to Sybille Russell for her family recipe for Danish glögg (page 138), to Sarah Ingram Hill for the sloe gin and champagne cocktail (page 138) and to Caroline Davenport Thomas for the mulled cider (page 139).

The Christmas muffins (page 146) come from Sarah Wilkin, and homemade granola (page 147) and rosemary ricotto (page 210) from Francis Hamel Cooke. Janie Stewart-Malir provided the recipe for sorrel eggs (page 153). Ray Smith from the River Cottage team cooked something similar to the pork and chestnut terrine (page 216) when he was teaching with us at Perch Hill, and Sarah and Montagu Don demonstrated the loin of pork with fennel (page 240) at the school too. Aurea Carpenter first cooked me the Elizabeth David slow-cooked lamb (page 244), which she'd learnt from her stepmother Jill. I first ate the delicious date and toffee pudding (page 249) with Emma Bridgewater – the original recipe for this came from Adrian Gill.

As well as Tam and Jane, who got submerged in the process of making this book almost as much as I did, huge and loving thanks to Adam, Rosie and Molly for tolerating being surrounded by Christmas for far too long last year and all the usual maelstrom and chaos that goes with living with me. Hopefully our Christmas this year will run like an Aston Martin: fast and furious, but absolutely smooth.

About the author

Sarah Raven is an expert on all things to grow, cut and eat from the garden. Her most recent book, *Sarah Raven's Garden Cookbook*, was named Cookery Book of the Year by the Guild of Food Writers. She is a passionate teacher, running cooking, flower arranging and gardening courses at her East Sussex farm. She is also a presenter on BBC's *Gardeners' World* and writes for the *Daily Telegraph* as well as for several leading magazines. Sarah is married to the writer Adam Nicolson and has two daughters and three stepsons.

About the photographer

Jonathan Buckley has been collaborating with Sarah Raven, taking photographs at Perch Hill, for ten years. His work has been widely published in books, magazines and newspapers worldwide. He was named Photographer of the Year and Features Photographer of the Year by the Garden Writers' Guild in 2006.

First published in Great Britain in 2008

Text © Sarah Raven 2008
Photography © Jonathan Buckley 2008

The moral right of the author has
been asserted.

Bloomsbury Publishing Plc,
36 Soho Square,
London W1D 3QY

Bloomsbury Publishing,
London, New York and Berlin

A CIP catalogue record for this book
is available from the British Library.

ISBN 978 0 7475 9510 6
10 9 8 7 6 5 4 3 2 1

Photography: Jonathan Buckley
Design: SMITH, smith-design.com
Victoria Forrest, Lesley Gilmour
and Namkwan Cho
Index: Vicki Robinson

The text of this book is set in
Neue Helvetica.

Printed and bound in Italy
by Graphicom.

FSC
Mixed Sources
Product group from well-managed
forests and other controlled sources
Cert no. CQ-COC-000015
www.fsc.org
© 1996 Forest Stewardship Council

www.bloomsbury.com
www.sarahraven.com